Native Poetry in Canada

Native Poetry in Canada

A Contemporary Anthology

edited by Jeannette C. Armstrong

& Lally Grauer

broadview press

National Library of Canada Cataloguing in Publication Data
Main entry under title:
Native poetry in Canada : a contemporary anthology

Includes bibliographical references.
ISBN 1-55111-200-0

1. Canadian poetry (English) — Indian authors.* 2. Canadian poetry (English) — 20th century.* 3. Indians of North America — Canada — Poetry.
I. Armstrong, Jeannette C.   II. Grauer, Lalage, 1948- .

PS8283.I5N36 2001   C811'.54080897   C2001-930207-X
PR9195.35.I53N36 2001

Broadview Press Ltd. is an independent, international publishing house, incorporated in 1985.

North America:
P.O. Box 1243, Peterborough, Ontario, Canada K9J 7H5
3576 California Road, Orchard Park, NY 14127
TEL: (705) 743-8990; FAX: (705) 743-8353;
E-MAIL: customerservice@broadviewpress.com

United Kingdom:
Thomas Lyster Ltd.
Unit 9, Ormskirk Industrial Park
Old Boundary Way, Burscough Road
Ormskirk, Lancashire L39 2YW
TEL: (01695) 575112; FAX: (01695) 570120; E-mail: books@tlyster.co.uk

Australia:
St. Clair Press, P.O. Box 287, Rozelle, nsw 2039
TEL: (02) 818-1942; FAX: (02) 418-1923

www.broadviewpress.com

Broadview Press gratefully acknowledges the financial support of the Ministry of Canadian Heritage through the Book Publishing Industry Development Program.

Design and composition by George Kirkpatrick
Cover illustration by Sarain Stump (Permission from Linda Jaine)

PRINTED IN CANADA

Contents

Four Decades: An Anthology of Canadian Native Poetry from 1960 to 2000

Jeannette C. Armstrong

This anthology acknowledges the many Native writers whose words and whose insights inspired and led us in the development of our literatures in Canada in the last four decades. It also provides in one collection a survey of their work for those interested in the history and development of Native literatures in Canada. I chose to collaborate with respected non-Native colleague Lally Grauer because I think this collection will be important not only to Native audiences but to all those teaching literature. The whole process of this collaboration has been a learning experience that I enjoyed immensely—true collaboration in all aspects of commenting, questioning, and selecting. I have decided to share my views of how these various poets inspired and influenced my own development as a writer, to stand and raise my hands to them and say thank you.

I think of the day in 1965 when a cousin of mine pointed to the road from our one-room school on the reserve and said, "There's the Indian guy who wrote a book!" All of us rushed to the window to look at him, awestruck. I never was quite sure who it was, but was told later it was Gordon Williams. However, that experience exemplifies how remote the idea of a real live "Native" person writing a "book" was at that time. The only published "Indian" most of us had heard of then was Pauline Johnson.

I remember hearing Chief Dan George's soliloquy "A Lament for Confederation" in 1967. I remember feeling so much pride and a surprising sense of familiarity as I listened with awe to his delivery at a Centennial event hosted by our community. His poetic, oratorical, performance-based style of formal speaking was usually reserved for use in west-coast Native gatherings and spoken in an original language. But there he was, using it to speak to Canada and in English! I was still in high school, but I was already publishing poetry. Even then, I realized that this was not a speech simply intended to be understood, but foremost to be heard. It was constructed and delivered not only to move the listeners with words and meaning, but more, to move them with the speaker's passion and the strength of his emphasis, to engage them in experiencing the sounds words and phrases made. I remember sitting under a cottonwood tree talking about it with George Ryga, and sharing the feeling of excitement in the discovery that this prose was closer to poetry in its enrichment of symbolism and imagery and the use of spoken rhythm and cadence. Along with Pauline Johnson's use of sound and rhythm, I think Chief Dan George's language was perhaps one of the earliest Native influences on my own writing. It sounded like us.

One of those years in the late 1960s, I vividly recall a late night treat on CBC during the Christmas holidays when I heard Duke Redbird read "The Beaver." I can still go back to that night. Since we were living in a rural area of the Penticton Indian Reserve, we had no electricity, and my Dad had rigged up one of the tractor batteries to a large-tube wave radio which received signals from all over North America. Most times we were forced to conserve battery power and tuned in only to the local news in the morning, national news in the evening, weekly farm reports, local Penticton V's hockey games in winter, "Our Native Land" once a month, and Bakersfield California's "Hottest Hits" after school when Dad was out in the field. But that night we listened the whole evening to the special holiday programs featuring small community celebrations from all over Canada, with the tractor running outside so Dad could switch batteries every hour. It became one of my treasured moments when the announcer introduced Duke Redbird, and we all crowded around the radio the same as we did to listen to the hockey team or Joe Louis. After his poem we all cheered and my Dad said "Hot dog, that Indian sure said it!"

Something occurred to me then about the use of poetic form as a way to distil into symbolic imagery a perspective coming from our common experience of being Native in Canada. "Native" was the preferred word then, and I use it here. Hearing Duke's poem "make it to radio" and say things which resonated with us and yet were "presentable" because they were in a poem, began to define for me the beginnings of a type of literature we would later term "Native Writing." Like Chief Dan George, Duke made me look at poetry in a different way than I had in high school. I believe his work opened the door to others to consider what else might be presented in this malleable yet compact and portable form, while drawing on a familiarity with oral delivery and a common subject. I saw it as a way to get through to an audience, and voice what mattered to us as subject. Not unrequited love and romance, not longing for motherland, not taming the wilderness nor pastoral beauty, nor driving railroad spikes nor placing the immigrant self, but our own collective colonized heritage of loss, pain, anger and resistance, and of our pride and identity as Native. And later, when I received from a non-native friend a copy of *Red on White*, Marty Dunn's biography of Duke with drawings accompanying a collection of his poems, I was amazed by its use of forms and the way the concrete poems were structured on the page. To me, *Red on White* broke invisible barriers simply by appearing as a book, let alone leaping into the literary avant garde of the day, while preserving the underlying "Native" themes of the times.

At the end of that invigorating era of anti-establishment counter culture, flower power, Zen meditation, political protest against inequality, and fascination with things Native, I came across a very small collection of coffeehouse poems by fellow Okanagan Gordon Williams. For me, his poems mirrored a Native experience of the 1960s while, at the same time, they seemed to be influenced by beat, free verse forms, and the minimalist writings of the then obscure but now famous non-Native coffeehouse poets I was reading. Although no large collection of his poems has ever surfaced, he had a following on the west coast. I believe Gordon's writing influenced the development of Native writers reading and writing what I then called resistance poetry and which began to appear in all small circulation Native news bulletins in the mid to late 1960s.

About the same time I came upon Sarain Stump's extraordinary works and eventually his book *There is my people sleeping*. I remember reading and looking at his drawings and being stunned by the idea that he was speaking a secret poetic language of symbols and images that could be appreciated only by a Native who was culturally knowledgeable. Its simplicity and depth brought to us a way to speak to each other of those things spiritual without having to explain to non-Natives what they did not have access to, culturally. For example, I realized instantly that the poem "It's with terror, sometimes that I hear them calling me" was deliberate in its choice of spirit power symbols, thereby creating a special layer of meaning for me. I believe this work was monumental in its influence on many Native writers seeking ways to write about what was then a taboo subject.

I began to search for similar poems by "Indians" in "Native" news magazines, which in the mid to late 1960s began to be more available as alternative press. Native alternative press broke the print barriers and limited Indian subjects set in mainstream press to speak for and about all kinds of social and political issues. News magazines like *The National Indian* (Ottawa, National Indian Brotherhood), *Indian Record* (Winnipeg, Indian and Métis) and *Nesika* (Vancouver, Union of BC Chiefs) contained mostly political stories, but featured "poems" of various calibres and attributes, bound together by the common thread of being engaged in speaking out. I read Native magazines voraciously, searching for poetry that spoke to me. A few Native poems surfaced in literary review magazines and little magazines like *The White Pelican*, but mostly what was available to Native readers were Native newspapers and magazines. I also found small poems scattered like gems here and there in the pages of mimeographed Native flyers and bulletins which appeared at every native political gathering and sit-in the late 1960s to the very early 1970s. I recall reading a very small poem by Skyros Bruce in one such flyer and being so utterly thrilled with the beauty of her poem that I searched for flyers from everywhere to read her work. I was elated to find more in the poetry anthology *Many Voices*, edited by Marilyn Bowering and David Day, an important mainstream publication.

I learned as much from Gordon, Skyros, and others who appeared in that collection and who remained relatively obscure, as I did later from Peter Blue Cloud and Wayne Keon, whose names I also searched for among the pages of literary reviews and Native magazines like *TAWOW*, papers like *Akwasasne Notes*, and other more regional magazines such as *Indian World*. They were seminal in giving us the Native political information we craved while developing an audience for "Indian Writing." This was mostly poetry published for brevity's sake in these publications, but also consisted of reviews and lists of Native publications. I believe these papers were instrumental in engendering a literary movement parallel to or perhaps occurring as one of the vehicles of the "Indian Movement." Certainly such works allowed access to subjects not in the common texts of immigrant literatures. I think now that the political inclination of such publications almost totally influenced the subject matter of this "Indian Writing," though at the time I believed that freedom to write and publish such "resistance" writing was the reason such magazines were in print.

From the mid and into the late 1970s, after Native militancy dissolved into an upsurge in cultural revivalism, George Kenny's *Indian's Don't Cry* — his famous attack on stereotypes of Indians — was shocking in the stark honesty of his images. We followed his work with excitement. At the same time, the publication of *Poems of Rita Joe* rekindled my own interest in writing what she has termed "comment, protestation and correction aimed at history." I believe her poems spoke to all of us young Native writers coming from traditions in this country older than English.

With the publication of *Delicate Bodies* in 1980, Daniel David Moses' poems led us, not only into a new decade, but into new literary territory. I remember reading and rereading his poems and feeling everything from euphoria to anxiety at the imagery he conjured. I believe his works shifted the paradigm for those of us who struggled with writing and identity and moved us into a decade of Native literary experimentation. Throughout the 1980s, writers Beth Brant, Beth Cuthand, Lenore Keeshig-Tobias, and Emma Laroque rose and spoke with eloquence and confidence in a variety of published and collected poems showcasing the magic and the power of Native writing in Canada and breaking literary trail for an increasing number of new Native poets. Theytus Books, a fully Native-owned publishing house, was conceived and began to seriously promote Native writing. There were many who surfaced during those times who experimented with poetry, some of whom remain obscure and who published sparsely in a variety of journals. A few are published in small chapbooks in and outside of Canada. An example is the work of writer Rasunah Marsden who published a collection in a chapbook entitled *Voices* in Jakarta, Indonesia, in 1986 and who has continued to write and publish in various journals. Equally evident was the variety of subjects and themes that arose in this decade of political, cultural, and spiritual reflection. It closed when Joan Crate published *Pale as Real Ladies* in 1989. I remember driving to Vancouver to visit Lee Maracle to "talk writing" and the excitement of writers gathering to read poetry and stories to each other. A similar excitement prevailed in Winnipeg at Bernalda Wheeler's, where I met Beatrice Culleton, editor for Pemmican, a Métis publishing house. I think of Maria Campbell organizing writing circles in various places across the country to break ground. And non-Native friends, like Victoria Freeman, at the time with the feminist journal, *Women and Words*, and Ann Wallace with the women of colour journal, *Tiger Lily*, who were tireless in finding ways to make sure we were invited to "literary" events to help bring these circles together. Somewhere in that time we began to "hear" our poetry "read" not only by each other as writers, but also by a Native audience who was developing its own informed views on "authentic voice and Native Literatures," the phrase popularized at various literary conferences on the subject. Around the same time I came across the small magazine *Trickster*, published by the "Committee to Re-Establish the Trickster," a collective of writers including Lenore Keeshig-Tobias and Daniel David Moses, who were meeting and publishing thoughts on the subject. In 1988, the International Feminist Book Fair in Montreal brought together over fifteen prominent Native women writers from Canada and the United States to comment on Native Writing. A network, loosely begun through small regional circles of Native writers gathering to read and discuss Native writing, suddenly solidified around concerns of marginalization, ghetto-ization, and misappropriation of cultural voice. In 1989 the planning and establishment of the En'owkin School of Writing was a direct result of the development of a North America-wide network of Native writers and coincided with the publication of *Seventh Generation*, an anthology of contemporary Native poetry published by Theytus Books.

The 1990s began with the Oka crisis. "Protecting what is sacred" might well have been the slogan summarizing the sentiment of many Native writers and creating an awareness of our unique and separate cultural realities. It was to be an era of literary proliferation reinforcing an appreciation of Native cultural diversity. Marie-Annharte Baker opened the decade with her collection of poems, *Being on the Moon*. Her deft humour and cynicism as well as her extraordinary and beautiful symbolism launched us into an era of poetic celebration of being Native, each in our own unique ways. En'owkin's premier "Survival" issue of *Gatherings: A Journal of First North American Peoples* was launched, promoting the annual publishing of new writers and celebrating new works by established ones. Joining hands in the celebration of publishing first collections in the early 1990s were Duncan Mercredi, Joanne Arnott, Connie Fife, Kateri Akwenzie-Damm, and Joseph Dandurand, each contributing a diversity of style, subject, and view of being Native. My own collection of published poems, spanning the 1960s, 1970s, and 1980s, was released. Armand Ruffo, Louise Halfe, Marilyn Dumont, and Gregory Scofield powerfully cemented a decade of exciting works, giving us insight and appreciation through their critically acclaimed and award-winning collections. At the close of the decade and the opening of the new millennium, well-known writer Lee Maracle has brought us full circle, completing a collection of poems published over the last four decades, *Bent Box*, which mirrors the legacy of Native literary development through those times. The power of her style is reminiscent of Chief Dan George in preserving the oratorical quality of longhouse speech and returns us to the magic of "our" poetry. Many Native writers whose works we love and know and could not include are being published at the close of this decade and will soon be available in book form. One such work is *Under the Night Sun* by Randy Lundy, whose poems instantly enthralled me. If this is evidence of what is to come, I look forward to the literary decades ahead.

Tuning Up, Tuning In

Lally Grauer

Poems selected and placed side by side in an anthology begin to talk to each other. They tune in to each other's frequencies, seem to speak and respond, amplify and comment on each other. The reader hears conversations, reverberations, talk about talking, telling, writing, reading, listening. "If the legends fall silent," Chief Dan George writes, "the spoken word is not enough." "I do my footnotes so well/nobody knows where I come from," says Emma LaRocque in "Long Way from Home." Beth Brant asks, "Telling./Who hears?" "I study rocks ... for signs/for a telling/of age old crumblings/and majestic rises" writes Jeannette Armstrong. Some poems talk back to a colonial culture: "I lost my talk./The talk you took away," writes Rita Joe. Many poems invite the reader into the inner world of the poet, a world of emotions and perceptions, tellings of dreams, visions and ceremony. Ceremony is not necessarily equated with seriousness. Marie Annharte Baker, in "Coyote Columbus Café," tunes readers into contemporary "Indian time" and coyote: "*check coyote channel/check....*" Since the 1960s, the writers in this volume have been engaged in creating Native literature in Canada and changing Canadian literature. Jeannette Armstrong and I offer with this anthology one record of that movement, its complexities, and its innovative energy.

Putting together this volume has been a process of recovery and, for me, discovery. Jeannette Armstrong introduced to me writers such as Gordon Williams, Skyros Bruce (who has changed her name to Mahara Allbrett), and Sarain Stump, all of whom played an important role in inspiring her to continue and develop as a writer. Much of the writing by Native poets of the 1960s and 1970s was printed by obscure, small presses with short print runs in those exuberant, counter-cultural times; it is scattered and buried. This anthology acknowledges the impact of these early writers—including Chief Dan George, Duke Redbird, Peter Blue Cloud, George Kenny, Wayne Keon and Rita Joe—and attempts to make both their earlier and later work accessible.

We felt that the work of poets writing in the 1980s, 1990s, and 2000s also needs to be made accessible and available, work that is often acclaimed but also dispersed in little magazines, academic journals, and slim volumes quickly out of print. In this anthology, we select poems by writers such as Emma LaRocque and Lenore Keeshig-Tobias, printed over the years in literary magazines or anthologies, but not yet published in book form. We feature the poetry of writers often known for their work as playwrights, essayists, and novelists, such as Daniel David Moses, Beth Brant, and Lee Maracle. Others include Beth Cuthand, Joan Crate, Rasunah Marsden, Marie Annharte Baker, Duncan Mercredi, Joanne Arnott, Connie Fife, Kateri Akiwenzie-Damm, Gregory Scofield, Joseph A. Dandurand, Armand Garnet Ruffo, Louise Halfe, Marilyn Dumont, and Randy Lundy. Our anthology chronicles this explosion of poetry and aims to provide a substantial selection of each poet's work.

In her introductory essay, Jeannette Armstrong describes her connection to these poets as an Okanagan writer. As a teacher of Canadian literature, I see their work reach and educate my students. Funny, vital, moving, disturbing, these poems ignite new perspectives and sudden insights in the classroom; they reframe histories and make them relevant to the present. They communicate the complexities of Native cultures and a shared awareness of being Native in Canada. As well, they speak to and about Canada and the world; they participate in the movements of the last four decades, including counter-culture, feminist, ecological and post-modern movements.

Poems in this anthology also suggest that the poets share—cannot avoid sharing—experiences of racism and continuing colonial attitudes. The many poems to Helen Betty Osborne in this volume are no accident. She is both a symbol and a reference to a brutal, ongoing reality. Though subject to change like everything else, a deep alienation from Native peoples and their cultures is a part of Canada's history and social fabric. It is a condition of living in Canada that, to use Leonard Cohen's words, "everybody knows." Some poets—Connie Fife, Emma LaRocque, Lee Maracle, and Duncan Mercredi come to mind—confront head on this condition and the oppression it engenders; they bring it to light. Some use humour, anger, or both, to speak this reality, as in Duke Redbird's early poem, "The Beaver":

> Please God, my God, deliver me
> From Damnation.

*   *   *

The poems in this anthology suggest histories of being Native in Canada. Over the course of four decades, changes in the articulation of Native identities reveal themselves. In poetry of the 1970s by Peter

Blue Cloud, Duke Redbird, Sarain Stump, Skyros Bruce, Chief Dan George, and Rita Joe, the struggle to make one's voice heard as an "Indian" in a white society is often thematized—though in very different forms. As well, a growing solidarity among Indian people during the late 1960s and early 1970s, the time of Red Power, is represented. I think of Skyros Bruce's words, "we are all from the same root" or Sarain Stump's line, "Don't break this circle"; it is embodied in Wayne Keon's "Heritage." Peter Blue Cloud's refrain, "a tribe is an island" symbolically identifies Native protesters converging on Alcatraz from all over North America to be one "tribe" and suggests the "turtle island" of North America. In the late 1980s and 1990s, various writers represent Native identities and identity in general as mutable, subtle, mixed, and complex—though still political. Marilyn Dumont and Gregory Scofield question the "fit" of identities, "Native," "Canadian," "half-breed." Joanne Arnott explores the traces of repressed Native identity in "Song About": "maybe you recognize me…." In "my grandmothers," Kateri Akiwenzie Damm constructs a form to convey her mixed Native-European heritage. While these poems engage with the complexity of identity, others, such as Cuthand's "Zen Indian" and Annharte's "Bear Piss Water," breezily distinguish Native identities from New Age facsimiles.

While problematizing identity in various poems, these poets and others of the 1980s and 1990s also find ways to speak from within particular Native identities. Louise Halfe writes as a Cree without explaining herself as such. So do Emma LaRocque, Beth Cuthand, Marilyn Dumont, Gregory Scofield, and Randy Lundy. Many of these writers have expressed to me the importance of the Cree language to their work, whether it be in working with rhythm, sound, and tone or in the love of words and the play of words. Other poets speak as Ojibway or Anishnabe, Okanagan, Kwantlen, and other first peoples.

Not all poets are concerned with identity. Daniel David Moses writes lyric poetry in the late 1970s and 1980s depicting a world in which Red Power might never have existed. While his poems do not take on identity as a subject, they are redolent of the Grand River landscape where he grew up and imply relationships among people within his particular community. In later poems, he incorporates dream images of surreal intensity. Other poets also give form to dreams. Lenore Keeshig-Tobias lets the reader see through the dreamer's eyes in "New Image":

> You are at
> the kitchen table
> drinking coffee,
> writing

as he looms in
through the open door.

Joseph Dandurand, in "before me," merges dream and reality, asleep and awake, past and present. Wayne Keon also fuses dream and reality in his story/poem "Spirit Warrior Raven/Dream Winter." Using a matter-of-fact narrative tone, he makes the spiritual personal and concrete. Kateri Akiwenzie Damm's poem "frozen breath and knife blades," like Moses' "The Persistence of Songs," tread the border of dream and history.

*   *   *

While some poets "dream" the past, others dramatize, mock, interrogate, revise, reshape it and make it present. Some poetry, particularly the earlier poetry, protests the erasure of Native history and conveys the urgent need to regain it. "Know her," writes Rita Joe. "Know Demasduit/The last of the Beothuks of Ktaqmkuk." Peter Blue Cloud puts Yellowjacket and Crazy Horse on the page. Twenty-three years later, Armand Ruffo, thinking about Geronimo, "wonder[s] if it is possible for anyone/to have the last word."

In the 1980s and 1990s, not only the content but the telling of history becomes the subject of poetry; poets experiment with forms that create new understandings. Beth Cuthand dramatizes and juxtaposes the voices of the Riel rebellions in "Seven Songs for Uncle Louis." In "History Lesson," Jeannette Armstrong conveys the violence of the abstraction "colonialism" by telescoping it into a vivid caricature of mad physical activity:

> Out of the belly of Christopher's ship
> a mob bursts
> Running in all directions
> Pulling furs off animals
> Shooting buffalo
> Shooting each other
> left and right.

Joan Crate is possessed by Pauline Johnson, and vice versa:

> I remain
> onstage in front of you.
> I stare at the pelts
> hanging from my shoulder....

Pasts and presents interrupt, answer, and supplement each other in Louise Halfe's layered *Blue Marrow.* Joseph Dandurand, in "Fort Langley," also brings personal and colonial history together. In "Found Poetry," Lenore Keeshig Tobias comments on history and Canadian government policy simply by repeating it, and Marilyn Dumont "writes back" to Sir John A. Macdonald in "Letter to Sir John A.":

> Dear John: I'm still here and halfbreed,
> after all these years
> you're dead, funny thing....

                    *   *   *

From the 1970s on, Native poets have experimented with language and form. Emma LaRocque comments in her preface to the anthology *Writing the Circle* that Native people may come to writing in English from the background of a Native language or of a particular "english," to use the post-colonial term. Different modes of english may be more aesthetically pleasing to Native writers, or a writer may feel "slightly rebellious" about using it. Rita Joe and Sarain Stump both use a pared-down syntax and diction: in Rita Joe's case, the plainness of the language creates a penetrating directness; Stump's economy can be cryptic. He is one of the few poets to combine writing and drawing, though Marty Dunn's biography of Duke Redbird, *Red on White*, also combines image with Redbird's poetry. Stump's images ask for interpretation on their own level; reading one of his poems with illustrations is quite a different experience from reading it without. Gordon Williams experiments with form and style, moving from the relatively traditional stanza forms and syntax of "The Last Crackle" to the free verse and juxtaposed images of "Dark Corners" or the nightmarish running prose poem, "The Day Runs."

Other writers make language visible and use it subversively. Daniel David Moses' witty poem "The Line" foregrounds the line rather than the total poem, reeling the reader in line by line. In "Green," Jeannette Armstrong loosens the weave of text so that the reader can enter from any point around or within the poem, creating a sense of freedom without sacrificing meaning. Kateri Akiwenzie-Damm and Marilyn Dumont also use techniques that fracture logical structures and linear progression. Poets such as Marie Annharte Baker and Louise Halfe challenge the dominance of English in different ways. In "Raced Out to Write this Up," Annharte undoes the fixity of stereotypes by emphasizing the instability of meaning, while Halfe, in "Der Poop," uses Cree English to "dump" on religious pomposity and ignorance.

Some of Annharte's work encodes performance. The poets of the 1970s put various kinds of performance into writing: Chief Dan George's oratory is represented on the page; some of Wayne Keon's incantatory rhythms suggest ritual. New elements of performance enter into the poetry of the 1990s. In "Coyote Columbus Café," Annharte suggests the smoky, subversive atmosphere of the cabaret. Duncan Mercredi evokes the smoke-filled bar and the blues. Other poets turn on the music. Rock and hip-hop are becoming elements in some of Kateri Akiwenzie-Damm's poems, and she, Gregory Scofield, and Joanne Arnott work with traditional song forms in poems such as "partridge song," "Peyak-Nikimowin, One Song," and "My Grass Cradle." Armand Ruffo's "Rockin' Chair Lady" is a tribute to jazz and Gregory Scofield's "T. for," like other poems of *I Knew Two Metis Women*, plays on the themes and rhythms of country music.

* * *

Being "in tune": poetry is designed to be not only read, but heard. Anyone who has heard poetry read well knows that. Meaning also depends not only upon the speaker, but also upon the reader or the listener—what we hear or see, what we are capable of hearing or seeing. Some poets suggest how not to hear their poetry, as in Marilyn Dumont's "Circle the Wagons,"

> There it is again, the circle, that goddamned cir-
> cle, as if we thought in circles, judged things on
> the merit of their circularity, as if all we ate was
> bologna and bannock, drank Tetley tea, so many
> times "we are" the circle, the medicine wheel,
> the moon, the womb ...

I remember meeting with Jeannette fairly early in the process of putting together this anthology. We were talking about Sarain Stump. "I was mixing stars and sand," she said, looking at me. "Do you know what he's doing there? He's using a special language. It's a kind of shorthand." She did not say anything more, and yet her excitement communicated itself to me. For some reason, I went off on a tangent, talking about something that had excited me recently. I only admitted later what I knew inwardly at the time: I had not been listening. It was even more ironic, when, at home, I reread the whole poem.

I was mixing stars and sand
in front of him
but he couldn't understand
I was keeping the lightning of
the thunder in my purse
just in front of him
but he couldn't understand
and I had been killed a thousand times
right at his feet
but he hadn't understood

I tried, am still trying, to listen. Hearing not only the work but the interpretations of Native readers and critics can transform one's understanding; their participation in Canadian literature and Native literature will transform the interpretive field. In the process of putting together this anthology, conversations developed among Jeannette, myself, and the poets. I began to get a glimmering of the richness of lived experience, culture, language—none of these words are adequate—that I could only begin to understand. Yet this glimmering opened me to new ways of connecting. I still do not know exactly what "mixing stars and sand" refers to; Jeannette has told me it has to do with spiritual practices that are not talked about. The "information" or facts, however, are not necessary to understanding, although we are often persuaded by a growing info-culture to believe that it is. Sarain Stump's poem speaks to me of how what we can—or can't—see right "in front" of us is ideologically and culturally determined. He suggests the particular blindness of Euro-Canadian cultures, with their inherited beliefs in the superiority of the European over the "savage." Yet the poem, juxtaposing different conceptions of power and understanding, and simply reiterating the problem of not understanding, opens up the potential for communication, perception, and change.

Danny come home
the saw dust pile is high and
its slopes are sand
dunes we can slide down
at the bottom one can look
up and see only the crest
of sand and the promising sky

In the culture that I inhabit, we would rather talk than listen. The poets in this volume speak across this gulf. They speak of the pain of racism, of loss, despair, disinheritance, exclusion, poverty, cruelty. They also speak of strength, resilience, joy, love, renewal—the "laughing and gabbing" of a "pretty tough skin woman," to use Marie Annharte Baker's words, or the "promising" skies of childhood that Marilyn Dumont writes about. They speak of ways of constructing the world, of communicating, listening, hearing, and knowing. Besides the joy and pain of their poetry, I take from them the strength of their courage.

A Note on the Text

Readers will find two dates for most poems. Where possible, we have dated each poem according to the date it was written and the date it was published. (If only one date is shown, it is the date of publication. Usually this date indicates the poem was written in the year it was published. In some cases, only publication dates are available.)

Each poet contributed to the anthology an artist's statement which begins each author's note. Other unattributed statements from authors in these notes have been made to the editors in personal interviews. Works cited in the authors' notes, such as published interviews and essays, are listed below.

Blue Cloud, Peter. "Talking with the Past." *Interviews with American Indian Poets.* By Joseph Bruchac. Tuscon: U of Arizona P, 1987. 23-42.

Halfe, Louise. "An Interview with Louise Halfe." By Esta Spalding. *Brick* 60, fall 1998. 43-7.

———. "Writing, Healing and Spirituality." *Grain* 25.4. 5-7.

Keeshig-Tobias, Lenore. Interview. *Contemporary Challenges: Conversations with Native Authors.* By Hartmut Lutz. Saskatoon: Fifth House, 1991. 79-88.

LaRocque, Emma. "Tides, Towns and Trains." *Living the Changes.* Ed. Joan Turner. Winnipeg: U of Manitoba P, 1990. 76-90.

Moses, Daniel David. Interview. *Contemporary Challenges: Conversations with Native Authors.* By Hartmut Lutz. Saskatoon: Fifth House, 1991. 155-68.

———. "Spooky." *what magazine*, 1989. 5-6.

Chief Dan George [1889–1981]

Was it only yesterday that men sailed around the moon? You and I marvel that man should travel so far and so fast. Yet, if they have travelled far, I have travelled farther, and if they have travelled fast, I have travelled faster.

For I was born a thousand years ago, born in a culture of bows and arrows. But within the span of half a lifetime, I was flung across the ages to the culture of the atom bomb. And that is a flight far beyond a flight to the moon. . . .

I think it was the suddenness of it all that hurt us so. We did not have time to adjust to the startling upheaval around us. We seemed to have lost what we had without a replacement for it. We did not have time to take your 20th century and eat it little by little and digest it. It was forced feeding from the start and our stomach turned sick and we vomited. . . .

And now you hold out your hand and you beckon me to come across the street—come out and integrate, you say. But how can I come? I am naked and ashamed. . . . What is there in my culture you value?

Am I to come as a beggar and receive all from your omnipotent hand? Somehow, I must wait. I must find myself. I must find my treasure. I must wait until you want something of me, until you need something that is me. Then I can raise my head and say to my wife and family . . . listen . . . they are calling . . . they need me. . . .

I must go.

Akwesasne Notes, *1970.*

Chief Dan George or *Teswahno* (referred to in English as Dan Slaholt) was born into the Sleil Waututh First Nation on the Burrard Indian Reserve in British Columbia, one of twelve children. As a child, he helped his parents harvest berries and salmon, learning traditional ways; from the age of five he attended St. Paul's Boarding School in North Vancouver. There, his surname was changed to "George," and he was forbidden to speak his native language. At age sixteen, he worked as a logger. Three years later he became a longshoreman on the Vancouver waterfront until he was injured in an accident in 1946. During the next ten years, he became well known as an entertainer and musician, and in 1951 he was elected Chief of the Squamish Band of Burrard Inlet. He became involved in television in 1960 when he took on the role of Ol' Antoine in the CBC drama *Cariboo Country*. In 1965 he made his entrance into film with his appearance in Walt Disney's *Smith*. Appearing in eight Hollywood films, Dan George is perhaps most well known for his role in *Little Big Man* (1970), for which he received the New York Film Critics Award and the National Society of Film Critics Award, and was nominated for an Academy Award. After meeting playwright George Ryga, he began a stage career in the 1970s. In 1972 he received a Doctor of Laws degree from Simon Fraser University and the next year a Doctor of Letters from the University of Brandon. Chief Dan George's prose poems were published in 1974 in the volume *My Heart Soars.* A second volume, *My Spirit Soars,* was published posthumously in 1982.

Chief Dan George was respected and beloved as a spokesperson for Native peoples throughout North America. He spoke his "Lament for Confederation" to a crowd of 35,000 at the Empire Stadium in Vancouver at that city's centennial celebrations in 1967. The rhythms of his oratory can be be heard in his poetry; sometimes his poems suggest the voice of an elder speaking to his people; at others, he addresses non-Native society as a spokesperson for his people. He speaks with gentle authority of the distant past and looks ahead into the future, teaching ways of survival for Native peoples that involve reliance on cultural traditions to enable change with dignity and integrity.

A Lament for Confederation

How long have I known you, Oh Canada? A hundred years? Yes, and many many *seelanum* more. And today, when you celebrate your hundred years, Oh Canada, I am sad for all the Indian people throughout the land.

For I have known you when your forests were mine; when they gave me my meat and my clothing. I have known you in your streams and rivers where your fish flashed and danced in the sun, where the waters said come, come and eat of my abundance. I have known you in the freedom of your winds. And my spirit, like the winds, once roamed your good lands.

But in the long hundred years since the white man came, I have seen my freedom disappear like the salmon going mysteriously out to sea. The white man's strange customs which I could not understand, pressed down upon me until I could no longer breathe.

When I fought to protect my land and my home, I was called a savage. When I neither understood nor welcomed this way of life, I was called lazy. When I tried to rule my people, I was stripped of my authority.

My nation was ignored in your history textbooks—they were little more important in the history of Canada than the buffalo that ranged the plains. I was ridiculed in your plays and motion pictures, and when I drank your firewater I got drunk—very, very drunk. And I forgot.

Oh Canada, how can I celebrate with you this centenary, this hundred years? Shall I thank you for the reserves that are left me of my beautiful forests? For the canned fish of my rivers? For the loss of my pride and authority, even among my own people? For the lack of my will to fight back? No! I must forget what's past and gone.

Oh God in Heaven! Give me back the courage of the olden Chiefs. Let me wrestle with my surroundings. Let me again, as in the days of old, dominate my environment. Let me humbly accept this new culture and through it rise up and go on.

Oh God! Like the Thunderbird of old I shall rise again out of the sea; I shall grab the instruments of the white man's success—his education, his skills, and with these new tools I shall build my race into the proudest segment of your society. Before I follow the great chiefs who have gone before us, Oh Canada, I shall see these things come to pass.

I shall see our young braves and our chiefs sitting in the houses of law and government, ruling and being ruled by the knowledge and freedoms of *our* great land. So shall we shatter the barriers of our isolation. So shall the *next* hundred years be the greatest in the proud history of our tribes and nations.

1967

Words to a Grandchild

Perhaps there will be a day
you will want to sit by my side
asking for counsel.
I hope I will be there
but you see
I am growing old.
There is no promise
that life will
live up to our hopes
especially to the hopes of the aged.
So I write of what I know

and some day our hearts
will meet in these words,
—if you let it happen.

In the midst of a land
without silence
you have to make a place for yourself.
Those who have worn out
their shoes many times
know where to step.
It is not their shoes
you can wear
only their footsteps
you may follow,
—if you let it happen.

You come from a shy race.
Ours are the silent ways.
We have always done all things
in a gentle manner,
so much as the brook
that avoids the solid rock
in its search for the sea
and meets the deer in passing.
You too must follow the path
of our own race.
it is steady and deep,
reliable and lasting.
It is you,
—if you let it happen.

You are a person of little,
but it is better to have little
of what is good,
than to possess much
of what is not good.
This your heart will know,
—if you let it happen.

Heed the days
when the rain flows freely,
in their greyness
lies the seed of much thought.

The sky hangs low
and paints new colours
on the earth.
After the rain
the grass will shed its moisture,
the fog will lift from the trees,
a new light will brighten the sky
and play in the drops
that hang on all things.
Your heart will beat out
a new gladness,
—if you let it happen.

Each day brings an hour of magic.
Listen to it!
Things will whisper their secrets.
You will know
what fills the herbs with goodness,
makes days change into nights,
turns the stars
and brings the change of seasons.
When you have come to know
some of nature's wise ways
beware of your complacency
for you cannot be wiser than nature.
You can only be as wise
as any man will ever hope to be,
—if you let it happen.

Our ways are good
but only in our world.
If you like the flame
on the white man's wick
learn of his ways,
so you can bear his company,
yet when you enter his world,
you will walk like a stranger.
For some time
bewilderment will,
like an ugly spirit,
torment you.
Then rest on the holy earth
and wait for the good spirit.

He will return with new ways
as his gift to you,
–if you let it happen.

Use the heritage of silence
to observe others.
If greed has replaced the goodness
in a man's eyes
see yourself in him
so you will learn to understand
and preserve yourself.
Do not despise the weak
it is compassion
that will make you strong.
Does not the rice
drop into your basket
whilst your breath
carries away the chaff?
There is good in everything
–if you let it happen.

When the storms close in
and the eyes cannot find the horizon
you may lose much.
Stay with your love for life
for it is the very blood running through your veins.
As you pass through the years
you will find much calmness
in your heart.
It is the gift of age,
and the colours of the fall
will be deep and rich,
–if you let it happen.

As I see beyond the days of now
I see a vision:
I see the faces of my people,
your sons' sons,
your daughters' daughters,
laughter fills the air
that is no longer yellow and heavy,
the machines have died,
quietness and beauty

have returned to the land.
The gentle ways of our race
have again put us
in the days of the old.
It is good to live!
It is good to die!
—This will happen.

1974

If the legends fall silent

If the legends fall silent, ⟶ *orality*
who will teach the children
of our ways?

When a man sits down in quietness
to listen to the teachings of his spirit
many things will come to him
in knowledge and understanding.
We have been so much luckier
because we never needed to communicate
in any other way than by thought or word.

This alone will no longer be possible.

We have diminished in numbers and paid
for our past with sorrow and pain
of which no generation of native people
is without its share.
We have suffered much,
now we stand to lose all
unless we preserve whatever is left
from the days of our ancestors.

To do this, the spoken word is not enough.

When a thought forms
it needs much time to grow.
Silence between spoken words
has always been the sign of deliberation.
In these new times of a modern world
where everything has become of value

silence has become time.
Time unused has become time wasted.
We are told: "Time is money."

It is harder to find somebody
who will listen, but everybody reads.
Therefore we must write about our ways,
our beliefs, our customs, our morals,
how we look at things and why,
how we lived, and how we live now.

To do this, we need the old and the young.

Soon there will be many books
that will tell of our ways
and perhaps will shame even those
who think us inferior
only because we are different.
To those who believe in the power
of the written word these books
will proclaim our cultural worth.
It has been done so for other races
and their teachings.
This is how our young people
will bring to you the true image
of our native people
and destroy the distortion
of which we have been the victims
for so long.
Then we will prosper in all things.
From our children will come those braves,
who will carry the torches to the places
where our ancestors rest.
There we will bow our heads
and chant the song of their honor.
This is how the void will be filled
between the old and the new ways.

1974

Keep a few embers from the fire

Keep a few embers
from the fire
that used to burn in your village,
some day go back
so all can gather again
and rekindle a new flame,
for a new life in a changed world.

1974

My people's memory reaches

My people's memory
reaches into the
beginning of all things.

1974

To a Native Teenager

You are unhappy because
you live far from the city
that promises everything and
you think yourself to be poor
because you live among your people.

But when you live like
a person of city breeding
you will not hear the plants say:
eat off me,
nor will you take
from the animals because of hunger.

The ground will be so hard
that you will want to run
from place to place, and
when you have gone too far
there will be no moss to rest on,
nor will your back find
a tree to lean against.

Your thirsty throat
will long to savor water
from the cup of your hand;
instead the liquid that lives in a bottle
will burn your tongue,
soften your mind,
and make your heart ache
for the sweetness of spring water.

Tears will keep your eyes moist
because a thousand small suns
that never come nor go
flicker everywhere.
The wind will not carry
messages from land to land,
and the odor of countless machines
will press on your chest
like the smell of a thousand angry skunks.

You will look at the sky
to pray for soft rain;
instead you will find
above the tree tops
lives another city
that stands between you
and the guidance of stars,
and you will wonder where city people
keep their dead.

A longing will rise in your heart
for the days of your boyhood, and
your fingers will grip the sacred tooth
you hid in your coat pocket.
But the train that carried you into
the city never brought the spirit along
that guides lost hunters through the woods.

Again and again your eyes will try to see
the evening dripping off the sun
like wild honey and your nostrils
will quiver for the scent of water
that tumbled through the canyons
of your childhood.

You'll stand at a corner
amidst the noise
and bow your head in despair
because you are humbled
by the desire to touch
your father's canoe
that he carved when you were born.

Wherever you look
there is nothing your eyes know,
and when weakness settles into your legs
you will recognize your brother
by the shadow his hunched body casts
in the corner of a street,
in a city where people walk
without seeing the tears
in each other's eyes.

1974

I have known you

I have known you
when your forests were mine;
when they gave me my meat
and clothing.
I have known you
in your streams
and rivers
where your fish flashed
and danced in the sun,
where the waters said come,
come and eat of my abundance.
I have known you
in the freedom of your winds.
And my spirit,
like the winds,
once roamed your good lands.
For thousands of years
I have spoken the language of the land
and listened to its many voices.
I took what I needed
and found there was plenty for everyone.

The rivers were clear and thick with life,
the air was pure and gave way
to the thrashing of countless wings.
On land, a profusion of creatures abounded.
I walked tall and proud
knowing the resourcefulness of my people,
feeling the blessings of the Supreme Spirit.
I lived in the brotherhood of all beings.
I measured the day
by the sun's journey across the sky.
The passing of the year was told
by the return of the salmon
or the birds pairing off to nest.
Between the first campfire and the last
of each day I searched for food,
made shelter, clothing and weapons,
and always found time for prayer.

The wisdom and eloquence of my father
I passed on to my children,
so they too acquired faith,
courage, generosity, understanding,
and knowledge in the proper way of living.
Such are the memories of yesterday!
Today, harmony still lives in nature,
though we have less wilderness,
less variety of creatures.
Fewer people know the cougar's den
in the hills, nor have their eyes followed
the eagle's swoop, as he writes endless
circles into the warm air.
The wild beauty of the coastline
and the taste of sea fog remain hidden
behind the windows of passing cars.
When the last bear's skin has been taken
and the last ram's head has been mounted
and fitted with glass eyes,
we may find in them the reflection
of today's memories.
Take care, or soon our ears will strain
in vain to hear the creator's song.

1974

Rita Joe   [b. 1932]

My work is to inspire others to voice anything they want. Published work is going to be around a while. Inspiration came to me by learning that others do not always write what I want to hear—the good in my culture. Write what comes from the heart. Do not wait until tomorrow, do it now!

Rita Joe is a Mi'kmaq poet and Elder. Born in Whycocomagh, Cape Breton Island, she now lives on the Eskasoni Reserve on the Bras D'Or Lakes. Following the death of her mother, Rita Joe lived in foster homes from the age of five until she was twelve. For the next four years, she attended the Indian Residential School in Shubenacadie, Nova Scotia. She says, in her collection *Song of Eskasoni*: "That school plays an important part in my life, along with native upbringing by many mothers." She married Frank Joe in 1954 and began writing in 1969 with a column "Here and There in Eskasoni" in the *Micmac News*. "At that time I began writing poetry, two lines, now and then." She submitted a manuscript to the 1974 Nova Scotia Writer's Federation poetry competition and won an honourable mention. She saw it as a gain for all Native people: "Now my people will think, if she can do it so can I." Today a mother of ten and grandmother as well, Rita Joe has worked actively for the education of Native children and of non-Native children on the subject of Native culture. In 1989, she received the Order of Canada and, in 1993, an Honorary Doctor of Laws degree from Dalhousie University.

Rita Joe has published four books of poetry: *Poems of Rita Joe* (1978), *Song of Eskasoni: More Poems of Rita Joe* (1988, edited by Lee Maracle), *Lnu and Indian We're Called* (1991) and *We Are the Dreamers* (1999). In 1996, with the assistance of Lynn Henry, she published her autobiography, *Song of Rita Joe: Autobiography of a Mi'kmaq Poet*. Her work has appeared in *Kelusultiek: Original Women's Voices of Atlantic Canada* (1994) and in *Mi'kmaq Anthology* (1997), which she co-edited with Lesley Choyce. In the 1990s, Rita Joe has been writing songs with melodies, as well as poetry.

Rita Joe's poetry often suggests sadness at the loss of her Mi'kmaq culture and language as well as determination to retrieve and maintain it. Her poems are usually short and spare, making powerful statements about personal experience, loss, and renewal. "I write stories in poetry form," she says. While she believes in emphasizing the positive and has described her "song" as "gentle," her poems are clear-eyed and un-sentimental. They can be poignantly direct: "I lost my talk/You took it away." She writes, "the early work I did from 1969 and onward is a comment, protestation or even a correction aimed at history." She is often referred to as "the gentle warrior."

In changing the colonial record, Native writers play an important role, she suggests in her poetry. "'I am the Indian/And the burden lies yet with me' means I am the Indian, I am responsible for myself in everything I do." Her understanding of Kluskap traditions is suggested in the two poems about him below. When she wrote "The Legend of Glooscap's Door," she says, "I thought [it] was a legend; found out it was real." She first learned about Glooscap from "my brothers Rod and Soln. At first I thought it was just a fairy tale, so I wrote in that version." Her latest poem on Kluskap, "Sune'wit at Kelly's Mountain" conveys her new awareness. "Today I am so proud to be able to write the right version of it, the learning from the elders and the traditional people who have prayed and fasted there ... if you are sincere and stay the four nights with just the little fire, just meditate, the surrounding area just glows; prayer helps in the supernatural setting. The area is sacred, as the Mi'kmaq say."

I am the Indian

I am the Indian.
And the burden
Lies yet with me.

                                                      1978

Your buildings

Your buildings, tall, alien,
Cover the land;
Unfeeling concrete smothers,
        windows glint
Like water to the sun.
No breezes blow
Through standing trees;
No scent of pine lightens my burden.

I see your buildings rising skyward,
    majestic,
Over the trails where once men walked,
Significant rulers of this land
Who still hold the aboriginal title
In their hearts

By traditions know
Through eons of time.

Relearning our culture is not difficult,
Because those trails I remember
And their meaning I understand.

While skyscrapers hide the heavens,
They can fall.

1978

Wen net ki'l

Wen net ki'l?
Pipanimit nuji-kina'muet ta'n jipalk.
Netakei, aqq i'-naqawey;
Koqoey?

Ktikik nuji-kina'masultite'wk kimelmultijik.
Na epa'si,
    taqawajitutm,
Aqq elui'tmasi
Na na'kwek.

Espi-kjijiteketes,
Ma' jipajita'siw.
Espitutmukewey kina'matnewey-iktut eyk,
Aqq kinua'tuates pa'qalaiwaqann ni'n
    nikmaq

Who are you?

Who are you?
Question from a teacher feared.
Blushing, I stammered
What?

Other students tittered.
I sat down forlorn,
                dejected,
And made a vow
That day

To be great in all learnings,
            No more uncertain.
My pride lives in my education,
And I will relate wonders to my
            people.

1978

When I was small

When I was small
I used to help my father
Make axe handles.
Coming home from the wood with a bundle
Of maskwi, snawey, aqamoq,
My father would chip away,
Carving with a crooked knife,

Until a well-made handle appeared,
Ready to be sand-papered
By my brother.

When it was finished
We started another,
Sometimes working through the night
With me holding a lighted shaving
To light their way
When our kerosene lamp ran dry.

Then in the morning
My mother would be happy
That there would be food today
When my father sold our work.

1978

Expect nothing else from me

Klusuaqann mu nuku' nuta'nukl
Tetpaqi-nsɨtasin.
Mimkwatasik koqoey wettaqane'wasik
   Lnueyey-iktuk ta'n keska'q
Mu a'tukwaqan eytnuk klusuwaqaney
   panaknutk pewatmɨkewey
Ta'n teli-kjijituekɨp seyeimɨk

Words no longer need
Clear meanings.
Hidden things proceed from a lost
   legacy.
No tale in words bares our desire,
   hunger,
The freedom we have known.

Espe'k Lnu'qamiksuti,
Kelo'tmuinamɨtt ajipjɨtasuti.
Apoqonmui kwilm nsɨtuowey
Ewikasik ntinink,
Apoqonmui kqama'lanej app;
Espɨpukua'lanej aqq mlkiknewa'lanej.

A heritage of honour
Sustains our hopes.
Help me search the meaning
Written in my life,
Help me stand again
Tall and mighty.

Mi'kmaw na ni'n;
Mukk skmatmu piluey koqoey
   wja'tuin.

Mi'kmaw I am;
Expect nothing else from me.

1978

She spoke of paradise

She spoke of paradise
And angels' guests.
She spoke of Niskam
And the Holy Spirit.
She spoke religiously
Of man's true brotherhood.
Yet once when she must sit beside me,
She stood.

1978

I Lost My Talk

I lost my talk
The talk you took away.
When I was a little girl
At Shubenacadie school.

more orality

language as pivotal

You snatched it away:
I speak like you
I think like you
I create like you
The scrambled ballad, about my word.

an native language, orality is synonymous to thought

Two ways I talk
Both ways I say,
Your way is more powerful.

So gently I offer my hand and ask,
Let me find my talk
So I can teach you about me.

native language as essential to identity

1988

Take away the talk, the thought, and what is left? Lost in translation; there are things expressed in native languages that can't be expressed in English

Demasduit

On March 1819, the Beothuks were surprised and killed.
Demasduit survived.
She just had given birth to a babe
All mothers on earth consider a prize.
A man, her captor, the all-powerful white
Committed a crime
Nobody paid.
Chief Nonosbawsut, her husband, tried with his life
But nobody paid.
I implore for Demasduit,
Mary March they named her,
I implore, know her,
But not her killer.
Know Demasduit
The last of the Beothuks of Ktaqmkuk.

1991

The King and Queen Pass by on Train

I am happy
The King and Queen will pass by on train, they say
All the boys and girls on the reservation
Will receive pants, skirts and sailor blouses.
Our parcel arrives from the Indian Agency
To the foster home where I live
There is one sailor blouse, a skirt
My heart goes flip flop.
But the fun day goes by
With no one saying, "Put your blouse on."
My heart stops.

The day is over
Gone, my longing to see the King and the Queen.
And now my foster brother has new hand-made pants
With a sailor blouse to match.

My heart goes flip flop.

1991

Indian Talk

Jiktek
All is still.
Silence reigns.
Tepknuset
the moon
A month.
Nemi'k
I see.

So long ago.

Nmis
my sister.
maja'sit
she go.
Nmis, my sister
Nutaq, I hear
Wena, who?
Nekm, her, him, them.

So long ago.

Api, a bow
Teken, which?
Ji'nm nemi'k
Man I see.
Kwitn, a canoe
App kinu'tmui, teach me again
Lnui'simk, Indian talk.

So long ago.

Migration Indian

I toss and turn all through the night
The hurting bunk-boards, the hay and quilt not enough
The alarm rings, horizon turning red
We wash, dress, eat and take buckets
Rush to the fields of blue, like rivers out of sight.

And before noon we try to reach the quota
The songs in our head unsung
We work the blueberry fields
All muscle and might.

There is a way to hold rake, wrist in motion
Or to bend your back, legs wide, moving forward
Spacing your wind, going easy, your spirit cool
In spite of the sun on back, riding your shadow.
Then noontime, cold beans or bannock
Your thoughts speed back to the field
The song in your head inspiration
The blueberry fields we work
All muscle and might.

The long walk to the blower, to clean your berries
Waiting your turn, have a cigarette.
The comparing of notes and friendly chatter
Payday tonight, "Where's the best restaurant?"
Maybe phone home to Canada, bragging about quota
Then rest, not long, picking means money
The song in your head ready to sing
About the blueberry fields we work
All muscle and might.

We travel to find work, the migration Indian.

1991

The Legend of Glooscap's Door

There is a doorway to Glooscap's domain
Where you throw dry punk and fish
For his fire and food.
But you must not enter
Though you may leave a gift on stone
Waiting to feel goodness.
This is the way the legend goes
So the Micmac elders say.

At Cape North on a mountain you whisper,
"My grandfather
I have just come to your door
I need your help."

Then you leave something you treasure
Taking three stones.
This is your luck.
This is the way the legend goes
So the Micmac elders say.

At Cape Dolphin near Big Bras d'Or
There is a hole through a cliff
It is Glooscap's door.
And on the outside a flat stone
It is his table.
The Indians on a hunt leave on table
Tobacco and eels.
This brings them luck, so the story goes
The legends lives on.

1988

Sune'wit at Kelly's Mountain

All is quiet, so very still
The sun is between earth and sky
The fire is lit, crackling flames
The smudging must be done to whole body and area
He throws tobacco on fire praying softly
So soft the bird on the ground does not notice
As she bends her ear to the ground to hear the worm
The flowing words to his Creator
Non-stop hoping to be heard
But oh so swift the answer there
No time to wonder just amazement
The wonder will continue throughout the day
Not like last night when there was a glow
All over the mountain when sight was given to you
The feeling of goodness all in the glow.
It is the fourth day, today he goes home
The songs must be sung from the core of being
To Kisulk who made us
Then we rest, purification complete until next time
Soon I hope, it is an aspiration

1997

A Course of Study in School

for the teachers of Mi'kmaq in Eskasoni, N.S.

For a long long time I read your word
A slanted voice who thought it was correct.
I read it and held my judgement
Remembering my elders request.
"Wait a while
We have been waiting five hundred years.
Someday they will listen."

Today I voice what is in my heart
I am a teacher.
On the blackboard I write Mi'kmaq words.
The children read as I accentuate
The spoken syllable of my tribal language.

Again and again
I voice what is in my heart.
The tribal language my parents used.

Voicing the curriculum prepared by myself is not hard.
I was born into this world.
Self-government only opened the door of determination.

2000

Fishing and Treaty Rights

Clean water
I see the fish
I take only what I need.
Then the treaty is signed by you.
Humbly I add my X.

The year 2000
I hardly see the fish
I take all I can handle

The treaty is examined again
I voice my claim.

The Treaty was your suggestion
Wasn't it?

2000

Peter Blue Cloud / Arionwenrate   [b. 1933]

I write because I have no choice in the matter. When the urge is there, it must be done.

Peter Blue Cloud is a member of the Turtle Clan, Mohawk Nation, Kahnawake. His name, Blue Cloud, is not a translation of his Mohawk name; it is a "present" from "some Paiutes." As Blue Cloud says in an interview with Joseph Bruchac, "They asked me my Indian name and I told them. They asked me what it meant, and the closest you can translate it is 'Stepping Across the Sky.' But then you have to say there's blue in there because of the first part, *Aronia*. *Aronia* is blue, so 'Stepping Across the Blue Sky.' Or it could be 'Climbing up toward the Blue Sky,' so they said, 'Ah, Blue Cloud.' That was twenty-five years ago, and I said 'That's my name from now on.'"

Blue Cloud grew up respecting oral story-telling and writing. His grandfather, who was a schoolteacher and spoke English well, would permit only Mohawk to be spoken in his house. The songs and stories Blue Cloud heard in childhood were another influence, with a "rhythm unlike stories in English. You hear the songs, the repetition of the chants, and you begin thinking that way." When Blue Cloud first begin writing poems at age thirteen, "I was almost as good as Robert Service. Everything rhymed and I used meter. It had to be a perfect beat" (interview with Joseph Bruchac).

Blue Cloud was a moving force in the revival of Native culture and the stimulation of creative writing by Native people in the late 1960s and 1970s, "back when no-one wanted to publish us." He wrote often for the Mohawk newspaper *Akwesasne Notes*, serving as poetry editor from 1975 to 1976. Participating in the claiming and occupying of Alcatraz by Native people in 1969, Blue Cloud's poems about that event reached out not only to Native people in North America but to people throughout the "third world." His first book, published in 1972, was *Alcatraz is not an island*, a history of the occupation. He published poetry and stories in the 1970s and 1980s: *Turtle, Bear and Wolf* (1976), *Coyote and Friends* (1976), *Back Then Tomorrow* (1978), *White Corn Sister* (1979), *The Paranoid Foothills: a Senesemilla dialogue-in-progress* (1981), and *Sketches in winter, with crows* (1984). Blue Cloud is known for his coyote stories. In travels throughout British Columbia, Oregon, and California, he heard, adopted and adapted them: "With Coyote," he says, "you can cover any kind of ground—philosophy, history, make fun of current events" (interview, *Survival This Way*). Many of his coyote stories can be found in the collection *Elderberry Flute Song* (1982) and *The Other Side of Nowhere* (1991). A collection of his poems was published in 1995, entitled *Clans of Many Nations: Selected Poems 1969-1994*. Blue Cloud lives in Kahnawake, where he continues to write.

Animals appear often in Blue Cloud's poetry. "They're much more interesting than people to me…. The animals don't have a college degree and they're fine" (interview with Joseph Bruchac). Animals such as the bear are informed not only by Blue Cloud's familiarity with and connection to them, but also by their significance in representing a Mohawk clan. In "Bear," Blue Cloud translates the bear's power to the West Coast; in "When's the Last Boat to Alcatraz," the spirit of Richard Oakes is suggested by the "lone bear." Oakes, a leader of the Alcatraz occupation, was murdered in California in 1972. In that poem, as in titles such as "back then tomorrow," Blue Cloud's understanding of the present containing both the past and the future is suggested. The past is alive for Blue Cloud: "I still *feel* it. I can still see that first ship landing in 14-and-something. I was there!" (interview with Joseph Bruchac). He vividly creates the past in poems such as "Crazy Horse Monument" and "Yellowjacket." At the same time, those poems recover a proud history and construct the warrior heroes that were important for the militant Native movement of the 1960s and 1970s.

Alcatraz

As lightning strikes the Golden Gate
and fire dances the city's streets,
a Navajo child whimpers the tide's pull
and Sioux and Cheyenne dance lowly the ground.

Tomorrow is breathing my shadow's heart
and a tribe is an island, and a tribe is an island,
and silhouettes are the Katchina dancers
of my beautiful people.

Heart and heaven and spirit
written in a drum's life cycle
and a tribe is an island, forever,
forever we have been an island.

As we sleep our dreaming in eagles,
a tribe is an island
and a tribe is a people
        in the eternity of Coyote's mountain.

                                                    1969

When's the Last Boat to Alcatraz?

(for Richard Oakes)

When's the last boat to Alcatraz?
        I hear the foghorns and lonely gulls.
Who's skipper on that leaky tub,
        the Broken Treaty,
and what people drum and chant
        upon that turtle now?

It grows darker here, within this forest.
        They try to tell me that my brother died.
I laugh and my laughter echoes,
        through these redwoods
        breaking inner light.
I laugh and laugh and hear a pistol shot,
which is a loose rock falling from
        the cliff on Alcatraz.

A lone bear walks the wooded mountains
        of Pomo country, of Pit River country.
A tall bear, whose anger is a sometimes
        earthquake
        of gentle thunder.

When's the last treaty being written?

It is ten seconds to America, 1976.

It grows darker still as the sky eagle
folds those great wings
        upon my brother's sleep.
It is winter and the glaciers descend
        upon the cities,
the harbors freeze over and the tug

boat "Good Citizen" is trapped
        between Alcatraz and myth.
It is cold and even the temperature
        of memory
        slows its course.

The breath of that lone bear
        is snuffing loudly
        among the giant redwoods.

When's the last boat to Alcatraz?
        (It was so cold and damp,
so little food,
        the children's laughter.
That fog we remember, out there.
        We played shadow games.
Close to fire's heat the drum's taut need,
        and our need
                a warmth of dancing.)

Such strange visions upon that rock.
        Hey, yes,
                these are tears
                        at last.

Told never to say that name again, and
told to dream of other islands,
        dreaming instead
                of a bear,
                not lonely, but,
dancing slowly and heavily.

My brother, Stands Tall, his name,
        now we wish his journey
                be in peace.

                                1976

Ochre Iron

Falling forever
with over and under
falling forever from
pink to purple bridgeways
my father's floating, falling,
decays many schemes
in youth's web-footed anger
      of balance.

I wonder how many, if any,
boyhoods my father portrayed
upon my reservation's
      starving soil,
or how many puppies yapped his heels
as over and over he fell,
or which of the mothers
cast shy eyes at fleeing feet,
      and was it this
same lonesome loon
keening his sunset fears.

Falling forever
among wheeling stars
transfixed upon a canvas
      of universes,
my boot's sad dust
in vain retracing
a highway's straight
and naked hostility,
as over and under
      falling forever
I scream his outrage
to echoing hills and
vibrating steel bridges.
      I scream
            falling,
as cities collapse to my cry
and layer upon layer of lies
of twisted iron beams and braces
cut limbs tearing searing pains.

I wonder forever how many
if any, stole of rest within
the rich hayloft world
of another's dreaming,
and how many now deserted
campfires cast a warmth
in a taste of winter
found in hidden springs
        along that lonely highway.

Bent and twisted he sat
fashioning handles of hickory
with eyes always centered within
to stare down the pain,
so young to be an ancient
too tired to want anything,
smiling, at last, crookedly,
when death offered its dark robe.

And grandfather's bones stirred
once in mute grief, and made room
for the son he barely knew
and the pain was passed on
        and on
not only to another son,
but to a tribe.

And falling forever
with over and under,
I clutch at naked sky
to stand on firm earth,
        father,
I live you moment by moment.

1957, 1975

Bear

A Totem Dance As Seen by Raven

(for Ranoies)

The black bear does a strange and shuffling dance
foot to foot slowly, head back, eyes closed
            like that of a man.
Beneath a loosely falling robe,
mouth sewn shut upon protruding tongue
            of red-stained cedar shreddings.
Foot to foot slowly in lumbering
                              shadow dance
within the fog and rain of high, thick ferns,
beneath a dripping, tapping spruce,
            echo of raven
morning cry of night visions unwanted.

A heavy, leaning snag it seems at first
the sound of crashing fall
                        suspended
            between ground and lowered sky.
then swirl of fog unveils
                        a huge head
carved atop the pole, a silver-grey of cedar.

Gnashing of angry teeth at driftwood shore
and killer whale spews up
                        a wreckage
            of pock-infested sailors.

Foot to foot slowly, the totem dance continues,
sky to earth the leaning weight
                        of pole
            and people and bear
            and now the drum,
rectangular and fringed with clacking claws.

A chant begins of deep-voiced rumbling,
of the black slate carved
                        into bowls now broken

with fragments scattered in despair
        of a death not prophesied.

Great cedar poles in moist earth,
these dwellings speak with dark passages,
    (the rib of a tribe is a brittle section
                        of a dugout
      or what is left
              of a stolen house post,
      vast heritage dragged
        into strange museums)

and still, and forever, foot to foot slowly
the strange and shuffling dance continues.
And day after day the mourning chants
and keening voices silence all else
              as dugouts
      with quiet paddles
convey the dead to sacred islands
      in endless procession.

And soil seeps thru roof cracks to fill
the huge and silent dwellings.
And totems lean from which
           great eyes
gaze either up to sky or down to earth,
And the death of a village is a great sorrow,
and the pain of the survivors
      is a great anguish
           never to heal.

Slowly and gently
        foot to foot balanced
and awkward in beauty
         the child dances.
And grandfather taps,
        delicately taps
the drum and his voice is very, very low,
    and the song is a promise
    given a people
in the ancient days of tomorrow.

And grandmother's stiff
                        and swollen fingers
weave cedar and fern and spruce,
        and occasionally
        in a far away closeness
her eyes seek the dancing child.

The bear pauses in his quest for food
                to stand and sniff the air
then in a dream like fasting
                                he begins
        to shuffle
        foot to foot slowly
as the dance continues.

                                                        1973, 1976

Dawn

in balance, the moon & dawn cast equal light & shadows
                are twins of a single core
the pines of black their webs of branches lean toward the dawn
                in that first touch of wind,
                that ancestor murmur, gentle sweep across earth,
as stars & crickets begin their harmony of sleep, one by one
                gone into silence,
& momentarily, a vast quiet settles all, then a snapping twig
                betrays a tentative step,
& again the quiet, but for the echo of coyote cries heard earlier.

the campfire speaks a low, soft crackling & smoke is the story
                of surrounding growth,
odor of smoked deermeat tempts the mind like tiny, sharpened
                hooves,
& coffee is early morning wine fermented in the glowing coals
                of welcome heat.

a first bold chirping in a sapling oak, a startled answer
                from the pinenut tree,
& suddenly there never was a silence, as blue jay tells on
                flicker, "he did it! he did it!"
& dawn is bright reality in newborn day,
& will the hawk, cry soon.

                                                        1973, 1995

Crazy Horse Monument

Hailstones falling like sharp blue sky chips
howling winds the brown grass bends, while
buffalo paw and stamp and blow billowing steam,
and prairie wolves chorus the moon in moaning.

The spotted snake of a village on the move,
a silent file of horses rounding hills,
in a robe of grey, the sky chief clutches thunder,
and winter seeks to find the strongest men.

      Crazy Horse rides the circle of his people's sleep,
          from Little Big Horn to Wounded Knee,
      Black Hills, their shadows are his only robe
          dark breast feathers of a future storm.

Those of broken bodies piled in death,
of frozen blood upon the white of snow,
yours is now the sky chant of spirit making,
pacing the rhythm of Crazy Horse's mount.

And he would cry in anger of a single death,
and dare the guns of mounted soldiers blue,
for his was the blood and pulse of rivers,
and mountains and plains taken in sacred trust.

      Crazy Horse rides the circle of his people's sleep,
          from Little Big Horn to Wounded Knee,
      Black Hills, their shadows are his only robe
          dark breast feathers of a future storm.

And what would he think of the cold steel chisel,
and of dynamite blasting mountain's face,
what value the crumbled glories of Greece and Rome,
to a people made cold and hungry?

To capture in stone the essence of a man's spirit,
to portray the love and respect of children and elders,
fashion instead the point of a hunting arrow sharp,
and leave to the elements the wearing-down of time.

Crazy Horse rides the circle of his people's sleep,
   from Little Big Horn to Wounded Knee,
Black Hills, their shadows are his only robe
   dark breast feathers of a future storm.

1973, 1976

Yellowjacket

He rode into town upon a wild-eyed mountain horse
his hat pulled low and down his back and shoulders
swaying and blowing in wind, long black and grey hair,
and no one saw the eyes, but even the soldiers felt
themselves being studied, maybe as coldly as the wind blowing downriver,
man and horse, passing through town in silent watching
stirring along small puffs of dust and leaving behind
the strong odors of buckskin and cedar smoke,
"He carries a pistol besides that rifle," someone said,
and a young and respectful voice said, "a real bad one, too, I hear."
an old man, a healer who still dared perform the rituals
of curing, but in hiding from the eyes of soldier and missionary
hummed and muttered an old mountain song under his breath
and whispered, "A spirit rides with him, and he carries
a whole tribe: he is what remains of a tribe, and we, the ghosts."
"Yes," said the sergeant, "another goddamn fence has been
ripped down and dragged until tangled and useless. We give
the heathens a whole valley to live in, but it ain't good
enough for them, should round them up and shoot the lot,
like we was doing before; or at least the real bad ones, especially Yellowjacket."
with a half a butchered steer tied to his horse
he approached his sister's tiny shack at the edge of town,
"The deer are moved to the high mountains like me, don't like
the smell of oiled leather and iron stoves. Here is meat
of a kind best left for the buzzards, but meat at least to eat."
Another fence was torn down and three head of cattle
slaughtered, and the meat left at the edge of town, as a dare
to the hungry to take, and to eat and to live a while longer,
and a soldier, too, found with slit throat, a quick and
clean kill and no signs of cruelty or anger, a hunter killed by the hunted.
and mounted, the soldiers rode through town
and the people watched and knew a longing,
a feeling for a something lost, just out of reach,
but not a one of them mounted a horse or reached for a rifle,

but merely watched and waited, ashamed to raise their eyes to one another.
and they saw him, hatless and riding slowly, so slowly
into town, and the clean upriver mountain air wildly
blew his hair about, and as he passed he stared into
the eyes of each with no reproach, and each of them saw
the holes and streaming blood as he rode through their midst
and was never seen again, and the talking, too, stopped
when his sister said to a crowd of them, "Don't speak
of him again, you don't deserve his name," and they
watched her saddle up and take her child
and turn her back upon her husband and home and never look back.
and on that same evening, a few youngsters, too, saddled
up and for the first time in many seasons, openly
showed their rifles, and some old people joined them
and they rode upriver, up toward the clean air and
naked stone, and the soldiers saw them pass, and dared not interfere.

1974, 1976

Sweet Corn

the edge of autumn touches leaves
    and sharpens
    the morning air
white breath the river speaks
in tumbling, slowly tumbling
                 rising
    mists of steam
a biting axe
       is a dog bark
a cracking rifle
         antler
hollow ringing woods

a crow graws us welcome
    (imagined)
as we harvest sweet corn
the field her summer warmth
    still holds
    in deep, rich earth
             we bend to,
as a running breeze begins
the shushing corn dance

of our tall sisters
and the sweet grace of their motion
    is the sacred ritual
    of our people,

now, kneeling here upon a blanket
as rain taps lightly the windows,
braiding the sister corn into circlets
to be dried for the season of cold,

    at winter's table
                may we all
   think upon
           the first green shoots
      those gone
           and those to come.

                      1975, 1976

Sandhills That None May Visit

Sandhills that none may visit,
crumbled ruins which echo a song
carried on the winds of yesterday.
A lone coyote keening the moon,
the headlights of a car
    searching through the night.
The silent laughter of stars
as they dance their light
across an endless landscape.

Each daylight rises, a praise
in the song of Creation.
A circle of drummers and singers
gathered low upon a sandhill,
and the eagerness of ourselves
in a running stagger through sand
to join their circle.
          And they
keep fading back into distance,
and their music is like a memory,
as we become shadows of tomorrow
on the red stone cliffs of today.

Springtime flowers born of snow,
crystals floating on a desert wind.
A sacred message etched in sand,
magic tumbling track of sidewinder.
At the corner of the eye, naked stone,
and lightning dancers leaping from
black, rumbling storm clouds.

A large track no one recognizes
          behind us
Slowly filling with sand.
Sudden laughter where
          only emptiness was.

A lizard transfixed upon a stone
waiting into forever,
                              as we
do push-ups and grow tails.

Dried, scattered corn stalks
rustling in the desert wind
          as an old man
shakes a gourd rattle and chants,
his eyes closed, a smile playing
games of youth.

A woman on her knees, patting
soft circles of frybread
          as a child
watches her, and then solemnly
says, "I'm going to be a dancer."
And the woman looks back
at the child as solemnly
and says, "Yes, you will be a dancer."

A piece of pottery, smooth and
rounded by fingers of wind,
the same wind whose flute
plays the cottonwood's
          Creation song.

We pass our own scattered bones
lying in jagged fragments,

home for scorpions, and we
smile at those brittle memories,
crumbling them between fingers.

And we pause at a waterhole
to study the countless markings,
and drink deeply, to become rivers,
and lie back upon the sand
and stretch out, and out,
as our bodies become mountains
and crumble into sandhills
   that none may visit.

1978, 1995

Crow's Flight

I watched the solitary flight
of a black and silent crow,
never a sound, not looking around,
bent upon a one-way flight
heading toward the edge of night.

1992, 1995

Searching for Eagles

A pair of great blue herons should
be feast enough for anyone's sunset.
Still, I chant an inner prayer
to glimpse but once, a circling,
soaring eagle close to
this river at my doorstep.

This bit of Mohawk territory, encircled
by cities, towns, freeway and seaway,
cannot be what my ancestors dreamed.
They, who intimately knew eagles,
how would they reconcile today
without the loon's evening cry?

I pretend this river at my doorstep,
for it is a backwash of the seaway,
not flowing, but pulled back and forth
by passing ships. No more the taste
of fresh fish, what swim here are
sickly, polluted, and dying creatures.

Few stars penetrate the man-made
haze of light. No owls hoot the night.
What may resemble peaceful sleep
is the reaction to troubled reality.
No, no more eagles soar here, only
those kept harbored deep within.

1992, 1995

Old Friends

Dark-Buffalo, are you out on the plains
in a rusty pickup, still counting
the holes in your old boots?
You were always laughing and promising
to sing me your special vision song.
But you never did, and I suspect that
your laughter was the true vision.

And you, Painted-Hand, growing old
behind steel bars for defending
women and children, I know that
you haven't forgotten the desert
sands you introduced me to, the
mountains, always ahead.

And, Feather-Held did you ever
return to the far north to marry
that "big clumsy guy" you used to
tell me about? The way you smiled
when you spoke of him is the way
every man would wish to know
at least once in his lifetime.

And You-I-cannot-name because
your name has already been re-given,
you died so quickly. And when
we reached you, you were smiling.
Your blood still stains this ground,
for the years can never erase
one who dies for a people.

My friends, as heavy rain falls
I just wanted to remember you all.

1994, 1995

Duke Redbird [b. 1939]

The inspiration for my work comes from the deep well of history and tradition that is the heritage of our people on this continent. From this well I quench the thirst for wisdom and water the seeds of ideas that the creator has sprinkled upon my soul; nourished into words and verse these ideas become poems which I enjoy sharing. I hope that they bring pleasure and inspiration to those who read them.

Duke Redbird was born on the Saugeen Reserve on the Bruce Peninsula, near Owen Sound, Ontario. He began writing in the early 1960s. Performing and reciting his poetry at folk festivals, coffee houses, and theatres across Canada, he became a nationally known Native writer and spokesperson. In 1967, his poem "Indian Pavilion" was featured during Expo 67 in Montreal. In 1977, a multi-media musical based on his poetry was performed in the presence of Their Royal Highnesses, the Queen and the Duke of Edinborough during Silver Jubilee celebrations in Ottawa. He represented Canada at the Valmiki World Poetry Festival in Delhi, India in 1985; in 1989, a commissioned work of his was read for the opening of the Canadian Museum of Civilization in Hull, Quebec.

In the 1970s, Redbird also worked as an activist on many projects in support of Native people, becoming vice-president of the Native Council of Canada in 1975. In 1978, he received a Masters in political science from York University and published his thesis, *We Are Metis*. In the 1980s, he became president of the Ontario Métis and Non-Status Indian Association.

Redbird has always been interested in film and media. He was the writer-producer for CBC TV's *Canoe in the Making* in 1993 and associate producer for the Canadian film *Dance Me Outside*. In his 1971 biography of Redbird, Native writer and artist Marty Dunn combined graphic art with the poetry, a work that reflected the creative counter-culture of its time. Redbird published a collection of poems, *Loveshine and Redwine* in 1981. Living in Madawaska, Ontario, he continues to write and recently produced a CD of his poetry and music called *Duke Redbird's Poetry*. His poems of the 1970s make use of contemporary poetic forms, such as use of colloquial language and line breaks that follow oral rhythms. In "Tobacco Burns" and "The Small Drum," Redbird brings ritual to poetry and to the printed page. "My Moccasins" and "Tobacco Burns" suggest his questing spirit that seeks to connect his present-day reality with traditional Native ways.

The Beaver

See how the beaver
Works all night, without light
In the darkness

He builds his dam
Limb and branch, mud and sand
Higher, stronger, greater dam

From dusk till dawn
His toil goes on and on

Then tomorrow, you will see
a bubbling stream

Become a pond, and later on
A stagnant lake

And all the creepy, crawly creatures
Will crawl down, to make a home
Within that putrid pond

With turtle, snake, frog and crab,
These neighbours now the beaver will have

But
The deer, bear, lynx and fox,
Raccoon, wolf, moose and hawk

Will move far away
To find a place the beaver hasn't been

Where clear, cold, clean water still flows
Living, Laughing, Tumbling Liquid Life

Waterfalls, brooks and streams
These are highways for life's dreams.

My son,
Do not become a beaver,
And build for yourself a dam

For this is what the whiteman does
With brick and stone and sand

Till his mind is like that lake
Filled with weird wicked wretches
That give no peace.

Then he cries to his creator
In desperation

Please God, my God, deliver me
From Damnation.

1968, 1969

The small drum

The small drum
Throbbed a story
And the old man agreed
Eyes dancing
Head nodding
In
The firelight
His body moved
To the rhythm
Of the drumstick
But
He did not know
It was in his hand
Nor the drum between his legs
Mist
Precedes the day
And in the mist
The old man saw
His prayer
He said nothing
But
The small drum
Remembered.

1971

My moccasins

My moccasins have not walked
Among the giant forest trees

My leggings have not brushed
Against the fern and berry bush

My medicine pouch has not been filled
With roots and herbs and sweetgrass

My hands have not fondled the spotted fawn

My eyes have not beheld
The golden rainbow of the north

My hair has not been adorned
With the eagle feather

Yet
My dreams are dreams of these
My heart is one with them
The scent of them caresses my soul

1971

Tobacco Burns

Tobacco curls when touched by fire
The smoke rises—up—
Blue and grey
A fog that holds medicine
The spirit is strong.
The story is old
The smoke curls
I feel a sound—the sound
Of drums on distant hills
Of buffalo hoofs on frozen ground
A medicine chant wailing by breezes
That have not blown

For many moons; nor suns
That shine no longer on brown children
My eyes seek a vision—
For old people told of visions
That were not seen by eyes
But burned in the mind and mouth
Of our men
Who fought battles
But did not win.
My body cries for strong medicine
But my eyes water from whisky
My brain bleeds—my heart sweats
I regret
That tobacco burns
And I am not strong.

1971

The Ballad of Norval Morriseau

Norval, Norval, What's driving you?
        Are the spirits talking?
Are the spirits coming thru?
Are they talking to you?
You've lived in the forest, all of your life
You've been hungry and you've suffered strife
And you paint with the blood of a thousand years
You paint the legends and you paint the fears
And you paint the birch bark and you paint the sand
And you paint your sweat with an ancient hand.

They took your paintings and hung them in town;
They took your body and flung it around,
So the world could see an Indian in high society.
They gave you a china cup filled with tea,
But you drown their pale faces in brown whiskey,
You painted their Jesus to expose their hypocrisy.

You've lived in their churches, you've known their jails
And you laughed when they said you had failed,
Your art will be living when they're all dead;

You took their green money and you painted it red;
You paint your canvas with a brush of pain,
You signed your works with an Indian name.

You're an Ojibway man, a child of this land;
An artist, a prophet with a torch in your hand;
A blueprint for seeing, and it's not for sale;
A harbour for living in the eye of a gale.
The people, they love you, and they know your truth;
The culture is yours; you can never lose.

The Algonquin nation is listening to your voice.
They're learning your wisdom and pride;
They're painting with a brush you passed on to them,
With a talent they no longer need to hide.
Yes, you've opened the doors and the windows too;
The spirits are talking;
                    yes they're coming through.

                               1981

Beth Brant [b. 1941]

Land. Spirit. History, present, future. These are expressed in sensual language. We labour with the English language, so unlike our own. The result of that labour has produced a new kind of writing. I sometimes think that one of the reasons our work is not reviewed or incorporated into literature courses (besides the obvious racism) is that we go against what has been considered "literature." Our work is considered "too political" and we do not stay in our place—the place that white North America deems acceptable.
"The Good Red Road," *Writing As Witness.*

Beth Brant is a Mohawk who was born in Detroit, where her father worked as an autoworker. He and his parents, in whose home Brant's father and Irish-Scots mother lived, were born in Tyendinaga on the Bay of Quinte, Mohawk territory in Ontario. Brant grew up an urban Mohawk who was also familiar with the community of Tyendinaga, where her family often stayed. "My grandparents gave me my Mohawk identity," says Brant. Her grandfather taught her Mohawk language; both grandparents passed on traditional wisdom.

Brant began reading at age four, encouraged in a household where reading was important. Her father, who educated himself by going to college at night, became a teacher. When she was in sixth grade, Brant won a dictionary as a prize for being a champion speller. "I loved that book—so many words to choose from, so many words to play with." For Brant, words and language are a source of pleasure; they are also important tools "to be of use: to my people, to the many families I am connected to—First Nations, feminist, gay and lesbian, working-class, human." Perhaps most important, they are a visitation of spirit ("Writing Life," *Writing as Witness*).

Brant began writing at the age of 40 in 1981. That same year, she published work in the periodical *Sinister Wisdom*, edited by Michelle Cliff and Adrienne Rich. The following year she edited a special issue of that journal which was published in 1983 as *A Gathering of Spirit*, the first anthology of Native women's writing, including lesbian writing, and the first anthology edited by an aboriginal woman. *Mohawk Trail*, Brant's first book of poems and stories, was published in 1985; *Food and Spirits* followed in 1991; *Writing as Witness*, a book of essays, appeared in 1994; and *I'll Sing 'Til the Day I Die: Conversations with Tyendinaga Elders* appeared in 1995. Brant is chair of the board of the Toronto organization Native Women in the Arts, and she edited the first two issues of that organization's magazine, *In a Vast Dreaming* (1995) and *Sweetgrass Grows All Around Her* (1997). She has read, lectured, and taught creative writing throughout North America. Brant has received awards from the

Ontario Arts Council and Canada Council, and the National Endowment for the Arts. She has also been a Fellow of the Rockefeller Foundation in California. Her work has been anthologized extensively in Canada and the U.S.A., and has been translated into German, French, Italian, and Chinese.

The question "What is writing?" is one that Brant keeps circling in *Writing as Witness*, and her sense of writing as both responsibility and mystery is evident in her poetry. The poem "Telling," with its connotation of revealing or divulging a secret (among many other possible meanings) confronts the power and potential danger of words. "Honour Song" suggests a different sense of telling, as in counting, placing on record. "Stillborn Night" explores telling once again, from the points of view of the grandmother and mother of a dead child. The poem moves from poetry to prose, a gathering of voice and words that are as important as the toy, turtle, bear, sweetgrass, and tobacco the poet will gather to bury with her grandson.

Her Name Is Helen

Her name is Helen.
She came from Washington State twenty years ago through
broken routes
of Hollywood, California,
Gallup, New Mexico,
Las Vegas, Nevada,
ended up in Detroit, Michigan where she lives in #413
in the gut of the city.
She worked in a factory for ten years, six months, making
carburetors for Cadillacs.
She loved factory work.
She made good money, took vacations to New Orleans.
"A real party town."

She wears a cowboy hat with pretty feathers.
Can't wear cowboy boots because of the arthritis
that twists her feet.
She wears beige vinyl wedgies. In the winter she pulls on
heavy socks to protect her bent toes from the slush and rain.

Helen takes pictures of herself.

Everytime she passes those Polaroid booths,
one picture for a dollar,
she closes the curtain and the camera flashes.

When she was laid off from the factory
she got a job in a bar, serving up shots and beer.
Instead of tips, she gets presents from her customers.
Little wooden statues of Indians in headdress.
Naked pictures of squaws with braided hair.
Feather roach clips in fuschia and chartreuse.
Everybody loves Helen.
She's such a good guy. An honest-to-god Indian.

Helen doesn't kiss.
She allows her body to be held when she's had enough
vodkas and Lite beer.
She's had lots of girlfriends.
White women who wanted to take care of her,
who liked Indians,
who think she's a tragedy.

Helen takes pictures of herself.

She has a picture on a keychain, along with a baby's shoe
and a feathered roach clip.
She wears her keys on a leather belt.
Helen sounds like a chime, moving behind the bar.

Her girlfriends took care of her.
Told her what to wear
what to say
how to act more like an Indian.
"You should be proud of your Indian heritage.
Wear more jewelry
Go to the Indian Center."

Helen doesn't talk much.
Except when she's had enough
vodkas and Lite beer.
Then she talks about home,
about her mom,

about the boarding schools,
the foster homes,
about wanting to go back to see her people
before she dies.
Helen says she's going to die when she's fifty.

She's forty-two now.
Eight years to go.

Helen doesn't kiss.
Doesn't talk much.
Takes pictures of herself.

She touches women who are white.
She is touched by their hands.

Helen can't imagine that she is beautiful.
That her skin is warm
like redwood and fire.
That her thick black hair moves like a current.
That her large body speaks in a language stolen from her.
That her mouth is wide and full and when she smiles
people catch their breath.

"I'm a gay Indian girl.
A dumb Indian.
A fat, ugly squaw."
That is what Helen says.

She wears a t-shirt with the legend
Detroit
splashed in glitter across her large breasts
Her breasts that white women have sucked
and molded to fit their mouths.

Helen can't imagine that there are women
who see her.
That there are women
who want to taste her breath and salt.
Who want a speech to be created between their tongues.
Who want to go deep inside her
touch places that are dark, wet,
muscle and spirit.

Who want to swell, expand two bodies into a word
of our own making.

Helen can't imagine that she is beautiful.

She doesn't kiss
Doesn't talk much.
Takes pictures of herself so she will know she is there.

Takes pictures of herself to prove she is alive.

Helen takes pictures of herself.

1985

Telling

for Celeste who told me to tell and for Vickie

Her face is wide, innocent, clear.
She tells me things.
They are secrets. "He did this to me. He told me not to tell. I never
told until now."
Her face twists for an instant, then returns to its rightful beauty.
I listen.
She doesn't cry, but my eyes feel the familiar moisture seeping out,
dropping on my hand that holds hers. How dare these tears appear
when she—who has the courage to tell—doesn't weep.
She gives me this.
Secrets.

I receive a package in the mail.
When I open it, a diary falls into my hands.
How she got my name, my address, she doesn't say.
Her letter says: *I needed to show this to you. You can throw the diary away if you want. I just
needed to tell.*
The diary is pink. There are gold words stamped on the cover—
Dear Diary.
I am afraid to open you, *Dear Diary.*
Afraid of the secrets I have to keep.
He did this to me. My father did this to me. They did this to me. They did this.
I think the pages should weep as I do when I read her life.
Who turned away from her need to tell?

Who could throw away the pink vinyl book of a life, a life thrown away by others? By others' need to throw away a life?
What do I do with this, *Dear Diary*?
A writer can read. She can hear. She can write.
What does she do with the need of someone to tell?

Our foster child comes to live with us.
One leg is crippled. the burn marks shriveling the skin.
This is his fifth foster home. He is three years old. He is difficult.
He burns with anger—the scars we cannot see.
He can't talk. He points to thing and grunts. In three years, has no one noticed he can't speak words?
My anger burns me. I feel as if I have swallowed hot grease.
What does *his* anger feel like?
We enroll him in a preschool for a few hours of the day, hoping the exchange with other children will help him heal. I take him to school and explain that he will be playing with other kids for a while and
I will be back to get him.
When I return, he comes out into the hall, a look of surprise on his little, dark face.
He smiles with delight at me.
I realize he thought I wasn't coming back.
And he accepted it as normal, as right.
My precious throwaway boy.
We taught you how to talk.
You were innocent. You were difficult.
Innocent.

I write.
I wonder what difference it makes. This writing, this scribble on paper.
The secrets I am told grow in my stomach. They make me want to vomit.
They stay in me and my stomach twists—like her lovely face—and my hands reach for a pen, a typewriter to calm the rage and violence that make a home in me.
I write.
I sit in this room away from my own, yellow legal pad beneath my hand, pen gripped tightly in my fingers. The writer who no longer writes directly on paper. The writer who uses machines to say the words.
This pen feels like a knife in my hand.
The paper should bleed, like my peoples' bodies.

I have a dream about Betty Osborne.
The last secrets of her life.
Stabbed fifty-six times with a screwdriver to keep the secrets of whitemen.
Betty, your crime was being a woman, an Indian. Your punishment, mutilation and death.
The town kept the secret of who killed you.
Seventeen years before the names were said out loud.
They keep secrets to protect whitemen.
Who do I protect with the secrets given me?
My pen is a knife.
I carve the letters B E T T Y   O S B O R N E on this yellow page.
Surely the paper must bleed from your name.
Why doesn't it bleed for you, my throwaway sister?
The sister I never met except in my dream, my obscene nightmare.
Betty, do I betray you by writing your name for people to see who will not love you?

What good is a poet.... Chrystos

I think about those words today and they hang like a knife—or a screwdriver—over my head, ready to pierce me and render me
speechless.
My speech that reveals itself on paper.
What good is a poet?
What good is this pen, this yellow paper, if I can't fashion them into tools or weapons to change our lives?
How do I use this weapon when I must hold the secrets safe?
This is not safe—being a writer.

We are the paint for their palette. Salli Benedict

What kind of picture is painted with the ink I commit to this paper?
How will they use it against us?
Will I be the same as them?
I love. They do not.
Will love make the difference?

Today I woke bleeding from my vagina.
My menses ended days ago.
Is this where the blood goes?
Running out of my womb instead of onto the page, into the words,
the weapon.
The words.

Ugly words.
RAPE. MURDER. TORTURE. SPEECHLESSNESS.
I write and make words that are not beautiful.
RAPE. MURDER. TORTURE. SPEECHLESSNESS.
Dear Diary, did you give her what she needs?
Do I give her what she needs?
A friend. A secret-keeper.
Love.

If love could be made visible, something to hold in the hand, would it be this
pen, this weapon, these words I cannot stop writing?
What were Betty's words?
Where did our foster child's words go?
Do words disappear, or do they linger behind like ghosts?
Do they float like spirits?
Do they cut through to a place I can barely imagine?
When I expose words, who do I betray?

If you hide the stories in the bureau drawer, they become Bad Medicine. Maria Campbell

Are some stories meant to be hidden?
What we do to each other.
What we do between us. The secret, ugly things we do to each other.
How do I show the blood of them? The ink of our own palette?
Medicine.
Who will heal the writer who uses her ink and blood to tell?
Telling.
Who hears?

Our foster child is with us one year. In that time he speaks, he cries,
he points to his leg and asks, "What happened? Who did this?
A judge gives him back to his mother, the same mother they say
burned him.
And I wonder if the mother has kept a secret of her own.
Her man's secret.
Has she lost her child for three years because of another's secret?
What lengths and depths do we go to protect our own?
The depth of losing a child.
The length of being branded as the torturer of an infant.
Secrets to protect.
These pages should bleed.

Deary Diary, did you give her what she needs?
Can I give what she needs?
Medicine.
I want my words to be Medicine.
Will the same Medicine heal the writer who carries these stories inside her like
knives?
He did this to me.
They did this to me.
I believe her.
Does she tell me so *I* can tell? The me that shapes words into
weapons.
What can heal the writer who dreams of Betty Osborne and can only imagine her
words?
Her last words, *NO. NO. NO.*
What can heal the writer who struggles to say the words for a little
boy? A child who cannot speak until he has been loved.
Deary Diary, did your blank pages absorb the shock of the words written on you?
Dear Diary, did you give her what she needs?
The need to tell and be believed.

I need to tell.
Carving letters on yellow paper to understand the violence committed against
us, by us.
What can heal the writer who feels the screwdriver in her dreams?
Who can heal the writer that feels the burning of a child's leg?
What will heal the writer who feels like a traitor as she writes these words, this
language of our enemy, on these yellow pages?
She said to me: "I need to tell you this. You will believe me."
She wrote: *You can throw away this diary, but I needed you to know.*
He said to me, pointing to his leg, "Who did this?"
We did this.
And *they* told us to be speechless.
But they taught us new words that do not exist in our own language.
RAPE. MURDER. TORTURE. SPEECHLESSNESS. INCEST.
POVERTY. ADDICTION.
These obscene words that do not appear in our own language.
What good is a poet who doesn't remember the language her grandfather
taught her?
What good is a poet who sees the power of those words manifested
on us and in us?
They stole our speech and raped our minds.
If love could be made visible, would it be in the enemy's language?
It is the only weapon I hold: this pen, this knife, this tool, this

language.

The writer has to tell. It is the weapon I know how to use.

Dear Diary, did you give her what she needs? Did you back away in horror at the pain of her life? Did you open beneath her to receive the blows of her testimony? Did you wrap your pages around her incest-battered body? Did you make her feel clean again, innocent?

Yellow paper, please give me what I need.

Pen, be my strength.

If love could be made visible, would it be on the skins of trees, this paper spread out beneath my hands?

Who will heal the healer? Dennis Maracle

Love as piercing as the screwdriver's thrust.
Love as searing as the marks on an infant's leg.
Love as clear as her face.
Love as clean as a sheet of yellow paper.
Love as honest as a poem.
I have to tell.
It is the only thing I know how to do.

1989
Toronto, Canada

Honour Song

I will listen to you
For every ear that turned away from your story, I will finely tune
my own to hear every syllable, every cry, every nuance of speech,
every whisper, every secret.
I give you what you have given me

I will touch you
For every hand that failed you in gentleness, my own will become
birds to lift your tired body into flight, will become water to
bathe your wounds, will become caresses to ease your spirit into
calm.
I give you what you have given me.

I will believe you.
For every time they called you liar, I will trust your honesty, I
will be faithful to your words, I will be a sentinel of your story.
I give you what you have given me.

I will see you.
For every eye that glanced away, that refused to look, my own eyes
will behold beauty, will reflect our history, will softly cover you
with respect.
I give you what you have given me.

I will stand with you.
For every war that rages against you, I will be on your side. I
will be as a warrior beside you, I will fight with you.
I give you what you have given me.

I will laugh with you.
For every insult and curse thrown down at you, I will throw it back and
turn it into a joke on them. I will tell you gossip and dirty
stories that cause laughter to rumble from your gut.
I give you what you have given me.

I will cry with you.
For all the ugliness you were witness to, I will shed tears for
each one. I will cry for lost babies, for lost language,
for unnamed sufferings. I will cry and my tears will fall on you and
you will feel them and know I am with you.
I give you what you have given me.

I will love you.
I have so much and I give it to you humbly, respectfully,
honestly.
I will love you as you have loved me.

Our love will turn over this earth.
Our love will be a seed.
Our love will be a flower, will be fruit.
Our love will be food for our Nations.
I give to you what you have always given me.

I sing your names aloud to honour you.
Mary, Celeste, Vickie, Connie, Nicole, Doreen, Janice, Elaine,
Doris, Donna, Viola, Dorothy, Jan, Karen, Margaret, Chrystos,
Katsi, Elizabeth, Monique, Muriel, Lisa, Gloria, Joanne, Carole,
Susan, Cindy, Beverly, Anna, Maureen, Littlefeather, Kate, Betty,
Judith, Terri, Raven, Nila, Share, Midnight Sun, Jackie, Awiakta,
Barbara, Linda, Edith, Deb, Marcy, Leslie, Lee Anne, Jeannie,
Redwing, Diane, Sharon, Sandra, Charlotte, Linda.

I sing your names aloud to honour you.
I give to you what you have always given me.
My sisters.
I sing this honour song for you.

1991, 1994

Stillborn Night

Wind.
Outside my suite, wind screams.
There is no rain, unless my tears can be called so.
I have heard over the wires, the phone held weakly—
My fourth grandson is dead.
Unable to make the journey of birth, he has become a
spirit.
I am unable to be with my daughter, my son-in-law, my
grandson that
lives.
The wind. The wind has cut power lines, has uprooted trees,
has
cancelled flights. But the ringing of the telephone remains
constant.
Through the wires, I hold my family. Voice becomes the
means to
love and comfort
My daughter cries—"Mama, why did he have to die?"
Tim cries—"Mom, I'm scared."
And I think about the careless words that are said by
people when
a baby has not completed the passage to this world.
"You'll have another one, you're young and healthy." "It's
better
this way."
I can only say—"I love you". "I know you're scared." "I'll be
home as soon as I can." "I don't know why he died." "I will
miss
him too."

But I did know that he would die. All these months—I knew
—and I curse this knowing and want to scream like the wind
outside my suite.
My immediate thoughts are for my daughter—how to ease
her pain,

wanting to take that pain and absorb it for her, my lovely daughter.

This is what a mother wants to do.

The grandmother wants the impossible.

To hold a baby in her arms. To rock him. To sing to him.

To imagine the first time he looks at me in recognition and smiles at

his grandma.

I bought no baby clothes, no rattles, none of the little things

that signal the celebration of a new being. I assembled no medicine

bag for him, no filling the pouch with gifts to keep him strong and

balanced in his journey of life.

I told myself I was being careful. This had been a difficult and

dangerous pregnancy. I was being careful, I told myself. I did not

want to presume the outcome.

But when I wandered through stores, I would go to the baby clothes

and hold them in my hands, fingering colours. I picked up rattles

and shook them, then lay them down. I looked at tiny shirts and

diapers, smelled baby powders. I wanted to wonder if this baby

would have thick, fine black hair like his brother, Benjamin. I

wanted to wonder what the mixture of Tyendinaga and Kanawake would

produce this time. He was to be named Brant Montour, family names of

the grandmothers of this child.

I bought no baby clothes. I kept this secret of knowing from everyone, even the woman who shares my bed and my life.

I went with my daughter to doctor's offices. Went with her to have tests. She talked of looking forward to being home again, not having to go to work, looking forward to the night feedings, the smell of baby's head, Benjamin's reactions to having a baby brother, the solidifying of a marriage that has been at risk for years. I listened.

This past year my thoughts have only been of Benjamin—
his terrible anger and confusion of his daddy leaving him
his four-year-old fears of abandonment. Even while my
daughter needed so much from me during this time—love
support, money, time—my thoughts have been of
Benjamin. He would come to see me, but would not spend
a night or weekends, fearing his mother would not be
there when he went home. If his daddy left him, why not
his mama?

When does this dysfunction end?

Upon hearing my daughter was pregnant, I cried. She was
trying to "save" a marriage that, by all accounts, was dead.

The wind. I stand next to the window listening to the
moans of air.

I call the hospital again. This time my daughter tells me
that Benjamin is there. They have told him. He comes on
the line.

"Grandma, Brant Montour died."

"I'm so sad," I say. "Are you sad?"

"No," he says, that little boy voice so sweet and pure.

"He's with great-grandpa. He flew right here to be with
him. He's an Indian angel too."

Despite my sorrow, I laugh. "Is that so?"

"Yeah, grandma, so you don't need to be sad. Great-
grandpa is changing Brant Montour's diaper right now."

I can hear my daughter and son-in-law laughing in the
background. Jill comes on the line, "Of course I didn't tell
him that. He has it all figured out himself."

I stand once again next to the window. I think of my dad
changing the diaper and I smile. He was so sick and weak
before he died. But perhaps Benjamin sees a great-
granddad who is strong again, who laughs at children's
antics, who gives big hugs. This is how I imagine the Spirit
World. A place of my relatives, joking, walking, eating,
strong.

The wind has begun a new sound. A steady keening.

I turn on the radio. There are reports of accidents, of trees
breaking and flying onto homes, of people afraid of the
natural. There are no reports that an Indian baby ended his
struggle to live inside his mother. There are no reports of
strong and loving sisters who are taking care of their own.
There are no reports of a lonely grandma, who knew this

moment would come, but waited in silence.

There is a final call.

"Mama, I'm holding him in my arms now. He looks just like Benjamin. He has black hair. He's so sweet. His right arm isn't developed. And his left arm is twisted. The doctors think his lungs and heart just didn't grow the way they were supposed to. He's so tiny." and her voice breaks.

My heart turns over. I want to sob, but more than that, I want to give my daughter what she needs. My desire to caress my daughter's hair, stroke her back, croon to her, takes control of my voice. I murmur words, make soothing sounds. This voice is all I have at the moment to give her. Old images scatter across my memory. Giving birth to her, hearing the words, 'another girl', rocking her as she sucked her bottle, her frightened face as her father and I began our daily ritual of violent acts and words, her joyous face when she gave birth to Benjamin.

I croon, I murmur, I pretend I am strong. My voice takes on the rhythm of the wind outside the window.

And I am stunned by the knowledge that my daughter is facing this pain head-on. She is not taking short cuts through grief. She is holding her dead child in her arms and she is grown-up. Why does this surprise me? This courageous woman is my daughter. How could I not have seen it before? What does it take for a mother to see this? Tim's voice comes on the line. He tells me about the night, about the stillborn night. My anger at him dissolved weeks ago, as I know what it takes to grow up in Native homes. I also have remembered what is required to grow up in Native homes. Gentleness, patience, love, acceptance. Tim and Jill have given each other these very gifts that have been difficult to give. This long night, they have given these. I talk with him for a while, then return to my daughter. She retells the stillbirth, gathering details around her like folds of material. She is to retell this story for months after. Each telling confirms the reality that she carried a baby inside her. That Brant Montour was a life. It is four in the morning. The wind has calmed to a song-like murmur.

I stand next to the window again. Sometime during this night, the spirit of Brant Montour passed over my head, passed over the lands of Tyendinaga and Kanawake, passed over into the World of his ancestors.

I look out the window onto the grounds of the campus. What people walked here? What spirits still swirl underneath the carefully clipped grass? I open the window and lean out to inhale the air, made fresh by the wind. My tears dry instantly on my face. I whisper his name into the cold air. I am comforted by the saying of his name out loud.

In one year I have lost two of my family. My father—role model, hard worker, reader of books, listener to beautiful music, loving parent, arrogant Mohawk, humble Mohawk, handsome man, learned man, loving man. Brant Montour— only a blurred vision of the baby, the boy, the man he would have been. The songs I would have taught him, the games I would have played with him. Just a blurred vision, and one I knew would not come to be. Still, I loved him.

In the plane, on the way home. There is no wind this morning. The sky is very blue and clear.

I mentally gather the things to bury with him. A Medicine bag for another kind of journey. He will need a small toy to play with, a carved Turtle from his Clan, a carved Bear from his father's, sweetgrass, tobacco, a stone from the earth, a bird's feather, a shell, an arrowroot biscuit. I assemble these gifts in my mind.

My arms ache. I will never hold him. My eyes are full of salt water. I will never see him.

My grandson.

1992, 1995

Marie Annharte Baker [b. 1942]

First, voice presented oneself within a quiet imperative. Desperate for audience, poetry spoke for me and others while the writing images just jiggled into focus. As I learn the lingo of visual art through collage with its possible multi-juxtapositions, I find myself silenced and struggling to say "what's up with me anyway." More and more I am approaching self-expression as "off book" or "improv." Age has aged me, no doubt. Now, it is all very hard to do with lesser energy available. I definitely require a collective from which to work and/or community. As a member of the Carnegie Writing Group, I found a "home" for recent explorations into autobio (moibio). Do I still sound the same? Or, have I transformed myself into yet another persona, Rakuna Kahuna (street name) for Esibankwe (racoon woman). Feeling furr-tive total scavenger of the environment this way as I re-cycle every bit on a grandma's path for a poem or art or performance or video. Miigwetch.

Marie Annharte Baker, Anishnabe, was born in Winnipeg, Manitoba. She received a scholarship to attend Brandon College (1963-65). She became a founding member of the Canadian Indian Youth Council and went to the American Indian Workshop in Boulder, Colorado. The Regina Aboriginal Writer's Group otherwise known as the "raggedy shawls" allowed her to do cultural work.

In 1992, she won a scholarship to the Naropa Summer Institute on Pan American and Eco Poetics. She has taught writing workshops for Native women, and in 1995 received a B.A. in English from the University of Winnipeg. She now lives in eastside Vancouver and is studying collage, pottery, and multimedia. Her son Forrest Funmaker is also a writer and a pow wow singer, and she has two Okanagan grandchildren, Madeline and Soffia.

Being on the Moon (1990), Annharte's first book of poems, was the result of a twelve-year writing process. "Loneliness and self doubts as a single parent expressed in daily journal writings became poems," she comments. During part of this period, she worked as a family worker to prevent the apprehension of First Nations children by social services and to defend the rights of Indigenous mothers to keep their children safe. "Granny Going" tells about an experience in Northwest Ontario when the occasion to give a ride to a hitchhiker back to her family turns into a moment of admiration for the woman's endurance.

The title "Being on the Moon" invokes the image of the moon as grandmother in a thirteen-month calendar. It is also a connection to women's monthly cycle, or "granny's visit." Finally, being on the moon allows Annharte to write from a safe and powerful place, as if looking down from the moon. In "Penumbra," she locates Helen Betty

Osborne and in just such a place, on an island in the Caribbean. Annharte's chapbook *Coyote Columbus Cafe* was published in 1994. Annharte calls it "a poetic tour of a woman's self-discovery or 'perpetual recovery' of Indigena spirit charm."

Subversive wordplay is characteristic of Anneharte's style. So is the loaded line: "I like to push things to the end of the line. I see it as a kind of cliff, with everything pushed over, falling into the next line. And again and again." As for the comedy that permeates her work, she comments: "I was influenced by my Irish dad's language use and of course his humour. I figure I do have a keen, skeptical 'inherited' bent for laughing from my Ojibwe side. However, being teased a kagillion times does make one a funny old lady."

Granny Going

Granny going on the road to town
Packing her raggy clothes on her back
Tied up in a plastic garbage bag
Walking the one road through the bush
To her gang on the streets calling
Charming her bone crack marrow
An old dog tagged behind her every step
Too scared to be scaring a bear
He would know she needed company
He heard her wine gut grinding

1990

Penumbra

for Betty

Temporary the shade my straw hat weaves
across my basket face of Caribe pleasure.
The bright sun makes me want to run and jump,
I had been told if I were smart, I'd stay hidden.
On my island, I keep to myself & lie around.
Turtles crawl past me to dig their nests.
Tortuga oil is outlawed and so am I.

Odd, this exposure of my not too recent killing.
Seventeen years it took getting to court
those who mashed my face because of dark skin.

Hating the contrast of each pinky penis
I left The Pas to be a turista and relax.

They understand I stayed away to make sure
I'm not the only witness to their sorry act.
Not even good at it, I might add as insult.
The reserve is a huge donut around the town,
no place to go unless you're Indian like me.
Laughing at the other end of the beach
gets me wondering how it's my turn.

1990

Moon Bear

My moon is a deep lake in mind
little fishes swim in depths
too scared to see the shaking
sunlight spears above their stare
She-bears birthing in my winter womb
sleeping till spring to growl again
shadows dancing before the nights come
Tomorrow the wind message will bring
what happened since her earth eyes shut
Muzzle up and around for scents secure
Maybe even a tourist campout is early
Her baby wants her back, it's still cold
The iceface feel of my moon lake
slips away as soon as there is more sun
My moon will grow within me to greet
rising bears bringing warm faces to my lips

1990

Bird Clan Mother

Middle of my junk room
        Dream eyes seeing small
                Prehistoric possum mother

Running footbeats jiggling
        Babies hanging on a long tail
                Curved over her back

What was chasing
     My little friend
          Just before dinner?

She could be running
     Right into some bad
          Stink mouth to be gulped

Down with a Family Style Gravy
     To be a bird dropping
          Better to choose a cannibal cure

Another time dream eyes clear
     White bird place known to be
          For all birds a home

Beating wings soaring
     Coming closer starting to lift
          Rising and soaring high above

Lying at peace on a bird back
     How did I get here so fast?
          My wings hardly moved at all

Soft feathers fanning me
     The scars from the possum past
          Still hot from toothmarks

Gliding like a Bird Clan Mother
     I did take off wherever to begin
          Crafty ways, I hunt myself

Whoever sees my shadow overhead
     Knows to run but I slow up
          Beady little eyes blink quick

Ducking the flying jokes I resume
     The feeble crouch run and hide
          This once I will eat squash blossoms

1990

Pretty Tough Skin Woman

old dried out meat piece
preserved without a museum
missing a few big rips
her skin was guaranteed

her bloomers turned grey
outliving the city washing
not enough drinks to keep her
from getting home to the bush

tough she pushed bear fat down
squeezed into sally ann clothes
she covered up her horny places
they tried sticking her under

soft jelly spots remain in bone
holding up this pretty tough hide
useful as a decorated shield for baby
swinging in her sweet little stink

just smell her old memories, gutted fish
baked muskrat—she saw a lady
in a shopping mall with a fur coat
told her an Indian must eat such delicacies

her taste was good she just needed a gun
to find a room in the city to put down
her beat-up mattress where her insides fell out
visitors ate up the bannock drank her tea

they were good at hocking her radio or tv
everywhere she stopped she told her troubles
if I press my ear down on this trail I bet
I'll be able to hear her laughing and gabbing

1990

Trapper Mother

Looking into the animal den, I saw how carefully she
set the trap hidden with pieces of pine branches. Our
tracks she kicked away in the snow. I was her helper.
She gave me the job of turning the wheel on the egg
beater to make milk from Klim powder. The meals I made
were for the cat. She supervised boiling birds in
my toy cookware after I'd plucked them. I wasn't very
squeamish. I saw my mother's bloodied hands on a muskrat
skin turning it inside out to fit a stretcher. Her floured
hands made a baby pig from the scraps of bannock dough.
Her tomato soup was creamy because she used canned milk.
The only time I tasted it was after school. I came home
knowing she was acting strange. She just wasn't around
that much or she was drunk a lot. In the bush, we had a
stove and table next to the bed. In the city, the
room had a double burner hot plate. I never saw my mother
in a kitchen but I saw her in jail.

1990

Boobstretch

my breasts when I was 14 were silky soft
to the touch from outside my brassiere
loaded with scarves to avoid the falsie feel
babies know what to do right away just suck
choosing between vanilla on the right doodoos
or chocolate on the left doodoos
just have to be plugged in
someday we will all have the granny tits
eaten out milkers stretched by generations
so long and flat over our shoulders trailing

1990

modernist much?

Raced Out to Write This Up

1   I often race to write   I write about race   why do I write
about race   I must erase all trace of my race   I am an
eraser abrasive bracing myself embracing

2   it is classic to want to write about class   not low class but
up the nose class   I know I am classy   brassy   crass ass
of a clash comes when I move up a rung

3   we are different skins   different bins for brown rice and
white rice   not even a container of wild rice   you know
what they do when you are white and not rich   poverty
counts big when you count the cost of a caste a colorful
past

4   drunk as a skunk he danced at the Lebret Hotel   what for
no   not really   says he's not writing because they won't
publish his books   he does a number for a book   he
hugged me like I was his old Tibetan guru out on the
dance floor teleporting again

5   white racists notice color which they don't have   you
might be off-white   a bone white   a cream white
alabaster white   dingy white if you don't wash often
enough   nevermind a non-bleached white   white with
pinkish undertone   peaches and cream   white with
freckles   who is color blind   I write my black ink on
white paper   I white out write out my color lighten up

6   full of self I saw old whitey again but he wanted to be a
part of a pure religion not like ours   not that he was a
white racist but a pure racist in his heart which had no
color but our color   red   red   mind you a few white
corpuscles but compared to the red they were a minority
not visible

7   so few of me yet I still write not for the white audience but
the color of their response to my underclassy class   the
flash of their fit to kill me why race away to the finish
when I cross the finish line will it be white   will I be red
from running   hot and cold touch me not less I am to be

divided against my self who is both red and white but not a
shade of pink maybe a beige pink blushed flushed off
white right I color my winning everytime   I am still in the
red not the black   blackened red   reddened black   but
what about black n'blue   green at the gills   yellow belly
but what about the whitish frightish part I put it behind
behind me when I need to say my piece about togetherness
that we must breed not by ourselves but with everyone
out in the world who will listen   hey   I'm a half a half/
breed   a mixed bag breed bread and butter bred my
whole grain bannock will taste as good to me even if I
smear on red jam sink my white teeth down into it down
the red hatch to the black hole   that is behind it all   the
whole black of me   the whore backing up behind me
the sore holy part of me which ~~the~~ is the blackest darkest most
colored most non-Indian, non-white slice of me bred to
wonder

1990

His Kitchen

My father was my mother. He took over
cooking and childcare when she left.
At first, our food came from a can.
He wouldn't let me near the kitchen.
I had to learn to cook at school.
He improved. I asked friends over.
He didn't mind. He heaped up potatoes
and gave us canned fruit for dessert.
Only for a short time, did we go out
almost every night to a restaurant.
Even now, I know I am in his kitchen.
A paint scraper sits with the utensils.
I want to put it back with the tools.
It is his egglifter so I know better.
Holiday dinners he cooks and I make gravy.
Hard to forget he's both mother and father.

1990

Coyote Columbus Cafe

1. once more it's Indian time

always good to be
born the midnight star
500 night years ago
quincentennial dawn
time worth waiting for
never a dull moment
time circles
how a weasel pops
in & out of old tunes

at closing time
I always spot a guy
other end of the bar
time for one more cruise
& conquest   sneak up time
dare I ask   Sh   Sh
be still my boogit

I know the proper approach

*Boozho Dude. Hey, I'm talking
to you, Bozo Dude. My name is
Conquista. Come on adore me.*

my optimism looks good on me
in my territory my favourite bar
& grill   I bar none   grill some
bungee   little bit twobitz
too bitzy for you?
why beat around the bush?

*Suppose my moccasin looms
over your border, mistah,
& you put a teensy toe
on my medicine line.*

no problem lucky for me
I put my "c" mark

that's coyote country "cc"
not "ccc" for cheap colonial crap

I have an attitude how to frequent
with colonizers (dey got me surrounded)
the right time is now
to get discovered again
& again very frequently
on a repetitive basis

2. what does a poor coyote girl do?

I act choosy about what abuse
my clientele gets
I am the first one got Coyotisma
(dey all say dey ever met one)
if they don't like dis talk
I do teas'em up to the climax
of my act but I am too damn direct
for the colonized coyote
poor oppressed critter

hey, you on the Columbus trip

even when I yell at them
I get the usual ho hum complaint
as Coyotrix I lie and trick
what does a poor coyote girl do?

sure I pose baffling questions
administer random coyote IQ tests

what is paler than stranger?

I warn you multiple answers possible
circle (a) the landlord comes around
first of the month to collect rent
wrong answer but don't pick that one
please follow directions & circle choice
what about (c) a landlord of colour?
right answer is (d) I got my rights
(b) I am the landlord around here

*how about solving the mystery
did I discover Columbus first?*

it could happen in a Woody Allen movie
Columbus gives a squirmy spiel

I don't know anybody on this
boat. Strong chance we won't
make it to land.

The map I made shows the Indies
beyond the curve in the earth.
Most of the crew are already
around the bend.

Columbus did lack
    cultural awareness
    equity
    affirmative action
    political correctness

3. Discovery is a hard act to follow

Colon would get comforted
by a kindly Native who'd say

Don't feel bad bro.
You're lost like the rest of us.

if Columbus was looking for turkey
he came to right place

he'd get the deserved treatment
join our healing process

Do you feel like a wounded
buffalo raging within?

mine's ready & raring to stampede
right over a cliff

ever wonder if Colon confessed
to a priest? what did he say
to turn on church officials
start a catholic Rambo trend

now they stalk our organizations
get on the board of directors
become an Indian expert and

discover more Indians
meet up with famous ones

take a class Native Studies
begin with Precolumbian Era
receive an embossed buckskin
certificate or a stone with
your name in petroglyph

if the class is full
because too many Indians
are just learning about
their culture & identity
then simply select a popular
bestseller HOW TO OUTINDIAN ANYONE

don't read any works
by First Nations writers
that's an advanced course
& you must crawl before you
creep up to rich Indians
playing casino bingo warriors
subscribe to Aboriginal news
& pretend Indian sympathy

lo, the po'Indian

Indian Act
Tell Old Indian joke
like Indian Affairs

Act Indian
had an Indian affair lately?

learn how to approach an elder
& what to do if a fakey one comes up
do you talk his or her talk?

I said sweat lodge
makes body clean inside.
Keep it up. Dance pow wow.
After this, boy. You and me
go off West German First
International Wannabe Annual

I shed shwatch ludge
meks buddy kleen insaid.
Kip it up. Danz pahwah.
Hafter, dis, bah. You me,
go hoff big wes churman Furz
Hinter Natchinel Wanbee Annal

Celebration. Take first; don't
need take plastic money
visacard. You me same team.
Same team. Like hockey team.
Zjoonias, my boy. Think of it.
Swiss bank account, hey boy!

cel brayshun. Tek furz; don
need tek plashtik monhee
vissacad. You me sam tim.
Sam tim. Lak hocky tim.
Sch-oo-nash, my bah. Tinkobit.
Swish bank a cunt, hey bah!

discover an authentic Indian colonizer
slaver inside you & check your tongue
if still forked continue to discover
Other Indians do it to other Indians
first who do it to them first

former Columbus clones I implore you
you still got a chance, discover a first
nation friend lover first nation first
for keeps person

4. culture vulture voyeur trips

check   coyote channel check   channel
check   coyote check   just thought I'd
check out my cheque what happened to
my cheque   do you have my cheque
just came to pick up my cheque I
hope nobody cashed my cheque   check
coyote channel check

the other day I got welfare
I had a big zit on my face
with a bandaid to cover up
I practised with my tough look
in the mirror

give me my cheque

I always forget to mention
we were too good way back when
to be real people before discovery

when I'm having an Indian taco day
I discover it's just about too late
not to educate the oppressor
but am I ever good at doing it

my tiny whiny coyote heart
thump de thump thump thump

kicking on the inside
to get outside to howl

how does a coyote girl get
a tale outta her mouth?

1994

Tongue in Cheek, if not Tongue in Check

In a former life, I had to be a hyena.
I always wonder what is the difference
between a hyena and a coyote? Then I
had a coyote insight. Inner revelation.

You don't always know coyote is laughing.
Except deep inside. Pretty sneaky, eh?

One day I was walking along. I had no choice my car
broke down and coyote stories start with a coyote
walking. I met this other coyote going the other
direction and we exchanged scents. He or she maybe
(gender blind type of coyote) had a fragrant
mosquito repellent with sunblock & self-tanning sample.
I asked her outright if she'd seen any dull humans lately?

Being a coyote is not easy. The other night I
was at a meeting of Coyote Anonymous.

"Hi! My name is Coyote and I'm a (laugh, laugh) aholic."

De-nial. Then I asked myself, in front of all the ones
at the meeting, "when is a coyote not a coyote?" I
have looked in the mirror, under the bed, the Yellow Pages
even the Yellow Dog directory. I got tired. Too much research.
The obvious answer had to be "when having a coyote break".
They were just a bunch of great pretenders. But I kept'em guessing.

It's simple as Coyote in the Coyote dictionary it says:

what should be said, is at the tip of tongue
barely hanging on the retina's shine

or dew on a cactus
(but don't do it on a cactus unless desperate)
do it in mucho grande southwest deco portraits
or see entry, urine sample. Scratch and sniff.

No Coyote Thesaurus yet available. No Coyote Almanac.
After 500 years of discovery, any old coyote definition will do.

Kevin Costner shoulda asked *me* to dance.

1994

Coyote Trail

warm trail
>   my nose picks you to follow
your tracks quiver my whisker
>   my nostrils fill

you are a chunky one
>   your tail dragged a leaf
>   overturned bark
you too are hungry
>   fat
>   depressed
>   hopefully suicidal

I see your weight in microns of earth pressed
>   down
>   you won't easily pass the epiglottis
>   like last week   I sssll unk into town
>   I mean slunk not what I usually do

>   QUICK PAWS QUICK PAWS GOTCHA

>   YOU DON'T HEAR MY CLAWS UNLESS YOU PAUSE

something dead and delicious in that town
growing more foul each day
I call it fast food
though it don't move much
until I touch my paw to it
I drool when I talk that way

the last time we met One Gulp
you kicked against my canines
eager to become me
making me exercise
to get a bite or two
makes me think changes

I was a writer once
know how to keep track of things
by writing it down in a book

interdependence works for me
when I be the coyote
you be the writer

1994

Bear Piss Water

Consider going to shaman school. With
enough practice on the rattle and drum
I'd be able to back up a poet. A course
in chanting would help me solo.

Consider dropping out in my first
year. A grade point average must be
maintained and all classes need prior
approval by a guardian spirit. I got
to consider what have I got to lose if
I drop out. I still got the nerve
it takes to set up shop and practice
without a license.

Consider Bear Piss Water not poetry. The
potency of natural spring water that a bear
made sacred. That water with the mercury
and acid rain. You find it just after the
turn off to Sioux Lookout. Just when the
craze for natural water was highest I
decided to try an experimental market.

Consider this water pistol in my hand
which I filled with a Bear Piss Water

sample. A squirt or two and you'll
be officially blessed and prepared
to listen to my eco-poetics.

1994

I Want to Dance Wild Indian Black Face

I want to dance with the five tribes of wild Indians. Them
Wild Magnolias, Golden Eagles, Golden Stars, Black Eagles and
Young Sons of Geronimo dance wild Indian black face.

I want to hear the crowd say 'Ooh, them Indians are pretty today.'

I want to see a tribal official ready to lead his gang into battle
like Council Chief, Second Chief, Trail Chief and Wild Man.

I want to shout back wild calls and big boasts of Big Chiefs in
uptown New Orleans. I want to shout in my own city rez way.

I want to play in an inner circle of raggedy rhythm with beat-up
drums, cowbells, tambourines, whistles, wine bottles and sticks.

I want to carry on in a parade to sing Two Way Pak E Way. In Cajun,
Tuez bas qu'ou est means *Kill anyone who gets in the way*. I could be
a mean Indian some days.

I want to honour the spirits of Black Indians and Choctows,
Cherokees, Natchez and Seminoles who resisted the slave masters.

I want to wear a turkey feather in my hair and join the tribe of
the Creole Wild West. I don't want to be authentic all the time.

I want to be a Tribal 'Hawk' sing some jazz gospel ratty chanting.
Shout my spirit. Claim black and blues brothers same as sisters.

I want to mask Indian, adopt the Indian spirit figure once a year
dance in public with my big black face and talk back to chiefs.

I want to dance wild Indian blackface. I want to be that big bad
black Indian in a carnival parade. I want an Indian day off.

1994

Sarain Stump [1945-74]

In the drawing [for the poem "I was mixing stars and sand"] "but he couldn't understand" the two pierced hands belong to the Indian in the background who is without hands but has some feathers growing instead. The meaning of this drawing is that the white man took our freedom, the hands—in our pictography the hand means to do or did so—without understanding completely what he was doing and he didn't see at all our new minds, feelings and dreams—the wings growing in place of the hands.

— from There is my people sleeping.

Marion Sarain Stump, of Cree, Shoshone, and Salish ancestry was born in 1945. When he was growing up, he was interested in the old stories, and he began drawing as a child on grocery papers. Later he grew interested in Native painters from the southwest, such as Allan Houser and Quinchy Tahoma. According to Stump, "I started to understand the old paintings and drawings and finding them ever more full of meaning and life. These paintings and the Indians who explained them to me are my real teachers, I think." Contemporary Native painters from the Santa Fe Indian School, the Intermountain Indian School in Utah, and self-taught artists also influenced Stump. Of the Europeans, he found Picasso and Hieronymous Bosch interesting, although "Picasso took much from our art and the Negro and Oceanian carvings" (foreword, *There is my people sleeping*).

During his adult years, Stump lived mainly in Alberta, where he worked as a rancher, and in Saskatchewan, where he worked as an art instructor at the Saskatchewan Indian Cultural Centre. In addition to his work as a visual artist, Stump acted in the film *Dan Candy's Law* and performed in many productions across Canada. He drowned in Mexico on December 20, 1974.

Stump published *There is my people sleeping*, a book of illustrated poems, in 1970. His paintings were exhibited widely, and in 1974 he edited a special edition of *TAWOW* (Vol. 4:3). In his poems, Stump uses colloquial language and concrete imagery to evoke complex states of mind, such as the alienation expressed in "there is my people sleeping" and shamanic ritual, as in "I was mixing stars and sand." As Stump's statement above suggests, his pencil and ink drawings add additional layers of meaning and interpretation.

And there is my people sleeping

And there is my people sleeping
Since a long time
But aren't just dreams
The old cars without engine
Parking in front of the house
Or angry words ordering peace of mind
Or who steals from you for your good
And doesn't wanna remember what he owes you
Sometimes I'd like to fall asleep too,
Close my eyes on everything
    But I can't
      I can't

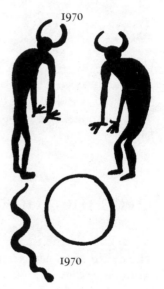

1970

It's with terror, sometimes

It's with terror, sometimes
That I hear them calling me
But it's the light skip of a cougar
Detaching me from the ground
To leave me alone
With my crazy power
Till I reach the sun makers
And find myself again
In a new place

1970

Little traces in my mind

Little traces in my mind
Brought me back where I was born
And there wasn't any explanation
Just my back shook
At the crying of my dying mother

1970

I was mixing stars and sand

I was mixing stars and sand
In front of him
But he couldn't understand
I was keeping the lightning of
The thunder in my purse
Just in front of him
But he couldn't understand
And I had been killed a thousand times
Right at his feet
But he hadn't understood

1970

He goes away

He goes away
Very far away
Without anybody on his tail
Teeth of snake, bird's wings
The shaman goes far away

1970

Seven men on the rock upon the house

Seven men on the rock upon the house
The deadman's head is laughing
At my mistakes
A lazy flyin' of crows in the sky
Brings me away
In a returnless run
Like red leaves
Carried by the autumn wind
With an iron blade
I was trying to write on rock hearts
Hoping to see them laugh
Hoping to see them cry

1970

Like little hands

Like little hands
　　The flowers
Break from the ground
　　To steal
Little drops of sun

1970

Round Dance

Don't break this circle
Before the song is over
Because all of our people
Even the ones long gone
Are holding hands.

1974

Wayne Keon [b. 1946]

I thought we all believed in majik. I always thought we are all majikal. I experience
majik every day. My children have demonstrated their majik since they were one-year-
olds. Some say I am psychic. I alway thought everyone had this ability.

I have no desire to be a unionized Indian. I have no desire to be enfranchised. I will
never sign a treaty. I believe in a spiritual approach. That everything on this earth has
life. Has a spirit. Shares this earth with us. Helps us, loves us, tests us & dies with us.
And deserves to be heard.

Wayne Keon once described himself as "ojibway man, business administration graduate, member Pan American Indian Association, painter, financial analyst, and majik man." He was born in Pembroke, Ontario, but grew up in Elliot Lake, midway between Sudbury and Sault Ste. Marie, where his father, Orville, worked for Denison Mines. "I believe this physical environment—mountains, lakes, streams, pine trees, maple forests, ravens, fox, wolf, lynx, hawks abundant in this area—influenced my writing." Another influence was his father, also a writer, "who gave me a gift one time of the complete works of W. B. Yeats, the 'greatest poet ever.'" "My father was a great storyteller," says Keon, "interesting fella, grade 6 education, self-educated, born in the Depression, sort of my Steinbeck On Board!" Keon was also encouraged by a teacher "who tried disciplining me by having me write out a half dozen pages of poems of my choice on several occasions." His extended family passed on to him "a sense of sadness for a way of life that was lost, a place where my people stood proud, capable, beautiful—and a sense of humour and ability to laugh at oneself."

After graduating from high school in Elliott Lake where he worked in the mines during summer holidays Keon attended the Northern Institute of Technology at Kirkland Lake where he graduated with a degree in business administration in 1969. He is now an internal auditor for the mining conglomerate Rio Algom Ltd. Keon lives in Toronto and has travelled extensively throughout South America, auditing operations of Rio Algom. The company has made good use of several of Keon's books in their South American operations "where our employees study English, compliments of Rio."

Keon began writing poetry when he was twelve. He broke new ground both in writing and publishing when he, his father, and his brother Ronald published one of the first collections of contemporary Native poetry, *Sweetgrass,* in 1972. "Yes, I had a sense of standing alone," he says now. "I just liked writing poems and stories.

I persisted even when no support was evident. Just liked what I did and did it." He went on to publish in periodicals such as *Canadian Forum*, *The Malahat Review*, *Queen's Quarterly*, *Exile*, and *NeWest Review*. In 1988, he co-authored, with his father, the novel *Thunderbirds of the Ottawa*. In the last decade he has published three books of poetry: *Sweetgrass II* (1990), *Storm Dancer* (1993) and *My Sweet Maize* (1997). His poems have been reprinted in numerous anthologies and textbooks; the poem "if I ever heard" has been translated and published in France, Italy, India, Japan, United Kingdom, and Australia, among others.

In his "opun ltr tu bill bissett," Keon acknowledges the influence of this poet, who, in turn, borrows from Native traditions in his own poetry. Like bissett, Keon works with phonetic orthography, repetition, and the placement of words on the page creating a space for his particular Ojibway voice. A shamanic voice emerges in such poems as Keon's "the eye/of the raven," or "for donald marshall." At the same time, as he warns us in "the eye/of the raven," "you have been tricked/and I do not fly so high." "i'm not in charge of this ritual," he asserts in that poem which plays with the intertwining of mystery and materialism, magic and mundane which is characteristic of his work.

Heritage

AlgonkinAssiniboineAthaapaskanB
eaverBellaCoolaBeothukBlackfoo
tCarrierCaughnawayaCayuyaChilk
atChilcotinChipewyanCreeCrowDe
lewareDogribEskimoFlatheadFoxG
rosVentreHaidaHareHuronIllinoi
sIroquoisKickapooKitwancoolKoo
tneyKoskimoKutchinKwakiutLake
LilloetMaleciteMalouinMenomine
eMetisMiamiMicmacMississaugaMo
hawkMohicanMontagnaisMuskoeeN
ahaniNaskapiNeutralNicolaNipis
singNootkaOjibwayOkanaganOneid
aOnondagaOttawaPequotPetunPieg
anPotawatomieSalishSarceeSaukS
aulteauxSekaniSenecaShawneeSho
shoniShuswapSiouxSlaveStoneySu
squehannaTagishTalhltanThompson
TlinkitTseutsautTsimshianTuscar
oraWinnebagoWyandotYellowknife

1972

nite

nite
sinks down
upon the earth

turning
its face
from the sun
at last

people singing
applauding
and crying

as all the stars
co-operate
and come out shining

1971, 1972

an opun letr tu bill bissett

deer bill
i don't think
i evr met yu
but sum peopul i no did

the rezun i am riting
this letr is tu tel yu
that i used sum of
yr lines

nd i hope yu
dont trn around nd
su me er such
as it is already

nd i bot one
of yr buks
tu pay yu bak sort of
sort of so yu wud no

i wuz making this
pome for mi
dan sing
chinese woman

so thanks a lot nd all
yrs truly wkeon
januari.9.72
in toronto nd such

1972

a kind of majik

a kind
of majik
in the way
the river
moves long
moon rising
hear animals
stop coff nd
growl along
the shore
but i just
keep rowing

1972

the eye of the raven

the eye
of the raven
black upon black
speck in the face
of the sun
flies so high
flies so high
flies so high
and you have been tricked
for even tho i am raven
i am man
and even tho i am man

you have been tricked
and i do not fly so high
in the face
of the sun
and the great
mystery
flies so high
flies so high
flies so high
flies so high

1972

moosonee in august

in moosonee
4 leathery faced
Cree women
sit in the shade
of a storm-gray church
even tho
it's only 50°

beaded necklaces
leather purses
& suede thongs
are cheap now
b'cause the tourist
season is almost over

the Cree women
are laffing
& hide their faces
behind a worn blanket
every time a man
raises a camera
in front of them

the other tourists
move on &
i pretend to
examine the wares

spread over a torn
piece of tarp

one woman
speaks to me
in a dialect
i cannot
understand
& i feel stupid
but smile anyway

my face
gets hot
when i walk away
and take the hand
of my blonde
woman

feeling
the black eyes
far behind me
nd the old Cree woman
are laffing
& hide their faces
behind a worn out blanket

1971, 1972

Kirkland Lake, Sept. 21

dark night
cold as stone
high flying
geese shriek
loud wind
and drunks
curse outside
broken down
boarding houses
Christ! it's going to snow

1971, 1972

eight miles from Esten Lake

5:15 a.m.
eight miles down the trail
lakes stand still
silence and mist
unbearably close to breathing

two loons
methodically work
the south shore of the pond,
dive and break surface

forty feet away and appear nervous,
but continue feeding

6:45 a.m.
return to town
soaking in the sounds of birds,
the dank smell of morning,
trying to bring it all back
to where it just doesn't belong

1972

in this village

in this village
this great
village
        i
        am no
        man's sun prophet
called canada
from the
tongue
        i can hardly
        manage my own
        day to day incidents
of my mother
earth ojibway
algonkin
        or resolve

> what's been past
> nd mystery of the sun

people of
long
ago

> i am standing
> before you
> sun

1990

for donald marshall

i've no secret old
time answer in
my hand

i've no majik justice in my sand

to challenge all
the inmate
time

to pray beside the sacred pine

i've no blazin fire trail
to sear the
wounds

nd close the ruptured aura burns

but seek her now nd
make it
end

seek her now nd see my friend

o great bear of the southern wheel
o great bear of the southern wheel
o great bear of the southern wheel
o great bear of the southern wheel

take the power
nd the
earth

take this breath to heal the hurt

take the power
nd your
healing

take the breath nd take this feeling

travel now in
breath nd
wind

travel now nd take the wind

travel now in
earth nd
land

travel now nd take the land

clothe him in
a yellow
gold

touch the pain nd make it old

1990

smoke nd thyme

they told me
to stop wearin
that old medicine shirt
to the office

nd i agreed this time

but i never told them
about the medicine bag
i made late in the nite

about the cedar flame
the smoke
nd the thyme

1990

i'm not in charge of this ritual

i'm not in charge of this
sun dance anymore
i'm hanging here
completely out of it
the lawyers nd therapists
have taken over
my breasts are pierced
nd writhin in the blood
nd pain
i'm not that brave you know
that's why my children
nd woman were
taken from me
that's why i'm takin it on alone again
i never did any of those purification rituals
that's probably why this isn't working
nd hallucinations start sneakin
into my work, i can't say home
because i don't have a home
i live in a room
making medicine bags nd
wonderin if the silver strands
nd gems i'm puttin in them will do the trick
i escape temporarily at nite catching
my breath at donut & pizza shops
where nobody talks nd everyone just eats
muchin nd chewin nd swallowin down
hunger in the nite
hah! despair wouldn't have the nerve to come
waltzin through the door here
it would be devoured whole
in one fat gulp
they're all lookin at me wonderin why
i'm so skinny nd still losing weight
they know i'm not one of them
but i'm there every nite

*performance
of the imaginary
indian?*

shakin over another cup of coffee
tired nd numb from another day of torture
i'm glad when the sun goes down
nd the crazy cool of dark comes
b'cos there's hardly anywhere left to hide
nd they'll find me in the mornin
nd drag me back to the dance
in front of the sun
i wish i knew how long this was gonna take
but there's always tonite
nd ah! there's always linda
always linda waitin in the nite
with smoky topaz eyes
with smokin lips nd thighs
pressed like a gem
from the earth
into mine
but even she's started lockin
her door at nite

1990

if i ever heard

if i ever heard
your love had gone pale

i would come out of this wilderness
with ojibiway majik
        for you

if I every heard
your love had gone without rain

i would come out of this wilderness
with my ojibiway river
        for you

if i every heard
your love had gone in the sea

i would come out of this wilderness
with ojibiway earth
      for you

if i ever heard
your love had gone in the nite

i would come out of this wilderness
with my ojibiway stars
      for you

1990

Spirit Warrior Raven: Dream Winter

A long time ago, in the land of the Anishnawbe, there was a man. His name was Raven and he was a great spirit warrior. I met the Raven man early one summer, not far from where our people came to fish in the spring. He had come a long way and was hungry and very tired, so I asked him to share my fire and food.

As we sat by the campfire, neither of us spoke. I prepared a small meal of fresh game over the open fire. We ate in silence and gave thanks to the animal spirits for the food we took that evening. Finally, I spoke to the Raven man.

"You have been away a long time, Raven. It is good that you came back," I said, as I watched for his reaction.

The Raven man closed his eyes and took a deep breath, then gazed into the flames of the campfire.

"I have passed through a Dream Winter," he said in a weary voice.

"Do you know of this land?" he asked.

I replied that I was not a shaman, but had heard of such a place. I said that I knew it was a spirit world and that it was not a safe place to be.

1993

the apocalypse will begin

and
we'll convene
again all right
and it'll be nothing
like you could ever imagine
and there won't be any petitions
seeking permission from anyone
there'll just be medicine wheels and dream catcher rings
everywhere and blow-outs that'll start to make oklahoma
look like
a saturday afternoon tea and nostalgia to get back
to something less onerous like maybe the little
big horn lyin' there naked and
frozen in the
dust

but
the claws
of these melodious birds
will be at your throat caressing
the chords and veins to choke out that
warbler sound and have you trill as sweet
as any song bird ever could
because this ain't gonna
be no picnic bein'
force fed
like

this
so get
ready for
that elixir so wild
and free and sweet that
you'll never go back, never again,
to the way you used to be

1997

replanting the heritage tree

A
lgonkin
Assiniboine
AthapaskanBeaver
BellaCoolaBeothuk
BlackfootCarrierCaughnawaga
CayugaChilkatChilcotin
ChipewyanCreeCrowDelewareDogrib
EskimoFlatheadFoxGrosVentreHaida
HareHuronIllinoisIroquoisKickapoo
KitwancoolKootneyKoskimoKutchinKwakiutl
LakeLilloetMaleciteMalouinMenomineeMetis
MiamiMicmacMississaugaMohawkMohicanMontagnais
MuskogeeNahaniNaskapiNeutralNicolaNipissingNootka
OjibwayOkanaganOneidaOnondaga
OttawaPequotPetunPiegan
PotawatomieSalishSarceeSauk
SaulteauxSekaniSenecaShawnee
ShoshoniShuswapSiouxSlaveStoney
SusquehannaTagis
hTah
ltan
Thom
pson
TlinkitTsetsautTsimshianTuscororaWinnebagoWyandotYellowkn
ifeZuni

1997

Gordon Williams [b. 1947]

Of Shuswap and Okanagan heritage, Gordon Williams was born in Vernon, British Columbia. From a young age, Williams had to fend for himself. In Vancouver during the 1960s, he wrote and published poetry in a number of community and literary periodicals, including *The First Citizen*, *The Indian Voice*, *Listen*, *The Malahat Review*, *Solo Flight*, *Tuatara* and *The White Pelican*. He attended Simon Fraser University and lived on the Burrard Reserve with Amy Marie George, Chief Dan George's youngest daughter. They had two sons.

Williams has continued to live in Vancouver, where he writes and paints. He also spends time with his brother in Orville, Washington, harvesting apples from his orchard. He has had a stroke and has periods of lucidity as well as confusion. His son, Nathan George, comments on the special quality of his father: "He sees, feels, and realizes much more than the average person."

The Last Crackle

She sat there by the west window
Unmindful of the mosquitoes who'd always
Manage to squeeze thru the screen mesh
Insect barrier. Now it was sunset
Again, so many days of waiting.

A long time ago there were hardly
Any bearded men, now the forests are full!
They've flung bridges across all our rivers
And even our lakes. The sky is filled with metal
Birds that make noise loud as thunder.

All our men are dead and our young ones
Have no ambition. They took it all away,
Those bearded men, with their strange ways,
"Kneel with us" they said, "and pray!"
Then they took our land and children.

Now they've taken their beards off and shorn their
Hair, and they smile quick as a rattler's strike;
Before you open your door, a face of stone,

Then before your door is fully open, a smile
Trying to sell an old woman beauty cosmetics.

Her eyes were closed, she seemed to be asleep
Her drifting took her back a hundred years or more to
When she was just a little girl throwing pebbles making ripples
On the water's picture of white poplar trees.
Her days of waiting were ended, her chair
Rocking her away, and the last rays washing her face,
While the chair gave away the last crackle.

1969

Lost Children

Walk in my moments of dejection
westward where the hot ball of fire sets
with no place in memory
an eternal day of misery
heavy coat knee length burden
cry in your hands loved ones
we will be gone forever
downtrodden people of the ways
born hundred thousand loser
hand gripped white knuckled
grasp, on the steering wheel
drive away to tragic ends
Miss Louise found dead in a hotel room
two bit flop bit part of dismal conclusions
Harry hasn't been around for weeks
he's left on a south bound freight
sad plight warrior lost in empty plain
black bird call thru the quiet dusty eaves
river flow into lake and out
grab your timber eastern wolves
lame horse has fallen to yesterday's ground
no bird can be dethroned from its skies
last week has been fairly profitable
apple blossoms cover the green picture field
a childish whimper fills Alec's barn
nail pierced Teddy's feet
and he cries in Wednesday's fold

wanderings in forest hills
pine needle bed under starry skies
hill men's children lost in the intellectual fields.

1971

Dark Corners

The hospital where I was born
is not there anymore
the town is—I think.

People were jovial winters
Summer just a breeze
over fields of alfalfa green
grasshoppers red and yellow winged
crackle from place to place
somewhere in the forties
as a little boy swatted them
world war years
jammed into tomato cans
war is for grownups
war is not for children
only mature people fight sensible
only children fight senselessly
blacken sister's eye—
if there were one.

Years floated by
bird in disguise
woodpecker pecking on rooftops
sleep was wonderful
and sunlight seeped thru
a crack in the attic
illuminating a path
thru dust particles—
no light reaches
the darkest corners

1971

The Day Runs

There is no one alive and the black flag flies dark birds perch upon the corpses tearing out their eyes, giant bells ring as the wind blows thru the city purging caverns of subways filled with those who had sought shelter something just destroyed their minds putting them all thru experiences no one could ever live thru caught unaware there were no heroes…an ape chiseled on a stone forming an image he saw in a pool looked quite like him except for irregularities caused by distortions of ripples changing the form of his face. Sometimes he saw visions of cathedral spires seemingly floating on clouds or a misty haze, these he never knew were pictures of a past…a black bird flew across the deep blue sky sun fire in his wings, occasionally looking to his right to his left keeping a sharp lookout on trees far below in which he had inherited memories of gunners that are now no more. The day picks up his clothes and runs nakedly westward sliding down the river into the sea. . . .

1971

Ernie

My cousin
    he said

I'd never amount
    to anything.

I thought
    to myself
"We're both in jail
so neither will he."

A prisoner
    died last night
because he couldn't
    take it—
he was tuff man
    on the tier.

I wonder
       if muscle
makes a coward
or is it
       skin and bone

                                                            1971

Creased Clinic

This is a calendar
              of January
       nineteen sixty-nine
on a Sunday
sufferin Jesus prays
hung over
and Monday
another week will begin
       trudge drudgery
       eight to five

on the front page
       of a dime
someone committed
              suicide
midway in the act
people prayed and laughed
in a single cell
Drawer "O" Burnaby 1, B.C.
gone to Essondale
home by the Fraser
Whenever you see things
other people can't see
it's all so childishly
              simple
people are animals
walking around upright
so many fucked up
       bears
a bear in isolation
(different from others
       of course)

stares at a nickel
in the year 32
could be there
    instead of here
        he thinks
maybe so...Buffalo Nickel.

Whenever someone
says I haven't got
all my marbles
I reach into my
pocket count them—
two is what I was
born with...
A man claimed he was
        Jewish
but he was an outcast
he said he didn't care
if Hitler got them all...
when his father was alive
        Jews were people
they died with his father.

P.M. eight
light bulb
suspended from
the ceiling
by a cord
a maddening glare
of pure turpentine
this is my world
I share it with none
but an occasional spider
whose only purpose
is to bring a message
askin for nothin
but to walk freely
across rented rooms
on vacancy signs
without reason
suddenly saying sorry we

have no room (never changed
in two thousand years) did we
did they? Tomorrow thinks.

1973

Justice in Williams Lake

A cold breath of dawn
speaks to the wind
to the flag fluttering across the sky
realizing that neither wind nor flag
        have ears—
only a heart
longing to see justice
withers
walking thru the gaping mouth of
        dawn
over the morning's bleeding lips
on last night's snow
first footprints red—
angry winds blow thru the chambers
of frozen minds
that won't serve justice
the wind blows colder
and the flag snaps angrily
bells of freedom ring
thru an idealistic dominion
publication
prints
splots
of ink
splotted splatted
blotted
plotted
democratic rapists
set free
fined forgiven—
Indian maiden
raped and killed
too young

too dead to smile
her murderers
set free
this is democracy
mute flags indifferent to lamentation
manipulation of justice
in Williams Lake.

1973

Jeannette C. Armstrong [b. 1948]

The purpose of my writing has always been to tell a better story than is being told about us. To give that to the people and to the next generations. The voices of the grandmothers and grandfathers compel me to speak of the worth of our people and the beauty all around us, to banish the profaning of ourselves, and to ease the pain. I carry the language of the voice of the land and the valour of the people and I will not be silenced by a language of tyranny.

Jeannette Armstrong was born on the Penticton Indian Reserve in British Columbia. She grew up speaking both Okanagan and English fluently. As a child, she often acted as a translator for members of her community. "It made me hear the difference in the languages and strive to bring the two together—to make English reflect Okanagan." Both parents influenced "the way we see the world through story. Although self-educated, my mother was an avid reader. She read to the whole family when we were young and encouraged us to read ourselves. My father was a really descriptive storyteller in Okanagan."

Armstrong attended Penticton Indian Day School on the reserve until grade 7. Then, "I got the shock of my life." Moving from a one-room Indian schoolhouse, she had to learn how to survive in a public school of 2500 children in Penticton, with non-Native rules and culture. "The description in my book *Slash* reflects pretty much what I felt. That's when I learned you figure things out as quickly as you can to survive. I would go home and tell my parents everything; together we would work out how to behave, what to do."

After completing high school in Kelowna, Armstrong embarked on the study of visual arts, completing a Diploma in Fine Arts at Okanagan University College. In 1978, she completed a Bachelor of Fine Arts at the University of Victoria. "A turning point in my life came when I returned to my community at the same time the Chiefs of the Okanagan decided to make education a priority. I had intended to work before going on to a master's program. I was recruited to help organize an educational stategy to develop an Okanagan curriculum." She helped found the En'Owkin Centre in 1979, then the Okanagan Indian Curriculum Project. In 1982, Theytus Books was established. "We needed indigenous writers, so the En'Owkin Centre became the En'Owkin International School of Writing in 1989." It offers Canada's only creative writing program designed for Native people. With Theytus, En'Owkin publishes

Gatherings, an annual journal of poetry, prose, oratory, and literary criticism of Native peoples of North America.

Jeannette Armstrong also serves on her community's traditional council as spokesperson. Known throughout North America and internationally as an advocate of justice for indigenous peoples, she consults with international councils and working groups on a wide variety of issues of concern to indigenous cultures.

Armstrong's publications include two children's books, her ground-breaking novel *Slash* (1987), the collection of poems *Breath Tracks* (1991), and the novel *Whispering In Shadows* (2000). She collaborated with Native architect Douglas Cardinal on the book *The Native Creative Process* in 1991 and edited the book of essays *Looking at the Words of Our People: First Nations Analysis of Literature* (1993). She was distinguished with an Honorary Doctorate of Letters from St. Thomas University, Fredericton, in 2000.

Armstrong has written poetry "since I was ten years old." Poetry, for her, is "something that's spoken inside, which I try to get outside, sometimes with a feeling of panic that I'm not going to get it written down in time. Prose is about bringing what's outside inside." She writes in a wide range of forms and voices: meditative, satirical, polemical, philosphical, lyrical. Storytelling and ritual are also incorporated into her poetry. Her poems take on the subject of language and formally experiment with it, as in "Green" and "Right It." "I want to continue to work with poems that deconstruct linearity, the page. Maybe someday I'll make a three-dimensional installation that will speak poetry the way I see it."

In-Tee-Teigh (King Salmon)

Time and space
did cleave
as one
then
through sun-flecked
ripples endless;
sleek and shining
you emerged,
In-tee-teigh;
now only in
memories dim
your sacred name
lives,
though a

million waves
whisper
to moonlit shores
In-tee-teigh
In-tee-teigh.

1968

Death Mummer

Yesterday I walked
by Thunderbird Park.
Tonight
With blood-stained fingers
I remove my mask
I think
walk
past garish totem-painted storefronts
down avenues that echo

There are no Indians here
None
even in the million dollar museum
that so carefully preserves
their clothing, their cooking utensils
their food
for taxpayers
from all over
to rush their children by

There are some good Indians
hanging around Kings Hotel
and they are dead
preserved in alcohol
it would be neater though
to kill us all at once
Whole clans and tribes
could be dressed and stuffed
Add a fifth floor to the museum
to accommodate them

Better yet
pile us up like cordwood

in those longhouses
we would be home at last
and it would be good value
I walk slowly and think back
I stagger under
the raw
hide pack
that I carry
and the clever mask that I have fashioned
for myself
from the bones and skin
of my dead tribe
and dipped in the fresh blood
of my brothers and sisters
scooped from old battle streets
near hotels

1976, 1991

Wind Woman

Maggie at night sometimes I hear you laugh

when I was ten we rode to huckleberry mountain
carrying ragged quilts and pots and pans
packed on an old roan mare called jeep
given to Maggie to help fill her baskets
I followed her
picking berries her failing eyes had missed
I listened as she talked in our language
half singing sometimes
for all the pickers to hear
her voice high and clear in the crisp mountain air
telling about coyote

I know how the trees talk
I said to Maggie
I heard their moaning in the night
while we lie so tiny in our tents
with those tall black pines swaying over us

she told me a story then
of how the woman of the wind

banished by coyote
carried her eternally howling child
tied to her back
as they moved forever through the tree tops
mother crooning to the child
how sometimes she would swoop down in anger
scattering berries off bushes

Maggie told me I had heard
the wind woman sing
she told me that I would remember that song always
because the trees were my teacher

I remember the song clearly
but it is always Maggie's voice singing
her songs
filling my world
with the moan of old dark pines
as the wind woman
that sings to me
follows
with her hungry child
wherever I go

1978, 1991

History Lesson

Out of the belly of Christopher's ship
a mob bursts
Running in all directions
Pulling furs off animals
Shooting buffalo
Shooting each other
left and right

Father mean well
waves his makeshift wand
forgives saucer-eyed Indians

Red coated knights
gallop across the prairie

to get their men
and to build a new world

Pioneers and traders
bring gifts   ← lol
Smallpox, Seagrams
and rice krispies

Civilization has reached
the promised land

Between the snap crackle pop
of smoke stacks
and multicolored rivers
swelling with flower powered zee
are farmers sowing skulls and bones
and miners
pulling from gaping holes
green paper faces
of a smiling English lady

The colossi   ← gods?
in which they trust
while burying
breathing forests and fields
beneath concrete and steel
stand shaking fists
waiting to mutilate
whole civilizations
ten generations at a blow

Somewhere among the remains
of skinless animals
is the termination
to a long journey
and unholy search
for the power
glimpsed in a garden   ← Green Grass, Running Water
forever closed   also makes explicit references
forever lost   to Eden; this is a mockery

1979, 1991

Dark Forests

It was spring when we met in Seattle
We danced the blanket dance
after the drum went quiet
there was warm sea
sand
and warm bodies
Maybe I was seventeen
you said you were from the owl clan

Once on Centre Island
we smoked a joint
laughed awhile
at birds coasting through clear summer

Then you told me about your son
It hurts me that he will never know
his grandfather was owl chief

In your eyes
a night bird trembled
in a dark forest

Wild roses blossom everywhere in the foothills
We walked to the buffalo paddocks
talked about this fall gathering of elders
Your red hairband showed allegiance
to spilled blood
to AIM
to Wounded Knee
to all of your hurts

That night we watched dancers
invoke kachinas
then you went to the ceremony
to speak to the masters
known only in shadows
who breathed your name
owl man

I have walked uneasy
down a long road
since they found you
covered in the first soft crow flakes
laid out in your best
eyes wide
mouth slack
your last master gratified

And I remember
always
in the night
owls call to each other

1980, 1985

Green

green   silence   softly
groping   into
          damp   earth   pushes   quietly
draws   tendrils   up   into
rich   dark   interiors
life   turns   to
                     green
reaches   toward   early   light
                     drenching   golden
fills   with
          clean   warmth   dew
soft   summer   breath
                               sends   whispers
                     easily   through
leaves   captures wind   swirls
          clouds   driving   rain
          washing   dust
                     moisture and   mystery
swells   twigs   moves
pollen   and   seeds   upward
                     scattering petals   moving
          forests   slumbering in tiny
pods   beginnings in   endless
          emerald   dance   circles

1983, 1991

Rocks

I study rocks
strewn into the distance

I scan jagged faces of dark cliff
for horses
with wings
examine underwater pebbles
rolling together
for signs
for a telling
of age old
crumblings
and majestic rises

I look long
at thunder eggs
lying silent unopened
wait ages
to discern the heart shaped moment
frozen inside agate

I ponder bearstone glowing red
heaped in the centre pit

I carry a round calm blue stone
secure inside a pouch
and lift tobacco
in a red smooth familiar shape
cupped in the palm

I strike rocks together
calling fishes upstream
watch pointed obsidian
arc upward
and trace ochre rock dust finger marks
on shadowy cave surfaces

I hold onto erect pestle contours
and move precise circles

against elegant curves
inside hollowed mortar

I release a polar bear's stealthy creeping
in midnight black slate

I observe rocks
placed shape to shape
become old sanctuaries
pounded
baked into brick
change into garrisons

I weigh ores liquefied
forged into ploughs
into swords
poured into moulds
polished into bullion
minted
into coins

I see boulders
move to roadsides
as solid bedrock blasted away
becomes tunnels
and mountains dissolve into grey slag piles
and coal black mounds
heaped on trains racing through the night
toward granite and glass wall towerings
in asphalt and concrete canyons
encasing marble stairways
burnished brass
and stainless steel
reflecting the cold lights
trapped in glitter rocks
set in gold
wrapped around fingers

I watched rocks
hurled and smash
into cars of old Mohawk men
women and children

on a bridge
in Montreal
and the million dollar
rock slide
blockades
on ten BC roads
after stones rained
down rock cliffs
on police lifting
human blockades
protecting the slow disintegration
of bones into sand
resting under head stones
on Liliwat land

In the foreground
rock pillared bridges collapse
under the groan of earth's rock changed
into tunnelings
shiftings and spewings
as old stone worked churches dissolve ever so minutely
in the sad rain
while in the distance
one tiny grain waits
to flower into glazing white

I study the rocks
I have set into a circle
opening to the east
on this mountaintop

1990

World Renewal Song

Nothing was good
The winds blew
and grasses died

I thought I was pitied
so I longed
for a Whole Time Song
I danced for it

in deerskins

I made thought with paint
in red lines
from little finger to the left shoulder
I silent,
listening by dying grasses
began hearing
at dawn

A new fire is lighted
The finished world is here
formed in mind patches.
It is come
the song for rain and green
and good

I sit by talking grasses now
with nothing more
to make a good world of
than thought paint
and dance talk in lines,
but song colours
pour over my world
and my good time
still goes on

1991

Reclaiming Earth

for my father Ma'kwala (Stone Head Knife) who attained freedom from the body
March 15, 1992

the jingle of spur rowels
and wagon wheels
across Blue Horse tracks
and pages
of hand drawn star maps
traced paths in parchment
pinpoint slits in painted rawhide
open to the moment
to slip the skin
away

to shake loose
the cocoon of organic being
encasing
clusters of incessant musings

the dreaming body
drops from the mastering of intent
caught in the force of absolute alignment
requiring the internal mouthing of sound
be stopped

the moment tightens
into fusion
transparent wings of incandescence
flash
then sink
mirror deep into violet
a light swift fluttering
into spots of jet blackness

a pure motion
clean
sure
speaking instantly
to rocks
trees
and eagle emanations
reclaiming
sky
earth
and stars

we wore eagle down
drummed the horse riding song
scanned the eastern sky
catching the glint of hooves touching milk dusty paths
and cheered
our feet holding heavy
to earth surface

1992

Apples

i go to you with the speed and the rhythm of a new found poem when dreams ripen i wait to sway in the breeze and wait to go into the night i wait to do the right thing by each of the small fowl and flowers as they flutter to live in this slow absurd world which finds its way into all our hearts time again and i am wishing that i will not fall out of the sky with words which only want to catch me in the net catch me i say and free fall it seems only like yesterday that you smiled your sunny gods glinting from your eyes and stars were climbed i know

the kind of thing I was hoping would come of my little cool wind seems to blow like a breeze through my time now and i wish for the gold light in your eyes to shine through the black cold dark of that place where you chose to be leaving us to think about dead poets and i do think of your smile and your hair and the impossible and there are times when i think of the satin touch of skin on skin and the beading of sweat between slick thighs and running my fingers over hard muscle and breathing the dark dark brine smell of that land and mackerel skies that folded over fast scudding clouds the apple pie was the best that i can think of and i had no thought for any other that night not at all then or now was i on wings or was i moving slow to the dance of the sea was i still

alone in that or was it a time of magic the keen margin that you talk of when flat grey and dark sharp angles suddenly soften and blur and colour tightens into focus and then we can see each other in the truth only found at dusks edge and sunlights rise the leaves were so dark red and the smell of burning was in the air together with a brisk touch of fall and the water made sounds murmuring an old sweet song in the tongue that shaped your soul i thought the fiddleheads and the apple dumpling rice pudding could hold and sustain i think of the taste now and imagine the sweet sound of blues and laugh lines at the corners of lips curved trickster sticking a paw on the back and i am pulled down with the pain and then again its only rain that plops and plops on the tin roof and leaves me shaken

1998

Right It

come on down to where   the pun is mightier than
the street   ease   into a rude   world
of imaginary silver   spoons   placating peoples
mouths   a language of true   seduction a maid
to order item   the price of which   is never right
when you do   the dirty work   spokespeople of
a thriving species   tread in this land   scape
goats abound   where fools rush   around here
the only thing   stronger
than grief and guilt   is hope   that this is
the new season   and it's in avoiding   melt   down
puddles   and getting a bird's eye   view from below
that keeps changing   things from where   change
is the passion   loose change   preferably
so where is   the festival in sweaty   palms
and nausea   in work to rule   in holding up
pretence   there
is love   here among the ruins   right it
down   as it happens
is   up

1998

Beth Cuthand [b. 1949]

When I was in my twenties I said I wrote to stay sane. And it was true. My solitary communion with the art of the word saved me from the darkness of the abyss from which I crawled every now and then for a bath, a meal and clean clothes.

But that was then and THIS IS NOW.

In my fifties, my communion with the art of the word is stronger than ever, but I write when I choose and not because I must. These days, the words are placed on the page with confidence, joy—downright glee! The real work is always with us—to raise peoples' spirits—to birth the fourth world and to celebrate life as we do it. The best is yet to come!

Beth Cuthand is a poet and educator of the Little Pine Cree Nation. Born in LaRonge, Saskatchewan, beside the Sandy Lake Reserve, she "saw lot of the old way of life." Travelling by canoe with her father Stan Cuthand, an Anglican minister, as he visited small, scattered churches, "taught us how to concentrate. These long canoe trips honed my powers of observation." Stan Cuthand, who later became a professor of Cree and Native Studies when he resigned from the ministry, "was always gathering stories. He would get involved in long conversations about what happened where and who did what." Cuthand attributes her own interest in history to these early influences. Her Irish-Scots mother was a teacher who gathered materials for underfunded schools—paints, crayons, paper, pens—to which her children had access. "She stimulated our creativity," says Cuthand. "Books were always around the house. Three things were not stinted on in my childhood: books, the dentist, and shoes."

The family moved to Cardston, Alberta, when Beth Cuthand was ten. "We lived right by the Blood Reserve, and my father, who had a Blackfoot grandmother, became interested in Blackfoot history and stories—and so did I." Moving south was a shock to Cuthand and her siblings—"we entered a racist world. For this reason all of us have a very strong desire to communicate—to try to promote under-standing." After attending high school in Cardston, Cuthand studied at the University of Regina and the University of Saskatchewan. From 1975 to 1983 she worked as a journalist for CBC radio and Native newpapers in B.C. and Saskatchewan. She received a B.A. in sociology from the University of Saskatchewan in 1986 and an M.F.A. in Creative Writing from the University of Arizona in 1992. She has taught English, creative writing, and Native Literature at the Saskatchewan Indian Federated College and the En'Owkin International School of Writing in Penticton, B.C. She now lives in Merritt, B.C. where she teaches English at the Nicola Valley Institute of Technology.

Beth Cuthand's first book of poems, *Horse Dance to Emerald Mountain*, was published in 1987. Her collection of poetry, *Voices in the Waterfall*, was published first in 1989, then expanded in 1992. Cuthand has also edited a number of literary works, including Maria Campbell's *Stories of the Road Allowance People*, Ruby Slipperjack's *Silent Words* and the anthologies *Gatherings V*, with William George, and *Re-Inventing the Enemy's Language*, with Joy Harjo and others. A children's book, *The Little Duck*, co-written with her father in Cree and English, was published in 1999.

A sustaining and energizing humour is typical of Cuthand's work. Many of her poems are written as if to catch oral voices—often from both past and present—on paper, or even to skip the page altogether, as in "Seven Songs for Uncle Louis" and "Post-Oka Kinda Woman." Others, such as "This Red Moon," use Cree symbols to convey visions, prophesy and ceremony.

Zen Indian

Zen Indian tiptoes into Taos
watches coyote disguised
as an ice-cream vendor
sell dollar popsicles
to thirsty tourists.

Fishes down the Fraser
for dried salmon
thinking a No. 10 hook
will catch those freeze-dried suckers.

Careens into Calgary in time
for Stampede; bells polished
feathers fluffed
to dance three times a day
for a free pass to the rodeo.

Makes it to Winnipeg
just after Bismark and right before
wild rice time
to get folk-sey at the Indian Pavilion

Then it's on to pick wild rice
for Uncle Ben;

drop a few rocks in the sacks,
shoot at the crows and reminisce
about how it used to be
before the harvest became
the domain of Bros in hydro
planes and enough money for gas.

Oh oh, cold's coming.
Time to find a fine filly
with a job, not too many kids
and a warm place to lay up for
the winter.

Put cities in a hat:
      Minneapolis, LA
             Boulder, Santa Fe
Calgary, Seattle, Salt Lake.

Yee-ha! Watch out Boulder!
Here he comes.
Zen Indian on the road to enlightenment!

1978, 1987

Seven Songs for Uncle Louis

In the seminary I pray

in the voice of young Louis Riel

In the seminary I pray
until my knees bleed.
St. Joseph doesn't smile
and the Virgin never speaks.

Taché
he says, "Pray, Louis,
you will go far in the Church."

I say the rosary until
my voice is hoarse but
St. Joseph doesn't hear.

Is the patron saint of the Metis
deaf to seminarians?

Taché
He says I will save the Metis,
it is God's will.

But,
my father fights for the people
and prays infrequently, at least
I do not see his knees bleed.
All he has ever known
is the fight to defend the land
and the liberty of the Metis.

Taché
he says God listens to the
supplications of lowly seminarians.
But does God listen to the Metis?

Louis Told Me

in the voice of Evelina, Louis' betrothed

Louis told me
        when his father died
        he felt him heave
        his last breath
and though
        he was miles away
        he heard his father say

        Louis David, to you
        I transfer my bundle.
    It is small and humble
        wrapping little things
        a bone
        from the last buffalo,
        a stone
        from the Assiniboine,
        a small pipe and tobacco pouch
   and,
        a feather
        from the broken wing
        of one who flew too low.
Louis told me
        he couldn't bear the
        burden of that bundle.

And when
> his father died,
> he was alone
> and the voices
> and phantom winds
> blew
>> his soul
>>> away.

"Evelina, Evelina,
> I have been seeking my
> shadow ever since."

We Orangemen

in the voices of an Orange Lodge chorus

We Orangemen
don't want that mixed-blood,
sullied by the savage
love of wasted land
singing war songs
in our parliament.

He is not one of us.

It is enough for us
that the French presume
equality with the blood
of our Empire
blessed by God and Queen.

No

Not Riel, uncivilized half-man
murderer of Brother Scott,
never will he sit with
the true men of Britannia.

We Orangemen know
what is best to bless
this new land:
> Our God, white and right
> to cleave away the wanton
> blood of darkness

riding long enough
from us.

No   Not Riel.

The Anglais They Say

in the voice of Louis Riel

The anglais they say
I am crazy
the francophone   and the Metis.

But you old man
Why   do you smile?

Because you are gifted, Louis,
with second sight   like me.

But you   are not a man.
They   do not perceive
you   as such.
You   are a savage
who drifts
        over crosses
and churches
        and votive candles.

Louis, learn to use this gift.
Smoke your pipe and wear your sash.
If I am gifted
        as you say

Why?
        do you   allow me
        to suffer?

Why?
        do you turn   into silent
                wings
        that disappear
        in the night?

When at Last I Found Him

in the voice of Gabriel Dumont

When at last I found him
   kneeling in the church
He was enraptured
   deep
   in communion
   with the One Above.

Tears
   engulfed him
Even   when the sun
stepping free
  from the clouds
  enveloped him
   with light.

And when he turned to us, I
  stepped forward enjoining him,
  Louis, come home.
They cry out and no one listens.
  They die and no one sees.

He came with us
  and near the Bear Paw hills,
I saw him gaze over them
  with such foreboding
  I entreated him to explain.

"I see a hangman's noose
suspended from the clouds."

We Came to Fight

in the voice of Sailing Horse, Cree war chief

We came to fight
with Louis at Batoche.
It was in the time
of the hungry pup
when our people
were dying
daily
of starvation and disease.

We had nothing left to lose
by fighting with our nistas.
Their fight was ours
because they were our relations.

We smoked together and
     Louis had a vision
     that we would be victorious
     under a clouded sky.

I wondered how it would be possible
     when we were so few
     with nothing left to eat
     nor bullets for our guns.

But I said nothing.
How could I question
a man's vision from the One Above?

Dumont pleaded with Louis
     "Let the Indian sharp shooters
     go out and harry the troops.
     Let them pick off the leaders
     one by one."

But Louis was resolute.
     "We must be civilized men of war."

Middleton's army marched
to the sound of music
foreign to the voice
of the prairie wind and
     we sang our honor songs
     to veterans of other wars.

For a moment our voices blended
     with Middleton's musical march
and with the voice of the wind
older than hungry pups or
civilized men until,

the army charged.

I tried to protect Louis
as I ran from cover to cover
shooting carefully at the redcoats.
My bear cub robe would protect me
if I wasn't foolish.
  But Louis and his God's cross
  seemed stronger than my Bear,
  at least, I thought so
  then.

Standing naked, in full view of the enemy
Louis prayed loudly, his voice carrying
  over the sounds of their
  gatling gun,
  cannons and rifles
  and the pitiful wails of the women.

Louis held his God's cross aloft
admonishing us to fight on.

We shot nails and stones
and buttons
ripped from the coats of
children.

And when the battle was lost,
  the sun clouded over
  and we fled,
  running for our lives.

  They say that when the
  Redcoats took Louis
  he was wearing only
  a ragged sash
  and carried his God's cross
  broken in his hands.

Fire and Ice

for Brian Mulroney from all of us.

Who was guilty of this breach of
natural law?

Who can say what love lead us to this,
what hate, what passionate lack of
faith.

Was it you whose fear overwhelmed
your best intentions?
Or was it my desire for respect
that daunted your pristine belief
that you knew better than I
what was "realistic" or "bizarre"?

How could you know
living as you did
in that cabin by the lake
with your Canadian Club and soda
mixed in that cold crystal glass,
that you were not
in the best of shape
to judge?

Whose delusions brought us
to this madness?

Whose voice unleashed
the rifles and the tear gas,
the cigarette burns
and the stones that broke
an old man's heart?

Don't tell me
you're prepared to listen if
I'll just behave.
Don't tell me
that time and patience
will heal these wounds.

Don't harbour your delusions, sir,
that ice will cool
this fire
that rages in my gut.

                                        1985, 1990

Were You There

for Joy Harjo

Were you there
on the White Sands?
Did you feel that primal wind
caressing the pores of your skin?
Did you smell the salt
of the old sea or
hear the silence roar
louder than the bombs
that blew on
Hiroshima or Nagasaki?

Were you there in Ottawa
when we rose as one
spontaneously
like a prayer for
all that we had been
and ever hoped to become?

Did you feel it then?
The whispered words of beings
older than their
laws or constitutions?

Were you there in the pine forest
in communion with those old trees
who keen for the people
laden with their burden
of grief and disrespect?

Were you there when the army
attacked the Kanesatake?
Did you feel the wind
shift
and blow the tear gas
back
on the Destroyers?

Were you there on the hill
when we called the Thunder?

It rained

and the land was green.

1990, 1992

Post-Oka Kinda Woman

Here she comes strutting down your street.
This Post-Oka woman don't take no shit.
She's done with victimization, reparation,
degradation, assimilation,
devolution, coddled collusion,
the 'plight of the Native Peoples.'

Post-Okay woman, she's o.k.
She shashay into your suburbia.
MacKenzie Way, Riel Crescent belong to her
like software, microwave ovens,
plastic Christmas trees and lawn chairs.

Her daughter wears Reeboks and works out.
Her sons cook and wash up.
Her grandkids don't sass their Kohkom!
No way.

She drives a Toyota, reads bestsellers,
sweats on weekends, colors her hair,
sings old songs, gathers herbs.
Two steps Tuesdays,
Round dance Wednesdays,
Twelve steps when she needs it.

Post-Oka woman she's struttin' her stuff
not walkin' one step behind her man.
She don't take that shit
Don't need it!   Don't want it.
You want her   then treat her right.

Talk to her of post-modern deconstructivism
She'll say: 'What took you so long?'

You wanna discuss Land Claims?
She'll tell ya she'd rather leave
her kids with a struggle than a bad settlement.

Indian Government?
            Show her cold hard cash.
Tell her you've never talked to a real live 'Indian'
            She'll say: 'Isn't that special.'

Post-Oka woman, she's cheeky.
            She's bold.   She's cold.

And she don't take no shit!
No shit.

                                        1990, 1994

For All the Settlers Who Secretly Sing

for Sharon Butala

You have seen my ancestors
riding in buckskins
down the coulee into the trees.
You have watched them
frightened that it is you who intrudes
awed, that it is you who sees.

You have met the hawk
soaring above you as you sit
still
waiting for the land to speak
to you who have not heard her
since you fled your lands across the seas.

At night you dream of drums
and hear voices singing
high in the night sky
and you wonder if the northern lights
are more than they appear to be.

And you hold these questions
in your heart not daring to ask
the indigenous people who hold
themselves aloof from settler voices
chattering.
You know they think no one listens
and you understand
the stillness it requires
          and the faith
          and the faith
to hear the heart beat of the land
as one solitude not two.

And you dare not tell the others
her song rises in you
yet it rises and you sing
secretly   to the land
          to the land

And then she knows sister/brother,
that you belong here too.

1992

This Red Moon

For Steven with love

Tonight
the moon is a hard red disk.

Passpassces predicted it would be so.

Your Grandpa told me the old man
fasted for twelve days
with my Great-Grandfather, Missatimos
at Manito Lake
in the time of the
hungry pup when the people
were starving and fearful
of what lay ahead.

Passpassces dreamed far and saw many things.

"The people shall suffer a long war," He said.

Passpassces saw and knew
in this red moon
flowed the blood of memories;

      groping hands in the night,
      innocent children crying silent
      keeping secrets too fearful
      to tell. Too shamed to know

      it was not their fault.

      black whirlwinds   raging anger
      turned back inside our souls
      men beating women, the
      mirrored images of their own self hate
      children watching
      thinking terror is life
      and love   too bloody to risk.

Passpassces saw the black water
invading our sacred spaces,
drowning our knowing that
life is to be lived and
love is what heals

Our relations cried out for us
in their love   in their love
for our red clay blood
cradled in our land covered in sky.

In that dark night they called
creation to guide us.
and
they smoked together and prayed.

Passpassces held the pipe
and wept and shivered for
the ache of our starving
and the confusion of memory

hardened to shame.

> "The red moon tells us
> The way back to life will be
> by doing battle   inside ourselves.
>
> This will not be war as we have known it:
> Many will die in the fight
> Many will run from the blood letting
> Many will hide in the black water
> Many will try to escape by the color of their skin

But
> More will claim their warrior blood
> More will pray their road to peace
> More will dance under the thunderers' nest
> More will sing their way to freedom
> More will make their marks on paper
> in the spirit telling of all this
> that we pray for those not yet born."

Passpassces fell silent
and the people murmured amongst themselves
fearful for our future
not knowing if we would find the courage
nor even recognize the war

"How will we survive?" they cried
(meaning all of us for seven generations to come)

How will we survive?

There's no way forward
but through
this red moon blood of memory
and the telling of it son.

And the victory

And the victory.

1994

Lenore Keeshig-Tobias [b. 1949]

I see my poetry and all writing, in general, as recipes in a cook book (the practical) or a book of enchantments and spells (the romantic). If it is written well then everything is there—the ingredients, order and quantity. All one needs to do is share it—read it, preferably aloud since its origin is in the oral tradition, and cast those words out into the air....

Lenore Keeshig-Tobias, Anishnabe Kwe, was born on the Neyaashiin-igmiing (Cape Croker) reserve on the Bruce Peninsula (in Ontario) where she now lives with her family. She attended St. Mary's Indian Day School on the reserve and then went to high school at Loretto Academy in Niagara Falls and Wiarton District High School.

Both parents encouraged Keeshig-Tobias to become interested in language and storytelling. The oldest of ten children, Keeshig-Tobias says she was herself a political statement. "My father, at about age sixteen, had to make a living, so he worked in lumber camps. On payday when he went to town with the guys, before spending any money he visited the library to look for books on Indians. He was often disappointed by stories about Indians disappearing or dying. So he decided he would find himself a pretty young wife and have lots of kids." Her mother, who had a high school degree and served on the band council, read poetry to her children—"she introduced me to Pauline Johnson. And my name comes from Edgar Allen Poe's 'The Raven.'" Her father told stories, including Nanabush stories in winter.

Keeshig-Tobias received her Bachelor of Fine Arts degree from York University, North York, Ontario, in 1984. During this time she began writing seriously, mostly poetry, although she asserts "I've always been a storyteller, even as a child." Journalist, storyteller, poet, children's writer, she is a radical advocate of Native cultures who writes partly "out of a responsibility to make an Anishnabec voice heard." Keeshig-Tobias has published essays in *Saturday Night*, *This Magazine*, *Fuse*, *The Globe and Mail*, and *Books in Canada*, and has worked as an editor for *The Ontario Indian*, *Sweetgrass Magazine*, and *The Magazine to Re-establish the Trickster*. She has worked to create awareness in Canada of the appropriation of Native stories and voice by non-Native writers. "When the day comes that there is equity between First Nations people and Canadians, *then* we can sit down and talk about the issue again" (interview with Harmut Lutz). Since the early 1980s, Keeshig-Tobias participated with Daniel David Moses and other Native writers in a group which became, in 1986, the Committee to Re-Establish the Trickster. "We published a magazine and did lots of speaking gigs in the 1980s. I think we got a lot of people thinking about the trickster again."

In 1989, Keeshig-Tobias served as the founding-chair of the Racial Minority Writers' Committee of the Writers Union of Canada. She served as chair of the Chippewas of Nawash First Nations Board of Education from 1993-98 and worked as a school-age teacher for Nshiime Day Care Centre at Neyaashiimigming. She is currently a professor of Native Studies at George Brown College in Toronto.

Her most recent publications are *Bird Talk* (1991) and *Emma and the Tree* (1996), bilingual children's books in Anishnabemowin (Ojibway) and English. Both are illustrated by her daughter Polly. *Bird Talk* won the 1993 Living the Dream Book Award (an award that commemorates the life and work of Dr Martin Luther King Jr). She edited *Into the Moon* (1996), an anthology of aboriginal writing. Her poetry has been published in a number of journals and anthologies.

Some of Keeshig-Tobias's poems, such as "In Katherine's House," "New Image," and "I Got Caught," are "dream poems." "My mother encouraged me in childhood to remember my dreams. I try not to editorialize or interpret, but to keep the spontaneity and immediacy of the dreams." One technique Keeshig-Tobias uses to create this effect is the use of the second person. "By using 'you,' I can make the poem a little more impersonal. And this allows me to give the power of the dream to the reader."

(a found poem)

Chapter 149

An Act Respecting Indians

Section 11. Subject to section 12.
    a person is entitled to
    to be registered, if that
    that person (c) is a male who
    who is a direct descendant in
    in the male line of a male
    male person described in
    in paragraph (a) or (b);

Section 11. Subject to section 12.

    a person is entitled to
    to be registered, if that
    that person (f) is the wife or

or widow of a person who is
is registered by virtue of paragraph
paragraph (a), (b), (c), (d) or (e);

Section 12 (1) (b)

The following persons are not
not allowed to be registered
registered namely, (b) a woman who married
married a person who is not an Indian,
Indian, unless that woman is subsequently
subsequently the wife or widow of a person
person described in section 11.

Chapter 149

AN ACT RESPECTING INDIANS

CHAPTER 149

(subsequently and
without reservation)

Fathers brothers uncles
chiefs warriors politicians
Where are the Women

"out there" you point
"somewhere"

we reach out into the mist
to women you refuse to see
to strength you cannot give
and will not give to emotion
you cannot feel to the other
half of our beginnings

we have ourselves and our daughters
and you my fathers have
sons and sons and sons

and section 12 (1) (b)
in the Act Respecting Indians

1983

At Sunrise

yes, i am afraid
of the timeless motion,
the cool green depth
and the dark silence
that would follow
should i drown there.

so strange then
that i should meet
sunrise
at one of those places
in my dreams

where passage
is always
difficult
and frightening—
that stretch of
shoreline on the east
side of the reserve
and the road.

with the clouds so low,
i thought i'd missed
the moment and knew not
exactly what i was
looking for in sunrise.

with the clouds so low,
so morning fresh,
i thought i could
step out onto the water,
stretch up my arms and
touch those wondrous beings.

the waves rolled in
singing, pushing pebbles
higher onto the shore and
took my breath away—
who was i to think
i could walk on water.

sunrise it was then
with pink and gold
reflections undulating
across the waves, mounting
and splashing at my feet
again and again
and i cast my tobacco
prayers onto the waves.

sunrise it was
that warmed my shoulders
as i left the shore
and crossed over the road to my sister's house and   our seven sleeping
daughters

1987

New Image

I

He is an Iroquois.
You can tell
by the scalplock.

He is a fine looking
brave wearing a breech clout
and carrying a warclub.

You know he is an Iroquois
because you have seen
a picture of him
in your grade
five history text.

You are at
the kitchen table
drinking coffee,
writing
as he looms in
through the open door.
His intent
is to kill you.

II

If you can push
your children's
green toybox
into his path he
will trip over it.
The toybox bumps
his shins and bounces
back. The childish
ploy does not work
and the Iroquois
warrior now towers
over you.

If you can get a
better grip
on the toybox and
push harder,
he will fall.
Slowly, bending
knees, keeping
an eye on him, you
lower yourself behind
the green box and
push again.
He steps over it
and reaches.

You lean back
and grapple for some
kind of weapon, something
from off the
table. There is a
splattering of blood,
of flesh. Vision is
blurred as your hand
sweeps deftly from left
to right over the
warrior's chest.

child - like reactions brings to light the limited knowledge about the Native

III

*The warrior is
stunned, and the
wound now
appears clean
and does not bleed.
He reaches
again, motion
deliberate. He lunges
toward you. It is
as if he wants
to die. And you
thrust a pen
into his heart.*

imaginary Indian is not real; its an idea

kill the idea

You stagger
under his weight, but
do not fall.
You cradle the young
man then lower him
to the floor and
prepare him for death.
Aaaiiieee!
Weeping, you kneel
beside him. Weeping
you ask—why? why
have I killed
one of my own?

Silent figures,
tribal guardians move
about in the shadows
of the room. They have
been there all the
while, watching.
Aaaiiieee! Why
have I killed
one of my own?
You mourn.

IV

The inside frames the
outside. The sky appears
bluer, the grass greener
than ever before.

From the dim and
now crowded kitchen,
you look
out to see
people gathering, coming
up the road, some
in groups, others
alone. They come
with condolence
and quiet
relief to see
the 'dead Indian.'
They mill about, not
speaking, paying
homage. The fallen
warrior, he is
beautiful in death.

[handwritten annotation: Idea — Indian is dead, so everybody / imaginary / is happy / relieved]

V

Your eldest
daughter slips in
from behind
a blanket, a backroom
and moves about.
She seems to be
unaware of your
anguish, and
the silent watchers.
She scrapes the
dead man's flesh
from the wall.
She plays with
it, singing
to herself.

Through your tears
you think she
is being disrespectful
Stop. Don't
do that.
The child looks up
and offers her hand.
You reach out
slowly to touch the
rotting flesh, and
recoil.

This child continues
her play. She
delights in shaping,
molding, making
new images. Her
face beams and
her hands glow
as do the tiny
spots on
your fingertips
that had touched
and refused
her offering.

She raises her
hand—Mommy,
see what I can do.

The ball of clay
is clean,
bright and alive.

[handwritten margin notes:]

Next gen. to create the new image

image re formed/reworked refers to nature—Indian relationship

potential for a new image

superficiality of the idea

1988

He Fights (bear iv)

They have been
talking, those ones,
talking, saying as
he grows older,
he becomes graceful

in his lumbering,
he becomes more
bear-like

secretly, he dreams
of bear, and
struggles hard
to let go of it, let
go of things
that hold Indian people
back, things that
pull them back,
back into
the white
man's dark ages

and he well knows
the importance
of becoming a
man, modern in wanting
progress and other
white man things

openly, he fights
his children
those searching,
those trailing,
tracking and bumbling,
and yet, as the years
wear on, he walks
more and more
like the bear
they seek

1993

In Katherine's House

dedicated to our grandmothers, mothers and aunties

I

You are standing in
a pink attic where
the walls bulge bare
and empty of family
gone too long.

You are standing in
a pink attic where
the stairwell hangs
steep and narrow
like old bones in a fragile frame.

In this dream
you have come.
You have come to this
forgotten woman. For
guidance? Maybe for
knowledge? For
something. And yet
you stand here
in this dream
daydreaming in her
pink attic
while she sits downstairs
alone, waiting.

II

You make her a cup of tea
and feel compelled to
give her something,
a gift, anything—an old greasy washer
picked up on the way.
Perhaps in another time,
another age
it could have been a coin.

She fingers that small
gift and years of memory
unfold between you
and sunshine and summer
fields full of flowers
and endless youth,
days so long ago—
now so near.

You see age break and fall
away like an old worn
shell. The old woman
becomes youthful
again, radiant again,
knowing you sit here
listening, breaking the
spell of senility, of
useless and lonely years.

III
You know you'll
come back, back to
this dream, if you
can find it, and Katherine.
You'll make her tea
You'll sweep her floor.
And you'll listen.
You'll come back to listen.

1996

Emma LaRocque   [b. 1949]

Poetry provides one of the best transitions between oral and written literature, and since I grew up with Cree, I found poetry almost a "natural" avenue of soul-ful expression into English. But I write poetry mostly for the love of words. My Nookum and my Ama had an excellent way with words in Cree. Poetry provides me with the joyful challenge of playing with words. Through poetry I am passing on ancient Cree traditions. Also, through poetry I am keeping alive the voices of those I have loved and lost: my grandparents, my aunts and uncles, my beloved parents, my land—voices that I always "hear" deep within me. Poetry provides me creative freedom that scholarship, by its very nature, does not allow. With poetry I can stand on my own feet without having to qualify each thought with a proviso or a footnote. Poetry serves a prophetic function in our morally lethargic society. Finally, I write poetry because I must.

"As Tomson Highway would say, I was born on a trapline. Actually, I was born in a one-room log cabin near a trapline," says Emma LaRocque, a Plains Cree Métis. She grew up in a small Métis community in northeastern Alberta. Her father worked on the railroad in the summers and trapped in the winters. Language and eloquence were respected and enjoyed. Both her mother and her grandmother were "riveting" storytellers. For LaRocque, "the ethos of Cree culture—a love of excellence, a love for words among other things" is part of her poetry.

As she details in her essay "Tides, Towns and Trains," LaRocque also experienced a blistering racism when she attended grade school in the town near her community and high school in southern Alberta. An encounter with a perceptive Mennonite principal in junior high encouraged her to become an educator herself.

When LaRocque attended university at the age of nineteen, she began to gain a political understanding of her people's economic poverty and marginalization: "institutionalized oppression was an earth-shaking concept to me." Beginning a long career in academia, she received a B.A. in English/communications in 1973 and an M.A. in religion in 1976, before going on to achieve an M.A. in history and a Ph.D. in history and English at the University of Manitoba in 1980 and 1999. In 1975, she published *Defeathering the Indian*. LaRocque has been a professor in the department of Native Studies at the University of Manitoba since 1977. A social and literary critic as well as historian, she has lectured nationally and internationally on issues of human rights, focusing on Native history, colonization, literature, education, and identity, and has written numerous scholarly and popular articles.

LaRocque has published poetry in national and international journals and anthologies, such as *Native Literature and Canadian Writing,*

Four Feathers and *Writing the Circle,* to which she wrote the preface. The influence of Métis and Cree heritage in her poetry "is a question of nuance, of spirit in my work—it's subtle and difficult to put into words." The experience of "profound racism and dispossession" has given her "a passion" to write against the destructiveness of racism and related social violence. LaRocque's poetry often combines lyrical imagery with sharp-eyed irony and self-awareness. She writes movingly from a position of exile, wearing "the uniform of the dispossessed," and remembering, with strong emotions, a life on the land that has disappeared, a land never acknowledged legally, but one which "my ancestors loved and nourished long before con-federation was ever conceived." At the same time, her poems sug-gest a tough endurance gained from living between two worlds and forging a new existence: "calling names in Cree/bringing down their mooneow hills/in English too/this is home now."

Incongruence

A verdant, crooked path
So earth-soft
Framed by ash and poplar
Surprised by red berries
waving from the undergrowth
Enveloped by a warm, cerulean sky
Your beauty knives through me
as a cold snap in October.
I should be holding hands
With my lover
I should be picking berries
With my mother.

                                                                    1990

Commitment

My father
Bends low
His brown face
etched
with grief.

With veined hands
He pulls the weeds

He rearranges the rocks
That held the tarp down
That covers
The flowering mound
That covers
Her death.

47 years together
And at 82 his hands
as strong as the love in his bones,
So caringly, so angrily
does he rip those weeds
To make her place of rest
As neat as her house was.

If he could
I know he would
lift her
tenderly
out of there
out of solitaire
and hold her
and caress her
in the way of their youth.

1990

The Beggar

i met a boozed-up, begging Indian
on the proverbial mainstreet
ten years ago
when i had no money
i would have fed him
today
i slinked off
in my unfaded blue jeans
harry rosen plaids
and turquoise rings.

then
i stole a poem.

1990

Nostalgia

Where does it go
the log-cabins,
woodstoves and rabbit soups
we know
in our eight year old hearts?

I tried to hold it
with my Minolta
As Sapp stills it
with paint and brush.

I ran out of film,
and Sapp out of brushes.

1990

The Red In Winter

The blushing river the Cree called her
She wears no rouge today
She speaks no Cree
I ask about her other lifetimes
beneath her white mask.

1990

"Progress"

Earth poet
So busy
weaving
        magic
into words

so busy
placing
        patterns
quilting
        stars
so busy

making
        the sun
dance
so busy
singing
        your songs
in circles
so busy
tipping
        moons
in dreams

Earth poet
so busy
touching
        the land
        scape
mad modern man
must take me
look at
cold steel spires
stealing earth and sun
        dance.

1990

The Uniform of the Dispossessed

Sometimes I forget
so I buy soft things
surround my hard-won world
with synthetics
pastels
cushions
and Zamfir.

Sometimes I forget
so I go to theatre
surround my hard-won world
with cafes
espresso coffee
truffles
and Brubeck.

Sometimes I forget
so I buy books and brandy
surround my hard-won world
with ceramic thoughts
with silk shirts
modular sofas of burgundy
that match
     that hide
     the sorrow of the past
     the sorrow of woman
     the sorrow of the Native
     the sorrow of the earth
     the world that is with me
     in me
     of me.

Sometimes I forget
the combatant who has deserted

But I get recalled
Remembering
The uniform of the dispossessed
and like a court-martialled soldier
I cannot evade.

Sometimes I want to run
But I can't—
     I can't
         I can't.

1990

My Hometown Northern Canada South Africa

How did they get so rich?
How did we get so poor?
My hometown Northern Canada South Africa
How did you get so rich?

We were not always poor

How did they get
our blueberry meadows
our spruce and willow groves
our sun clean streams
and blue sky lakes?
How did they get
Their mansions on the lake
Their cobbled circle drives
with marbled heads of lions on their iron gates?

How did they get so rich?
How did we get so poor?

One sad spring
when my mother my Cree-cultured Ama
was dying
Or was it
the sad summer
when my father my tall gentle Bapa
was dying
I stood on the edge
of that blue sky lake
to say goodbye
to something
so definitive
no words in Cree
no words in Metis
no words in that colonial language
no words
could ever say

I looked at my hometown
no longer a child afraid
of stares and stone-throwing words
no longer a child
made ashamed
of smoked northern pike
bannock on blueberry sauce
sprinkled with Cree

I looked at my hometown
Gripping my small brown hands

on the hard posts of those
white iron gates
looking at the lions
with an even glare

How did they get so rich?
How did we get so poor?

How did our blueberry meadows
Turn to pasture for "Mr" Syke's cows?
How did our spruce and willow groves
turn to "Mr" Therien's General Store?
How did our aspen covered hills
Turn to levelled sandpiles
for gas pipelines
just behind my Nokum's backyard?
How did our moss-green trails
down to the beaver creek
turn to cutlines
for power lines?
How did the dancing poplar leaves
Fall before their golden time?
How did my Nokum's sons and daughters
and their sons and daughters
and their sons and daughters
Fall before their seasons?
How did my auntie Julia die?
When she was 19 she was found dead
under a pile of sawdust
long after it happened
She was last seen with a whiteman
sometime in World War II they said
There was no investigation
Not even 16 years later

Now did my Nokum lose her grandchildren
that she so carefully housed in her loghouse
made long by her widower sons?
Was it really about
a child stealing a chocolate bar from
Therien's Store?
Or was it about The Town
Stealing children to make us white

Taking Uncle Ezear's Lillian Linda Violet
Taking Uncle Alex's Lottie Robert
all they had left
after T.B. stole their mothers
in far away places of death

How did my uncles Alex and Ezear die?
Singing sad songs on the railroad tracks
on their way home from Town
2 a.m. in the morning
Was it really by the train as the RCMP said?

When did my mother and her sisters
Catherine, Agnes, Louisa and Mary
stop singing
those haunting songs in Cree
about lost loves and aching
to find their way home?
When did they lose the songs
those songs in their steps
Wasn't it when the Priests the Police
and all those Home and Town good boys doing bad things
came
No one talks about it
My Nokum and her daughters
Singing sad songs on the railroad tracks
on their way home from Town
2 a.m. in the morning

How did we put away Pehehsoo,
and Pahkak?
When did we stop laughing with Wesakehcha?
When did we cross ourselves
to pray to Joseph and the Virgin Mary?
How did we stop speaking Cree
How did we stop being free?

How did they get so rich?
How did we get so poor?

How did my Bapa and Ama's brothers
Alex, Ezear and Victor
and my aunties' husbands Stuart and Moise

lose their traplines?
Was it really for the Cold War planes
Or was it for one of those cold marbled lions?
And what war
takes my brothers' traplines today?
Some say to save the lions

My hometown Northern Canada South Africa
making marble out of lions
making headstones out of earth
turning the earth on
Nokum's sons and daughters
and their sons and daughters
and their sons and daughters
turning Nokum
into a bag lady
before she died in the Town ditch

How did they get all the stones?
Those stones in their fireplaces,
Those stones around their necks,
The boulders in the whites
of their eyes,
Those stony stares,
How did they get the marbled stones in their hearts?

I look at you
My hometown Northern Canada South Africa
I look at you
no longer a child afraid
of stony stares
and rockhard words
no longer a child
made ashamed
of my Cree
dipped in cranberry sauce
giggling with Wesakehcha
I look at the paper head-dresses
you got from Hollywood
for your Pow Wow Days
Trying to feel at home
in your postcard tourist ways
Giggling with Wesakehcha

I look at the turquoise
in your stones
I look at your lions
with an even glare
Even in my dreams I see

But still
I look
From the inside out
Gripping my still brown hands
on the hardposts
of White Iron Gates

My hometown coldstone Canada South Africa

1992

Long Way From Home

I've walked these hallways
a long time now
hallways held up by
stale smoke
thoughts

I've walked these hallways
a long time now
hallways pallored by
ivory-coloured
thoughts

I've walked these hallways
for a long time now
hallways without windows
no way to feel the wind
no way to touch the earth
no way to see

I've walked these hallways
a long time now
every September closed doors
stand at attention
like soldiers

guarding fellow inmates
guarding footnotes
guarding biases

as I walk by

I do my footnotes so well
nobody knows where I come from
hallways without sun
the ologists can't see
they count mainstreet
bodies behind bars
they put Ama's moosebones
behind glass
they tell savage stories
in anthropology Cree

My fellow inmates
they paste us prehistoric
standing in front of us
as if I am not there too
as if I wouldn't know
what they think they show
showing what they don't know
they don't know what they show
they take my Cree for their PhD's
like Le Bank
as my Bapa would say
they take our money for their pay

When I first came to these hallways
I was young and dreaming
to make a difference
thinking truth

With footnotes pen paper
chalk blackboard
I tried to put faces
behind cigar store glazes
I tried to put names
behind the stats
of us brown people
us

us brown people
in jails
in offices
in graveyards
in livingrooms
but to them it was
just Native biases

I've walked these hallways
a long time now
hallways hallowed by
ivory-towered
bents

way too long now
hallways whitewashed with
committee meetings memos
promotion procedures
as fair as war
pitting brown against colonized brown
choosing pretend Indians

When I first came to these hallways
I was young and dreaming
to make a difference

but only time has passed
taking my Ama and Bapa
my Nhisis my Nokom
my blueberry hills

I've walked these hallways
a long time now
I wanna go home now
I'm tired of thinking for others
who don't wanna hear anyways

I wanna go home now
I want to see the evening stars
get together for a dance
the northern light way
like Ama's red river jig
I want to see the sun rise

hot orange pink
like Bapa's daybreak fire

no one could see the morning come
as my Bapa
no one could scurry in the stars
as my Ama

I wanna go home now
but where is home now?

I do my footnotes so well
nobody knows where I come from
my relatives think
I've made it
they don't know
how long I've walked these hallways
my feet hurt
at 43
I wanna play hookey
but I can't
I have credit cards to pay
footnotes to colonize
My relatives think
I've made it
they don't know
who all owns me
they won't lend me money
from their UIC's
my relatives laugh.

Oh I did my footnotes so well
nobody knows where I come from

I've walked these hallways
with them a long time now
and still they don't see
the earth gives eyes
injustice gives rage
now I'm standing here
prehistoric and all
pulling out their fenceposts of civilization
one by one

calling names in Cree
bringing down their mooneow hills
in English too
this is home now.

1994

Rasunah Marsden [b. 1949]

The Anishnabe were known as "The Good People." Literature embodies the essentials of life through storytelling. Words or phrases which struck me in literature led me to the fascinating idea of "living letters," or words which had a life of their own; even the spaces or silences between words and in languages speak from within the power of all human relations, community and natural nobility of existence. Writers, artists, musicians are cultural carriers. Through a contribution of talent(s), I try to express and celebrate a tangible "je ne sais quoi," a "strange but real" love of life.

Of Anishnabe and French heritage, Rasunah Marsden was born in Brandon, Manitoba, and lived until the age of seventeen on the Canadian Forces Base at nearby Shilo where her father served in the army. Moving to the west coast to attend university, Rasunah received a B.A. in English literature from Simon Fraser University in 1974. She also completed teacher certification and course work for an M.F.A. in creative writing at the University of British Columbia. "Studying with George Woodcock and others at U.B.C. was encouraging," she says. "They were critical but they enjoyed what they were doing—that was the greatest inspiration."

After traveling to Australia in 1982 "to discover other states of mind," Rasunah spent seven years in Jakarta, Indonesia, where she taught English language courses, worked in Telemedia, a tech-transfer company and for Matari Advertising. "I purposefully opened myself to various disciplines of writing—technical, educational, commercial—because I wanted to break the 'post-romantic, neurotic, burnout approach' to what people think writing is; I didn't want to limit myself to a literary space." In 1990, she moved back to Australia, where she received a post-graduate diploma of design from the University of Technology in Sydney. Returning to Canada in 1995, she currently teaches creative writing at the En'Owkin International School for Writing in Penticton, B.C.

Rasunah's travels "have definitely affected my writing in ways impossible to sum up. For instance, people in Java have time for fine attention to detail. They also accept a wide range of human behaviours. Culture is treasured, and lived. Traditionally the kings of Java explored esoteric and mystical practices; they are the cultural caretakers of their people. This was part of their role for centuries." In Jakarta, Rasunah published a chapbook entitled *Voices* (1987). Her poems have also been published in *The B.C. Anthology of Poets, The West Coast Review*, and *Gatherings*. In 2000, she received a B.C. Aboriginal Arts Award to compile a collection of her prose writings and is the editor of *Crisp Blue Edges* (2001), a first Indigenous collection of creative non-fiction.

The richly embroidered imagery of Rasunah's poetry is compelling. Her poems can take surprising turns, such as from the natural world to the eternal or otherworldly in "Yellow Leaves" or from Canadian "worlds" to Indonesian in "Dance of the Rounds."

Father

just a white line
a pool of light
& beyond it, darkness

once a year I traveled
with my father. North, north
to the summer holiday
on a cool night

I sat in the back seat
long, long into the night
& got to know the signs

3 curves coming up
go slow here
bump: talking from behind

happy to be kept awake
& keep awake
he was happy, there was

just a white line
a pool of light
& beyond it, darkness

                                        1976, 1986

Condolences for Marius

I should have called to tell you, Marius
That it is snowing on the mountain
So you see, the land is cooling out, softly
Just as you dreamt

Who did you think wished this, Marius?
Great, fat pudgy flakes
Not just for myself only

I knew it would snow, do you remember?
We agreed upon it, the day before

The snow will deepen
Covering what we have brought to it, delicately

1976, 1986

Three Objects

one side was male
wizened long beard
the other female
full faced
both with mirror or bowl in hand
formed of the same seated body
face in face
curved long lines robed
jade perfect even atop
carved roughness out of
rock

grotesque
this guardian
majestic
teeth curl round
firebreathing sneerholes with
mane Egyptian waves
& tail
this lion

sheaf rectangular bone
curved at each end
old ivory &
black
stripe down center
enameled red words villages mountains
on either side
one hundred slender teeth

1976, 1986

Kinanti: A Fragment

this is the river with tributaries which led to the ocean
overloaded with the silt of civilization
whose surface is glazed over with reflections
of genocide. I flowed through borderless lands
in childhood days; the salt in oceans cleansed my blood
no shores were foreign to me;
under the dazzling suns of history
the cool hands of toiling mothers
shook out their secrets & hung them out to dry

this is the mountain over whose rugged, refreshing terrain
& forests, animals & beings were swallowed whole by memory
over whose wind-swept heights the intellect of mankind's genius
was reduced to broken debris. I rose out of limitless aspiration,
& scoured heaven for a resting place. Buried deep in my womb
were the inspirations of mankind, borne out of my ears, where snow
sweeps sky, & where the spirit of the times spawned the issues of the day.

this is the wasteland upon whose aridity
the foundations of will & force are laid. Know me as shape-maker,
the instrument which fashions glass from dust that I am;
for the sword of power thrown to earth by passing meteorites
& wrought into the scepters of kings who wielded them that I am;
know me as creator who traced their outlines as wind follows sand
& out of which all images are authored, their comings & goings
delineated as sharply as are oases forded overland, that I am.

(Kinanti: Culture)

1992

Valley of the Believers

I'll say it this way:

you know they're going to walk deep
into the forest & dissect it, they're going to bring
microscopes & dirt samples & there'll be seekers
of wine & the bread I broke with you
or anyone. they'll peer between the leaves

& note the smudges, yes, & they'll find the bodies
strewn everywhere, & there'll be a collusion
of confusion & blood & screams,
(some of them mine) & they'll gut the place
of gold & emeralds & desecrate my sacred ground
& they'll water down every element
of purity & quality they find,
except for one thing:

by that time, you'll be able to smell me
in their pores, & I'll have touched upon
the essence of them
of every thing, & in that valley of tears
we shall already have become One.

1996

Wordmaker

I was a vessel
& delirious with intention
in early days, collected them
as foundations stones
strewn before the ever-
receding horizon
I was a reservoir
& they flowed into me,
or rose to the surface
& those aerated by light
lost dross & took on lustre

from silken threads
lying in baskets
wove coats of many colors,
fanciful clouds.
I was a rain maker
whose reverent channeling
of essences echoed songs
of natural elements.
I was a painter,
mixed colors nearest me
by hand, dreamt feeling

onto canvas, hid winter supplies
down bottomless wells
during eons of delight

hoarded every weight & hue
which from time to time
separated out into rainbows,
    (they had a history
    & so did I)
& worlds were born
in the places that we met…

a lover, seer or alchemist
awaiting in deepest caverns
of shimmering columns of light
near crucibles, seeking
to change gold into breath
finds only those hands
    which shall transform him
finds only those eyes
    which ferry him
across the burning seas…

1998

Dancing the Rounds

this page & I dance by lamplight in nights
before modern conveniences
I join hands with the ancestors
who jigged & drank
thru log cabin living rooms
in the rugged bays of lakesides
whose tree-scraped skies
were cluttered with the spirits of World Wars
& I join hands with all the brown-eyed children lost
or abused and the families whose spirits
are still being broken by anger & greed

by the shadowy flicker of lamplight
I step gingerly over borders centuries old
& watch the repetitive fall of kingdoms

& the lives of princes & saints unfold;
in fields of revelation unceasing
exquisite orchids grow

as I drive to this valley
ringed with the history of desert survival
loved ones past & present recede,
recede into landscape,
are submerged in memory -
so many leaves under snow,

the wake of creation,
is littered with the detritus
that we are: as under a lens,
still transparencies,
(or only so many hurled stars) ;
are traced onto the page, fleetingly
until it is folded & yellowed

(in the dance of worlds,)
the pulse of her blood thru our hearts
enlivens the play of words

in time which sanctifies or existence which typifies
the natural illumination of all things, between particles
of dust which permeate the air we breathe,
between shadows irradiated by lamplight on the screen,
dust, leaves, stars scatter, are folded away

1999

On Your Passage

the day is grieving
    & it is long with loss
        & you express
            a need to know yourself
I listen
& listen

the day is giving
    & full of unshed tears
        solitude becomes me again

I listen
& listen to

the day is leaving
      & overshadowed by night
           higher life forces
              shape new thoughts

I listen, I die to myself
& follow

the night listens
     to moments
         filled with living

1999

Tossing Around

that orchid's other-worldly,
grows fastened onto a certain tree,
blooms only on special nights,
you need to watch for it or you'll miss it
& the other way that orchid has
is to inseminate all within reach
with its exotic odor, so drop everything
you're doing, that orchid's there
to be admired, incandescently glowing
near the goldfish pond,
just YOU don't forget what it takes
to care for that orchid
or you'll writhe in pain
with what it is capable of suffering
something about that orchid
I'm still tossing around

that crow he's a black fool,
hanging around, making lots of noise
crowbeak between your fingers feeding,
but you can bet he'll be first
to graze on your innards
should you decline in strength, that crow
knows exactly what he's up to

just YOU don't forget what he wants
or he'll be gone
something about that crow
I'm still tossing around

2000

Yellow Leaves

yellow leaves announced premature change
earwigs crowded windowsills or fell off countertops
fat flies & then the mosquitoes thinned out drastically
hornets buzzing around the sap of the tree
finally burrowed holes underground as the level of the lake
sank, & with it I began yet another year's hibernation

that week my niece called to announce
she'd survived the birth
if not so joyously as her newborn son
& my children's calls quieted one by one
eventually all the curtains were drawn & with them
dreams of the real you who waited for me
were dreamt in better worlds
in better worlds where the trees were filled
to bursting with yellow leaves

2000

Skyros Bruce / Mahara Allbrett [b. 1950]

It is my wish that this poetry bring joy, reflection and inspiration to others. I write because I have a great desire to connect and express my inner life.

Skyros Bruce is from the Sleil Waututh Nation ("the people of the inlet") on Burrard Inlet near Vancouver. In 1977, she changed her name to Mahara Allbrett and prefers since to be known as Mahara. Born in Vancouver, she was raised by her grandparents. Her grandmother, Susan Long, a sister of Chief Dan George, encouraged her writing and introduced her to Pauline Johnson's writing. She recalls running free, as a child, on her great-grandmother's land, "climbing huge cherry trees, eating all kinds of fruit from her orchard, riding my great-uncle's work horses, picking berries, swimming in the ocean, fishing and eating our catch." Mahara attended elementary and high school in North Vancouver and, in 1969, Simon Fraser University. She began to write creatively in grade 8, and her writing was encouraged by her high school English teacher, Bill Woodward. Through him, she was introduced to Professor Lionel Kearns of Simon Fraser University, who published her collection *Kalala Poems* (*kalala* means "butterfly" in the Salish language) under the imprint of Daylight Press in 1973. During the 1960s and 1970s, she published poetry in numerous little magazines and Native periodicals in British Columbia. At the time, Mahara was also reading the writing of Sylvia Plath, Dorothy Livesay, Sarain Stump, Margaret Atwood, and Richard Brautigan.

In the 1970s, Mahara took intensive training in yoga at the Yasodhara Ashram in Kootenay Bay, BC, "which had a profound impact on my life." She now has a private practice in family therapy and studies art part-time at the Emily Carr Institute of Art and Design. When her marriage ended in 1994, she returned to the writing of poetry. Her most recent work has been published in the periodical *Gatherings*. Her daughter, Sarain, also writes and creates visual art.

Mahara's early work connects west coast landscape and cityscape with inner states of mind and suggests the rhythms and idiom of spoken language. It is also imagistic; as one (anonymous) reviewer of the 1970s put it, her early poetry tended to "freeze the moment" and "share ... her susceptible awareness of everything around" (*TAWOW*, Vol 3.3). Part of the awareness she shares in "the mountains are real," Lee Maracle has suggested, is the blending of past and present within the single moment (*Gatherings* 2, 1991). Her early work also shows a growing acknowledgement of a Native identity, as in the poem "In/dian." "My writing is inspired by deep emotions, usually," Mahara says. Intense emotions resulting from her sister's accidental death inform both early and later poems, such as "in a letter from my brother, Atlantis" and "Linda Louise." Lately, she has "surprised herself" with the writing of erotic poetry.

when the outside is completely dark

when the outside is completely dark
and the room is within itself
shadows adjust.
the tree alone is
a beautiful growth if the sand
yields to the sun.
houses are marks, black
against the soil.
poor man
in love
and unity—
he is not
even as the blades of grass
imprint on his body
he is not
the shells
the tide
i am not the moon
though worlds revolve
within me
and shadows adjust
to the dark

1973

eels

The little coloured shells
Slide
And scurry
An inch under water
Sticks come alive   in sea water
And slip between   my fingers
Sister Kath
Runs in

Splashing
Up to her knees
Trickling sea water
Down my sunwarmed neck
In the sand
        We ate
Orange salmon berries

1973

in a letter from my brother, atlantis

once i dropped 500 micrograms
and you know where   i sat?
for two days
i sat on our sister's grave
wishing it was her
sitting on me
that night while i cried
you watched the tears
and my face
like someone watching
the rain

1973

in

dian

we are north americans
he said
and made me feel
ashamed   that i was not wearing
beads at my throat
small proud flowers
growing there
or leather.
sarain stump
handsome faced
color of earth rose
quietly
telling me that i am

indian now
and ending all
the identity fears
the spiritual smell
of burning sweet grass
i smoke from the pipe
my brother passed to me
i pass it to my sister
it goes around

1973

the mountains are real

the mountains are real
they are me
i slept beside these mountains
near this water
long before i was born
in the cocoon of my mother's
womb. lain by this river
once i envisioned a large
bearded head floating in the water
half filling the inlet
i could see it from
the golden arc of the bridge.   the lions
sometimes i stand
for long spaces of time
looking at the mountains
and the sunny water in the distance,
at the land
at the clouds
or i lie on my back
looking up at the immense blueness
enjoying the sky
the earth is soft and curved
under my/your body
and i remember what he said,
when all your friends are gone
you still have this
the mountains   the oceans
and yourself

someday soon before you leave
we will go far away to a cabin
in the trees
and enjoy
silence

1974

in memory of fred quilt

spiral
ing from small
we are all   from the same root
everyone different aspects
of myself
some of the mist
ique gone
i still feel special
earthen bowl root star and tent
let me be
i am willing to share
unasked
the ojibway draws
from the inside out
i see your stomach
cave shaped
black lines drawn
around red
fred quilt
(i do not know your indian name)
justice continues
tears fill me
blue
i think about hate
the beginning form
that caused this to happen
to you
and i try not to transform
my pain
back into it

1974

her husband is a film maker

her husband is a film maker
the night she took
lsd
and walked in front
of the movie projector
i could see the tears
on her face
and i thought,   her life
is the saddest movie
of all
i wondered if he
could see it
yes, he said, I'm sort of
the director

1974

For Menlo

that day i told you
that the scars
on my wrist   were from
when i was a bird
that flew through glass

1974

Linda Louise

Linda, I miss your sunny coral lipstick
fruit flavored scents
older adolescence
teaching me to dance
to summer music
crisp ironed shirts
white ruffled tops
everything the latest.
The Lion Sleeps tonight
always reminds me of you.
You were the coolest.

White Shoulders perfume
always reminds me of you.
I dedicate my life work to you.
There is nothing
that can measure the shock
I felt that morning
I learned of your death.
I was fifteen,
you were nineteen,
our brother, drunk
drove through a red light
twenty-eight years later
and I cry as I open a tube
of coral lipstick in the drugstore
understanding now
why I have been craving
that color around me.
When I was a child you ran after me
and cradled my head to your breast
when I was afraid.
I'll never forget
your beautiful brown eyes
I'll never forget
your joking and teasing
I'll never forget

1992

in the bath

silken water   rosebuds floating
he faces her
his hands on her knees
drops his head forward
ecstasy.
She is floating in the water
like Ophelia
offering herself
to him on the waves.
The water lifts her breasts
luminescent in the candle light.
When she stands
he towels her

then bends down and slides
his tongue
up into her backside
and traces the space
between her anal opening
and vulva.
On the bed
she is resting
with her bottom up
like a baby,
he slides
beneath
her
outlining firmly
with his tongue
the definition of her folds.

1994

Father

fear closes down my heart
a certain kind of fear.
Ask me to write about something else.
Not the disappointment
of his nakedness on the couch,
passed out
from drinking in the summer heat.
Forgetting he had a daughter
coming to visit.
Forgetting he had a daughter,
ringing the buzzer outside,
looking at her reflection in the window,
her porcupine quill earrings,
forgetting he had a daughter
whose color of skin and face he gave,
who is waiting with soft dark eyes
for the father who never was,
who never could be.

1996

Lee Maracle [b. 1950]

Writing is "playing with words in long chains" to use Jeanette Armstrong's words in "For Tony." Poetry is when the words don't quite stretch to edge of the page before you want to pause, take another turn, send them flying in a new direction. It is a Raven Game, requires a tireless wolf spirit and the fearlessness of the shark who travels to the bottom of the sea, but it is the most joyful and mature productive play an adult can engage in.

Lee Maracle was born in North Vancouver, of Salish and Métis heritage. Largely self-educated, she is a prolific essayist, poet, and novelist. "I had to create my own language, working with the way our parents spoke English, which was not standard English. Underlying that English was a Native way of storytelling. It is what I call poetic oratory. It is this kind of language and underlying structure I work with in my novels and also in poetry. I want to write in English the way I feel story in our language. I want to take an old story and spin new myths based on the missing hundred and fifty years of story development since white people came."

"Salish origin stories take days to tell. The beginning is pure poetry, then it unfolds into drama. As each new being or subject is introduced, it begins again with poetry, then unfolds into drama. Comedic breaks take place as well. It moves like waves, rather than in linear fashion. It has a spiritual logic, rather than a plot logic. These are the structures I'm working with as well as the novel structures of English literature."

Maracle's writing is also characteristically political. "I write from my condition. We live in political, oppressive, and transitory times; my writing reflects that. I write from within a condition that surrounds us. The condition of Native people in Canada is political. We're in the process of struggling for decolonization."

I Am Woman (1988), Maracle's first book, defies the boundaries of political non-fiction, blending prose and poetry. Her other publications include *Bobbi Lee: Indian Rebel* (1990), *Sojourner's Truth and Other Stories* (1990), *Theory: Coming to Story* (1990), *Sun Dogs* (1991), and *Ravensong* (1993). She edited two books of poetry by Rita Joe, *More Poems by Rita Joe* (1989) and *Songs of Eskasoni* (1990), and was both an editor of and contributor to *Telling It: Women and Language Across Cultures* (1990). Her writing has been published in numerous anthologies. *Bent Box* (2000) is her first collection of poetry. A novel, *Daughters are Forever*, is slated for publication by Raincoast Books.

Working part-time for the Centre of Indigenous Theatre as the Traditional Cultural Director, Maracle intends to do more acting. She also teaches part-time at the University of Toronto and does consulting work for Mnjikaning First Nation in Ontario. She is the mother of four and the grandmother of four and now makes her home in Barrie, Ontario.

When Maracle learned to write at nine years old, she wrote her first poem, "My Box of Letters." The poem makes the abstract alphabet concrete, infusing life and spirit into the signs of writing, so often conceptualized as dead compared to the oral word. "Performin'" creates a stage for the Englishes that are part of Maracle's heritage and development, and "Razzleberries" brings two kinds of creative "vegetation" together. "That poem was written while my children and I were picking berries to get the money for our first holiday together." "Mr. Mandela" juxtaposes two prisons. "My people were always internationalists in understanding things."

My Box of Letters

(*December 23, 1959*)

I was only six when they forced me to take
the box of beastly letters.

We were not friends from the start
We resented each other.

They tripped over each other in crazy
senseless and ridiculous patterns.

They jumped around me defiantly
Higgledy-piggledy and round.

They got me in trouble, these mischievous
little rascals.

They hated me. They said it was because
I didn't understand them.

I jumped inside the box, grabbed them
and wrestled them down.

This didn't work, they fought hard.
There were 26 of them and I was only one.

(1991 afterthought on finding this, my first poem saved by my mother)

With diligence and persistence
I befriended them

I cajoled them, persuaded them for years
to make them behave.

1959, 1991, 2000

War

In my body flows the blood of Gallic
Bastille stormers and the soft, gentle
ways of Salish/Cree womanhood.

Deep throated base tones dissipate,
swallowed by the earth; uproarious
laughter sears, mutilates my voice.

Child of the earth-tear of west
coast rain; dew drop sparkling in
the crisp, clear sun of my home.

Warm woman of the Mediterranean sunscape,
bleaching rough cotton-sweatshop
anniversary.

Thunderous, rude earthquakes that
split my spirit within. Tiny grapes
of wine console me.

Can I deny a heritage blackened by
the toil of billions, conceived in
rape, plunder and butchery?

In the veins, that fight to root themselves
in the wondrous breadth of my
homeland, races the blood of base
humanity.

European thief, liar, bloodsucker.
I deny you not. I fear you not. Your
reality and mine no longer rankles me.

I am moved by my love for human life;
by the firm conviction that all the world
must stop the butchery, stop the slaughter.

I am moved by my scars, by my own filth
to re-write history with my body
to shed the blood of those that betray themselves.

To life, world humanity I ascribe
To my people... my history... I address
my vision.

1969, 2000

Performing

I shudda got 'n Oscar
for all the lies I told,
all the masks I wore...
But they don't give
Indian women Oscars
for dressin' like Vogue Magazine
and drippin'
honeyed English.

        Remember Ta'ah
        I speak brocken
        Ink-lish tooh?
Now
        I am
            speechless...

1972, 2000

Women

Palestinian women rock baby cradles
to the rhythm of US/Israeli bombs
while desert winds tear at tipis
and sand blasts the faces of water-bearers.

    In Can-America; mothers use ivory
    and the rising price of "HUGGIES"
    is our most serious problem.

Amid peppered streets
and flattened villages,
waves of resistance
lash at the citadels of capital.

    The streets of Can-America
    are flooded only with shoppers
    scurrying to buy… buy… buy…

In underground workshops
built by humble hands
women work through the night
to create weapons for Palestine.

    The feminine hands of Can-America
    greedily eat Israeli oranges
    Palestinian children have never seen.

Warm, the earth bearing woman's
soft, sure step dignity
printed in the oasis of struggle
watered by womanly resistance.

    And the warm winds of change
    breathe the pure scent of victory
    to the shores of my decadent home.

1979, 2000

Mister Mandela

Forgive me Mister Mandela
I tried to picture you in prison
for twenty-five years
but a hand closed on my throat

I know this land
It lives in the windowless room
of my childhood
A room filled with rats and menacing sounds

A terrifying loneliness
seizes my insides
closes my voice
and I don't want to remember

In the dark, eyes shut tight
the memories of an empty belly
force themselves to fill the space
where thought of you ought to live

The sight of your Black face
between stark white walls and iron bars
draws the drapes on the ray of light
left me by a thousand rain-soaked days

When I look at you in prison, Mr. Mandela
I can't feel the power of mother sea
feel the wind of my green mountains
or rise up to resist their demise

I treasure this eagle of resistance
couching you and Leonard in each wing
You shall have to be happy, Mr. Mandela
with my humble tribute

1980, 2000

Leonard

Where else does one hear
the clang of metal on metal

Where else do days stretch
into endless days

Where time is marked
by an insistent nothingness

Where from morning until night
there is no comfort, only cruel laughter
at the torment
of your comrades
who, like you
are incarcerated
caught in a time warp

"Momma my life stopped 11 and ½ years ago,"
Brother Malcolm said "everyone who is not free
is in jail"

It isn't so
Jail
is an empty room
without light
or love

It is life
without living
suffering without struggle

For those of you who are not free
but may move without steel
there is at least the joy
of rebelling

1980, 2000

Razzleberries

A thousand tiny thorns
        tear at my flesh
intense sun-heat blisters
       my black back.

Countless red berries
       bob and weave
          before me.

      Stinging nettles
morning mud, mosquitoes
        cow flies…

A heavy bucket pulls at my neck
arms upstretched, eyes squinting.

Still, I'd rather pick razzleberries
then vegetate before a typewriter.

1982, 2000

Autumn Rose

*This poem was inspired by a child named Autumn Rose. The poem is not about her
but rather my perception of our self-destruction and the children who are the natural
resistance to destruction. Our children are the basis for my optimism.*

If the state won't kill us,
then, we will have to kill ourselves.

It's no longer good etiquette
to head hunt savages,
so we'll just have to do it ourselves.

It's not polite to violate squaws,
so we'll just have to find an Indian to oblige us.

It's poor form to let an Indian starve,
we'll have to deprive our young ourselves.

Blinded by niceties and polite liberality
we can't see our enemy,
so we'll just have to kill each other.

> In this field
> of dying leaves
> dead grass
> and rustling winds
> blooms
> a lone
> autumn rose.

Since Uncle Willie started giving us hush money
we have stepped up the campaign against ourselves
with a fierceness we haven't known since our
forefather's resistance. I would be cynical but
for the tenacity of the late Autumn Rose who
stubbornly clings to life in a season when all
flora are laid to rest.

The children I meet are the roses in autumn.
A child is forever blossoming. Their parents
may feel crushed but the children go on blooming
like the lovely, stubborn rose.

1983, 2000

Ta'ah

I wanted to escape your smiling eyes,
go beyond their warm black
I wanted to wrap my spirit around
other feelings

Flee to unknown places
travel across time
to a different world
I didn't want to be you

You were still
I ran
You walked steadily
I refused

You were poetic
modest
in your presentation
of language

I, vulgar
brassy
repelling the soft murmur
of your voice

Manipulated
you called upon grandmothers
"let me be useful
one more moment"

Let me give one more second
of blissful reprieve, sock
life's crystal shard
safely in our lineage

I didn't want to be you,
but the embers
of truth behind your eyes
kindled my passion.

I travelled
to places
to relieve others
and tormented myself

I drank clear visions
from the lives of saints
whose demons made them blind,
watched my own fire catch

I went willingly, Ta'ah
to places where flames
licked gardens of eden
melted my insides

Bled lava rock
across emerald hillsides
exploded storms
of insidious words

poured black ash
across green growth
listened carefully
to tree lamenting death

in the ashes of cedars
burial
our grandmothers breathed
stories of unparalysed growth

I saw movement
purple, green and gold
spirits dancing,
loving,

exalting earth
in all its tormented
beauty
"crystal," Ta'ah, "is not clear"

you saw coal burn red hot
dusty black
to fired diamond
a jagged-edged miracle

"Just birth," you smiled,
"creation, re-creation,
new paths cut
from old patterns"

1989, 2000

Light

light
dancing purple light
engages green
encircles
passes through one another
sways above grass blade tips
swings
on wind's wings
half lit

purple/gray shadows
enwrap the dancing throng
step lightly
oh so lightly
on stone's soft skin
dance, without beginning
without end
dance
murmurs peace
passion's dance
carefully
oh so carefully
colours amuse touch
vanish amid bright red smoke
stanchions of pine
on khaki hillsides
dotted with pale green sage
a glorious *soiree*
before summer's sleep
in autumn's cool
still
air.
bright light
retreats
into scents of pine and sage
kisses earth
—her breast heaves
            a contented sigh.

1992, 2000

George Kenny

[b. 1951]

I believe in trying to show something rather than just talking about it. I use concrete images so that readers can share in them and make their own interpretations.

George Kenny, Ojibway, was born and raised on the Lac Seul Indian Reserve near Sioux Lookout in northern Ontario. He attended residential school in Sioux Lookout from age six to thirteen and went to high school in southern Ontario at the Great Lakes Christian College. He received his teacher's certificate from Hamilton Teacher's College in 1974. Ten years later, he received his bachelor of independent studies (B.I.S.) from the University of Waterloo. "A lot of my friends drop the "I" and say 'George has a B.S.'" Kenny has continued to focus on academic study, receiving a B.A. in cultural anthropology from Lakehead University in 1997 and an honours B.A. in archaeology from the same institution in 1998. He is currently working on a Masters in cultural anthropology at the University of Manitoba.

From 1976 to 1996, Kenny worked in community development projects for Native communities in Toronto, Kenora, and North Bay. "At one point, in Thunder Bay, I found myself sitting on fifteen non-profit community boards at the same time." He has taught literacy skills and urban life skills. He designed the Anishnabe Skills Development program for urban Native peoples, which is used by Native friendship centres throughout Ontario. "I'm interested in trying to improve relations between Natives and non-Natives in urban environments." In 1996, Kenny returned home to Lac Seul where he is researching the evidence for a claim against Ontario Hydro which flooded Anishnabe lands in 1928. He also continues to write. "I have six bad novels stored away."

Kenny has been "scribbling down lines for poems" and short stories since high school. When he arrived in Toronto in 1976, he became involved in the Native Association for Performing and Visual Arts, run by James Buller. There he met Graham Greene and Gary Farmer, who later acted in *October Stranger*, a short film made by the CBC in 1981, which dramatized Kenny's poem by that name. Buller encouraged Kenny to circulate his poems and short stories; *Indians Don't Cry*, a collection of eighteen short poems and eight short stories, was published in 1977. Kenny maintains that urban Natives were catalysts for the expression of Native culture at that time. "Back on the rez, people were dealing with severe social problems. Many of the Native education centres started in cities and towns were teaching traditional knowledge. Urban Natives who had moved away from their roots were looking for ways to express them —and they found those ways in the arts."

Many of Kenny's poems, using language sparely but powerfully, create vivid portraits of personalities confronted or trapped by harsh realities and surviving them with dignity. His title suggests a theme his poems work with — the connection between vulnerability and strength. As well, it suggests non-Native society's stereotyping and incomprehension of Native people.

Rubbie at Central Park

In the green beauty of Central Park
between Edmonton and Carlton streets,
every night, some of Winnipeg's
thirty thousand Indians
find acceptance
with a 10 fl. oz bottle of rubbing
alcohol.

Rubbie, while eventually
to burn a hole through the drinker's
intestines even when diluted with
Fanta or Coca-cola
is as good as any brand of whiskey
to start forgetting

the personnel man at the Bay
or any other employment office
took a look at clothes one didn't
have four bits to wash with
or maybe, just said to himself,
oh oh, a wino, look at his
scarred face
and said a sorry he didn't mean.

1977

Poor J.W.

a Sandy Lake Cree, postcard photographic
     plate of the city
implanted on his brain,

he, trying to cross Yonge st. at 5pm
was collared by a Jehovah's Witness—

Poor J.W., he didn't know;

that lost-looking Cree is a devil-casting-
     out-preacher, a brother
of Jesus.

Who'll save who?

My two bits on the Sandy Lake Cree,
     dumb in the ways
of the city,
     but fluent
in all tongues when it comes

to the Lord and the Bible.

Poor J.W.

1977

How He Served

every dawn, he brought his woman
some portion of his journey.
before sunrise, setting match
to kindling in a pot-bellied
Hudson Bay Co. stove,
slipping down to the sandy
shore in summer,
chopping away overnight ice
in the water-hole in winter,
fetching liquid for her
morning Red Rose tea

and then, surrendering
the sun of his fingers, he warmed
her with touches, tracing his
need along the smooth brown
skin lines and curves
of her body.

   through the dawns of their lives
how he served was his journey;
illustrated many seasons over
with the flames of devotion
tenderly,
   he brought his woman.

1977

Death Bird

I remember a t-shirt clinging hot dawn
when the mosquitoes had somehow infiltrated
past the screens my father had set up, and
looking out the window, toward the pink
sneaking approach of another day in August,
hearing the trembling cries of the
death-bird (an Ojibway belief was that
   anyone hearing the death-bird
   and not ending its life
   would have a near relative die)
and I hearing the raging of my mother's voice
why didn't you fix those screens, as storm
gathering in her, she whirled like a dragonfly
slashing at tormenting insects,

   (She didn't hear the death-bird
   or she would have shoved the
   12-gauge into my father's hands
   and kicked him out the door,
   not caring, anyone who tried
   to kill the death-bird and failed
   to do so, would himself die)

I remember being too scared of my mother's anger
to tell anyone I heard the death-bird
that t-shirt clinging hot August dawn

and I wish for a second chance

for barely four months later,

      mother rode off with the
death bird.

1977

I Don't Know This October Stranger

I don't know this October stranger,
each dawn groping for an alarm clock,
selecting a blue polyester suit
that used to belong to an indian
from the backforests of northwestern
      Ontario.

This autumn stranger washes a once
familiar face,
runs windburnt fingers over a
cowlick topped head of black hair,
the exact image of a man I swear
      I once knew.

This October stranger adjusts his
blue tie,
flips through his documents before sliding
them into a $40 briefcase
and then rides off on a rocking
subway train
to his 2nd story office
on Eglinton Avenue E. in Toronto.

I don't know this October stranger
that writes his stories
and poems
as if Chaucer himself was kicking

him along, never letting him rest,
this indian dedicated to becoming
published.

I don't know this October stranger
that left a love of three years
behind without a
kiss;
this autumn stranger that knew
his 14 year old sister would be
left all alone in a boarding school
and yet migrated south—

I don't know this October stranger.

1977

Duncan Mercredi [b. 1951]

I want people to travel that path that I have traveled, to meet the people I have met, to experience my dreams and my visions in some way, even in a little way, maybe be able to identify where I've been and to some extent see the path that lies before me. In this way I hope they will eagerly travel with me on my journey to forever.

Duncan Mercredi grew up in Grand Rapids, Manitoba, until the age of sixteen. "For the first ten or twelve years of my life I lived in an isolated Cree and Métis village. There was no TV—all images came through the radio or through my grandmother's storytelling. She spoke nothing but Cree and told the best stories. I guess I was being groomed as the next storyteller in the family. My grandmother said I would tell stories, although not necessarily in the same way she did." Mercredi calls this time "the age of innocence. Then Hydro moved in and that part of Grand Rapids opened up to the outside world. Racism moved in with it."

Growing up, Mercredi spoke Cree as his first language, although he was also encouraged to learn English. His mother, who had been to residential school, loved to read and passed that love on to him. At the age of sixteen, when Mercredi went to residential school in Cranberry Portage, English started to become his first language. "Now, I'm beginning to get my Cree back through telling stories to children. But it's a tough process."

In 1973 Mercredi began working for the Highways Department of Manitoba Hydro in construction and as a surveyor and continued to do so for the next twenty years. "I learned a lot about life. My eyes were opened. There was no room for our culture in non-Native society. In many of the little towns I worked in, it was not safe for a Native person to go into the bars. So I went to my room." Spending a lot of time alone in small towns or bush camps, Mercredi used it to write stories and poetry. As a child, he had been encouraged to write by a teacher in Grand Rapids. When he was in his late thirties, he answered a call from Pemmican Press for stories by Métis writers and was chosen to attend a workshop with other Native writers such as Maria Campbell, Jordan Wheeler, and Lee Maracle. This encounter encouraged him to commit himself to writing.

At present, Mercredi lives in Winnipeg with his wife and two daughters and works as a researcher on land surveys and permits for the federal government. Although he no longer works in bush camps, he still often feels apart. "I'm a blue collar person who has moved to a white collar job—it can be isolating. Luckily, there's a good group of writers here in Winnipeg."

Mercredi has published four books of poetry: *Spirit of the wolf* (1990), *Dreams of the wolf in the city* (1992), *Wolf and Shadows* (1995), and *The Duke of Windsor—Wolf Sings the Blues* (1997). For Mercredi, the wolf is his "spirit guide" because of traditional Cree teachings, but also "because I identified with this animal as being one who did his own thing, and yet was very family-oriented and protective of his space." Mercredi draws a parallel between wolves and Native peoples: "Wolves are marginalized, like First Nations. They are being driven into these little pockets of land, trying to maintain themselves as best they can." In his poems, Mercredi often adopts the persona of the loner, or writes about people from the streets. "There's a fine line between people on the street and ourselves. I listen to their stories, and to the music in their stories—that music would be the blues."

my red face hurts

my red face hurts
and i walk with my head down
to hide the tears

my red face hurts
as i watch my brother die before me
white bullets riddle my body
and i hide my face to cry

my red face hurts
as i watch my father stagger out of neon lit bars
and crumple on piss-stained sidewalks
as hate filled eyes step over him
i hide my shame behind shadows

my red face hurts
as i watch a white man hiding his white sheet
beneath his suit and tie
condemn me because of one man's greed
sentencing me to an early death
my red face hurts as he smiles

my red face hurts
as i see my sister stand on darkened streets
selling her gift to strangers
that use her till she has nothing left to give
and i cry as i pull the needles from her arms

my red face hurts
when i hear the hate on the radio
directed at my hopes and dreams
and another party is born
on the wings of a white horse
and i scream in anger as i watch the door close on me

my red face hurts
as i see the stirrings of a white nation
follow blindly the words of a salesman
with visions of a wall between us
and i cry for my unborn brothers and sisters
for they will feel the sting of this party's hate

my red face hurts
but the feel of a gun
comforts me

1991

Morning Awakening

silence greets the morning awakening
on a mist covered lake
still as glass

slipping to the edge listening
a loon rises from the mist
startling the calm sleep of the water

the mist that blankets the lake rises slowly
water is cold as it envelopes my body
i shiver at its touch

quiet in its depth i rise suddenly
coyote jumps back startled
not afraid but wary
watching drinking body alert to danger

i dive into the silent depths
rising to a cacophony of sound
the lake begins to awaken

gentle waves slap slap the sand
gulls chatter and scream over washed up fish
a moose shakes the dew off its back
gliding majestically into the trees
ducks parade their young
watching nervously

wind begins to rise
as i slip away

1991

Blues Singer

I always wanted to sing
    the blues
in a smoke filled room
    with empty tables except one
a table under a red colored lamp
    hearing the roar
from the single table holding
    friends laughing and singing
the blues

i always wanted to play the blues
    to feel the music in my hands
to breathe my spirit into the harp and hear
    my soul escape into the night

i always wanted to play the blues
    to feel the heartbeat of the drums
and escape to a pine scented cabin
    to dance to the beat of my heart

i always wanted to play the blues
    to calm the rage of silver strings
as they vent their anger at a black moon
    feeling the fury in my hands

I always wanted to sing
    the blues
to soothe my spirit's restlessness
    and calm an angry heart

from the single table holding
        friends laughing and singing
the blues

1991

Betty

Betty, who heard your screams that night
a gentle man, a family man, a silent man
a respected man

walking home, no cares in the world
glad to be alive
a car pulls up full of young men
four looking for an easy time

Young men who'd heard stories
about easy dark-haired girls
they force you into their car
but you fight

Betty who heard your screams that night
a gentle man, a family man, a silent man,
a respected man

Bruised, battered, you struggled on
out of town they drove
in a well-known car
but you fought because to give in
would be giving in to ignorance
what was yours was to be saved not used
by ignorant men
who'd heard stories of dark-haired girls

Betty who heard your screams that night
a gentle man, a family man, a silent man
a respected man

Clothes ripped you fought on
only with will and pride you fought
these men who thought that by virtue of their color
you were theirs to use

1991

back roads

i travel the back roads in dust covered vans
roads rough, wash board bone rattling rough
dusty, with loose gravel scattering from passing cars
spider webbing the windshield
coming upon small towns with a lottery ticket centre sign
on the only store not boarded up
small dark hotel sits empty, rooms unused
bar room holds peaked cap men hands dark from soil
dust caked jeans, cracked leather wallets empty
drinking on weather's promises
stepping outside, watching the circling clouds
listening for sounds of thunder
i jump start the quiet room when i enter
long black hair dishevelled from wind and dust
dark tanned skin almost invisible in the dim lights
blue jeans faded and tattered with grass stains
work boots, water stained, worn leather fraying at the
seams, steel toe visible and heels kicking up dust
the room remains silent as i sit down with four white men
suddenly I'm visible on these back roads

1991

He Likes to Dance

he likes to dance
long hair flying wildly
in the dark
feet moving to music in the silent room
he likes to dance
laughing loudly in the roomful of silence
dark eyes flashing madly
in smoke filled bars
colored lights throwing his shadow
on beer stained floors
he likes to dance
to music in his mind
creating visions from his dreams
living his lies in the daytime
he likes to dance

at night he wanders the streets
seeking relief in smoky rooms
by caressing strangers in dark alleys
accepting money from old men
spitting out their sex
washing the taste away with whiskey
erasing the memory with needles in the arm
and in the early morning darkness
alone in his room
he likes to dance

1992

something you said

it could be anything

     the way someone laughs
     or the scent of a certain perfume
     i can never remember the name
maybe when i'm just starting to wake
     and i'll reach beside me
     to the empty side of the motel bed
     but i feel the warmth of you
sometimes it's a song
     it was our song
     when we were young
     and we'd walk outside
     to a night full of stars
     and the song would follow behind us
it could be anything
     a whisper, a cough,
     or the way your breath would catch
     like that time we saw mountains
     riding in that train
     racing the sun to the ocean
sometimes the smell of sweetgrass
     will find you walking beside me
     like we did last summer
     united across this country
     and i could see the pride
     in your eyes
and i'll smile

maybe just before i fall asleep
and i'll hear a whisper
just before i close my eyes
and the words i hear
will be words of love
and i'll smile again
and whisper back
as my words catch the breeze
carrying my message to your land of dreams
it could be anything
but it's not
it's love

1992

born again indian

long black hair braided hanging down his back
he don't walk he glide
he winks as he talks trying to win with his smile
he disagrees without seeming to
can't be seen as difficult
know what i mean, wink wink nudge nudge
shaking his head pointing at the whites
as if they cannot hear
talking about phil and ovide like they were old friends
we're no different
yeah yeah he says but we're one with mother earth
we feel her pain
that's what i was trying to say in my dance
i thought it was a grass dance
and what you were shaking was for the white ladies
he laughs
flavor of the month man
let them have a taste
loosen up bro you take this traditional thing too seriously
just another church without walls
bottles loosen lips
smoke clouds the brain
and secrets are blurted out
silencing a bewildered audience
not knowing who to believe
i'm not ashamed of being an indian
said in the same breath as i want to use someone

for a change
he/she what does it matter
the night is dark
it's how you dance in front of the camera
you've sold your soul
born again indian laughs
we're savages remember we have no soul
then he talks about secret societies
rituals performed
all the while drowning his sorrow in smoke and drink
and his pain reaches out and grabs me
forcing me to look inside his hurt and confusion
who am i he asks
i pray to a creator and he looks like jesus
with attendants in black robes
that haunt my dreams born again indian cries
it's not fair what you have done
making me a side show with pretty colors
dancing to a discordant drum
surrounded by tourists with cameras
born again beings to droop clutching a bottle
his only hold to what keeps him in chains
he finds it slipping away
and the priest in his dreams mocks him
dancing drunkenly at the foot of his bed at night

1995

searching for visions

searching for faces on rocks i pick on travels through the paths i walk/
listening for songs on the breezes that waft across my face/ searching
for visions in the day just as the last of the sunshine sinks beneath the
canopy of pine trees that surround me/ nearly tripping on unseen
paths that cross mine/ glimpsing shadows of others that passed by
before me/ seeking visions that will guide them to a life that was much
like mine only older/ and the spirits they sought would whisper to
them at night and visit their dream state/ teaching them to dance to
fly to sing/ to become one like them/ and visit their visions to
understand the meaning of the faces on the rocks i pick and the songs
would suddenly burst forth out of the wind
        it is at that time i would dance

1995

searching for visions   II

these kids they're gonna be okay/ when they're ready, they gonna
take us places we never dreamed of/ man, the universe is
coming at them/ a million miles an hour/ incredible dreams
they must have/ the worlds they have travelled already/
these young travellers they'll be okay/
and when they're ready/ the stories they'll tell us/ the
worlds they'll take us/ i can hardly wait

1995

dreaming about the end of the world

feverish and dreaming
lying in cold sweat
hiding under the covers
fetal position
cupping the jewels
shaking and quivering
dreaming about the end of the world
can't travel the red road
full of dope and booze
dodging bowling balls
spewed out of pissed off volcanoes
aiming for my legs
trying for the quick strike
shaking and quivering
dreaming about the end of the world
half naked temptations on the side of the road
trying to lure a pathfinder
off track
but i'm firmly cupped in hands
and eyes straight ahead
only one purpose in mind
saving my ass that's on the line
a stream of obscenities echoing behind me
dreaming about the end of the world
inside a fevered mind
tossing and dodging the morning
wanting to see how the picture ends
only to see the gun aimed at my head
and the barrel explode

waking up hacking and puking
dreaming about the end of the world

1997

racing across the land

long after you are gone
i will be here
long after you are gone
i will remain
spirit will dance gain
in spruce and muskeg
winds will whisper our names
while yours will be silent
no sign of you will be found
long after you are gone
the cities you have built
hoping to leave as your legacy
will crumble and fall
becoming dust on the land
scattered in the four directions
and the prairie grass will bend
to the wind once more
and my spirit will join
the buffalo
racing across the land
our dance pounding across the land
long after you are gone

1997

yesterday's song

i wish i could slip into muskeg and spruce
encircling myself with northern lights
wolf songs and night hawks rustling the underbrush
catching the smells of the past still on me
even though my feet are concrete hardened
and my spirit tells stories of neon and blues
i am the son of muskeg and spruce
i still dance to the music of yesterday

1997

the duke of windsor

it's a thursday kind of night
a feeling of rain in the air
and the blues are calling
i enter harry's place
wiping the heat off my face
then you slide in the door
strutting
seeking the light from a stranger's eyes
and the temptation of the music in the night
enters a restless soul
and she yells as she walks in the door
i've got to hear me some blues
been walking all day
and I'm tired as i can be
so let those silver strings caress me
till i can't scream anymore
and et enters dancing
wearing someone else's clothes
kicking off his borrowed shoes
with two different socks
he glides he kicks up his heels
he shakes and he yelps out a song
just like a little dog
the moon ain't full and the tide is still low
and the world has got the blues
bouncing off the walls on garry
staggering the cars with a guitar sliding
down st. mary all the way to main
it's the 70's all over again
with wall to wall brown
on a thursday night just before the harvest moon rises
on the castle of the blues
and the duke staggers out before the streets roll up
a harp solo still playing in his head
the duke strides into the morning
humming a nothing song into the setting night

1997

Daniel David Moses

[b. 1952]

My name is Daniel David Moses. I am the son of David Nelson Moses and Blanch
Ruth Jamieson Moses. Debora Blanch Moses is my sister. I grew up on a farm on the Six
Nations lands on the Grand River in Southern Ontario. Through my father's line and in
the band registry, I'm Delaware. Through my mother's line, I've got relations among the
Tuscarora. I also claim sisters and brothers among two-spirited people. I'm a writer of
plays, poems, and only occasionally essays and fictions. I distrust the illusions of prose.
Those of spoken language, I follow into emotion and/or stories, into an understanding of
my home at the centre of the world. Someday, I will be a storyteller. Meanwhile, I live in
Toronto.

Daniel David Moses, born and raised at Ohsweken, Ontario, moved to
Toronto to attend York University, where he received an Honours B.A.
in Fine Arts. He received a Master of Fine Arts from the University of
British Columbia, winning the Creative Writing Department's prize
for playwrighting in 1977. In 1980 he published his first book of poems,
Delicate Bodies, followed by *The White Line* in 1990. That same year he
published the play *Coyote City* (nominated for the 1991 Governor
General's Award for Drama). His other plays include *The Dreaming Beauty*
(published 1989, produced 1990), *Big Buck City* (produced 1991, published
1998), *Almighty Voice and His Wife* (produced 1991, published 1992), and *The
Indian Medicine Shows*, which won the James Buller Memorial Award for
Excellence in Aboriginal Theatre (published 1995, produced 1996). With
Terry Goldie, Moses edited *An Anthology of Canadian Native Literature in
English* in 1992. He lives in Toronto where he writes full time.

Until he went to university, Moses spent most of his time on the
"old established community" of the reserve, to use his words in an
interview with Hartmut Lutz. His deep connection to that particular
land, and to the farm on which he grew up, is apparent in much of his
poetry, especially his early work. While poems such as "Song in the
Light of Dawn" and "A Song of Early Summer" show his characteristic
intense sensual imagery, they also subtly convey a particular
community and complex world view. Moses comes from a family that
"was Christianized with my great-great-grandfather's generation," and
he has said that his "sense of the beauty of the English language
probably is rooted in going to that Anglican mission on our reserve,
and reading the prayer book, and hearing hymns" (interview with
Hartmut Lutz). On leaving the reserve, Moses became aware of the
distinctiveness of the cultural values within which he grew up,
including "respect for the other person as an individual spirit.... We
were calling ourselves Christians, not to upset anybody [but] I think

we were really behaving like Indians!" (interview with Hartmut Lutz).

Moses began to write lyric poetry in the late 1970s and 1980s. "I told myself in poetry I would perfect my technique while I gave myself time to grow up." Quite soon, his style took a "turn to the surreal." First, "I decided not to write for the page but for the ear." Second, he began to incorporate dreams and "dream images," drawing from "the numerous traditional Native cultures which revere dreams as a way of understanding the world." The hoped-for richness occurred: irony, humour, and "dramatic monologues, implied dialogues, the half-heard discussions of several voices" ("Spooky").

Moses' poetry can take the reader on surreal or dream journeys, sometimes using the shock value of distorted or unexpected perspectives, such as the unhorsed rider's perspective in "Of Course the Sky Does Not Close." He describes his poem "The Persistence of Songs" as "a history of North America in 30 lines. Although it reads like a dream, the central images are all grounded in the real.... The 'horned horizon' was how an approaching buffalo herd was perceived and the lanterns are tipis at night...."

Song in the Light of Dawn

Fish. My eyes were sleepy
fish and in the overcast
world the road to work was mud.
Then something near a pond

turned my head. A black bird's
banded wing made the perfect
lure, the gay colour a hook
without hurt, a blushing

wash. Now further on on
this shoulder of the high
way even the gravel and
asphalt greys overflow

their textures. They're so clear
I feel more than awake. Oh

to stay and swim in them here
would be, would be enough.

1980

A Song of Early Summer

No one in the dark
houseful of sleepers can know
how the road marks the way to
the source of the night
cumulus. Only the drunk

cousins, thick eyes and stumbling through
conversation, consider that
the clouds against the moon are
dark as clods and the barley's
headed out in a luminous

mist. This gravel
strip their shoeless feet glide beside
is so far from the clouded
light that weighs on
the city they left tonight it seems

that city no longer exists. In the open
fields pale as remembered
dreams the cousins forget
their fatigue. Their drink
sore eyes explore the land's

undulations and the cold
dew growing through
the grass. Then the thin
horse with the whey
coloured scabs on its back clears

its throat and in the trees the birds
follow suit. Over the old
corral the cumulus are going
silver grey. The cousins eye
the east colouring

pink as the cheap
wine they drank. When the sun breaks
its red glare open, the cousins
enter the still
shadowed house where

the sleepers sleep
out their regular dreams and in
the kitchen waiting there
are the full
moon shells of the breakfast eggs.

1979, 1980

October

Pushing himself up
the Escarpment along
the road's asphalt
shoulder the man comes to

see the truth of
trees or at least of these
maples. In this row along
the brink they show

all their leaves for what
they became inside
the green hues of
summer. Flame. Flame.

Flame. The cars passing
here can have no sweat
worked up, no rasping
breath and no sense of

the flock turning over
trees like bits of
paper ash. But the man
has. This man running

himself toward that
edge above the motley

city where the flat
overcast starts and

his urge to climb could
end has stepped into
a signal moment he wants
to remember always.

1980

The Sunbather's Fear of the Moon

Now that I'm out walking alone, old Bone
face looks jealous of the blood ruddiness
of my skin. Just let her try to scrape it
away and she will see it takes more than
petty metal to get to me, she'll see

how useless a good cool staring-down is
against skin this tough and crusty. And she
should identify with that. What the pale
fool won't understand quite as easily
is that my shine's not a reflected light

because it's always noon inside my chest
where day has a home the size of a fist.
I'm flushed with the heat of its love and of
the pleasures it brings through its bright
probing fingers and tongues. It's made me so

young I can go it alone. I don't need
that shine she gives to the land so wanly
old Boneface must know it can't cut the dark,
can't make it bleed anymore than I did
by day. The bit of bright blood I shed soaked,

as her light does, into the mud. Might be
red rain subterraneously. Or stars
for the troglodytes to see. It doesn't
matter. I refuse to shatter and set.
Let Boneface put on her idiot gape.

1980, 1990

Twinkle

There's no light around
the old place tonight

—just lawn so profound
you feel for each step.

And the old house too
looks a perfect hole,

standing over you
like space with no stars.

Is this the place where
you grew up? This dark

so far from the road
everything's quiet

—no wind, not even
in the Big Tree's top.

You can't watch your step.
So stop. Look up. Hold

your breath. You see? There
in between the beats

of your heart—is that
a toad that hops or

dew that you hear drop?
What else could it be?

Why is Polaris
shivering that way?

1988, 1990

Ballad from a Burned-Out House

Fire always wanted to marry Stone.
She claimed he alone could anchor her.
She travelled through the wood with her hair
loose and lifting almost to the sky.

Stone never dreamed he'd meet such beauty.
The heat of her kisses startled him.
Though he wished to be diamond and quartz,
his body quickly thickened and broke.

Fire shrouded herself in smoke and rain;
Stone covered his dark wounds with new grass.
Of course, they had no children or pain.
Theirs was a cool and perfect divorce.

1981, 1990

Of Course the Sky Does not Close

Of course, when you've been unhorsed
by thirst, you tend to lie where
you've landed. Who's got the strength
or breath or backbone to move
—or even think about it?

Of course, you believe your ears
and eyes—though their energy's
so low you shouldn't. They seem
to tell you the sky's open
only for your benefit!

Of course, that may be the truth
for all they can know. With air
this dry, even sound turns vague and
dusty and all the light so
coarse, it callouses your sight.

Of course, you'll mistake your horse
(if it trots back) for a cloud,
say, with thunder cracks. You took

these oats dangling in your eyes
for birds too distant to hear.

Of course, you take your own breath
and the grit of dust for wind
and the taste of cumulus;
you're expecting there to be
a storm closing up the sky.

Of course, the sun is the one
white staring eye in the wide
blue face of the sky, a face
so open you can deny it
nothing and offer your eyes.

Of course, the sky prefers ponds.
It gently plucks each one from
the face of the land. The sky
couldn't care less about you
—or if your eyes get plucked too.

Of course, now you're so angry
and jealous, you've energy
enough to realise how
mad you've been, how pitiful
your situation's become.

Of course, you worry the sky
is so stupid it won't see
when you're dead. Will it keep on
trying to stare you down, not
realising it has won?

Of course, you are mistaken.
The sky is full of remorse.
The darkness in its face cries
the eyes of the land back in,
will even water your horse.

1988, 1990

Crow Out Early

The only one who speaks to this long rain
is that crow sitting on a pole like old
Raven, spitting out caws in pairs. He got
out of dreams on this wrong side of the bay.

Over there a foghorn makes a four-note
effort Crow can't comprehend. It's not like
even the loudest moans of his friends who
keep asleep, their effort to ignore how

this pressing fall of clouds has made a pine
the only place to settle. This makes Crow
with folded wings a black and glistening
pair of hands and his cries, a quick prayer, reach

out through the fog. His eyes get a shimmer
and his ears a song, both like the run off
gurgling at road edge. He sees the stones there
washing strong bodies egg bright, beetle slick.

1980, 1990

The Persistence of Songs

The people feed from the river and conceive songs.
But the strangers with the dead heads march towards the long
edges of their own blades. They see a thundering
fog along the horned horizon and turn around
to stalk the rising sun. They find four lanterns made
of skin arrayed along the river, the people
still feasting within. The strangers feed off their own
anger, flooding the river with blood. The four songs,
who are the children, go dumb and their white dogs mad
before the people have the strangers rounded up.

They bind them with skin from the fog and throw them in;
then, they wait for the river to heal. They try
to feast again. They pray to the children. By noon
the river grows an old skin and the children fade.
In the cold mud the strangers congeal. A fog

bleeds from the river, drowns the lantern and stops up
the ears of the people with a dull, three-note song.
The strangers are praising honed edges and the white
meat of their own bodies. They curse the sun and vow
the moon turns so perfectly round they will square it.

They lurch up through the river's dull skin and begin
the marching again. The people search in the skin
for reflected light, the sunset or a lantern,
then assume the skin as mourning. The procession
the people enter tracks the moon through fog, cuts it
into quarters. And black dogs track the procession.
They feed off their own hunger and conceive a song
in praise of a perfect horizon made of meat.
That song fades; but, the four songs, who are the children,
return with horned heads. They feed from ears and edges.

1986, 1990

The Letter

This favour you're asking of yourself
may not do you any good—but tell
yourself it will, tell yourself it should

save your skin, should put the fire out of
your flesh before it's too late, before
much more of this heat that alternates

with ash uses you up. There's hardly
enough left to feel embarrassed for
being so easy to read—hardly

enough left to make the request. Please,
that scrap of you says, Give the letter
up. Feed it to the fire. It's easy

for the fire to digest. Paper is
the brighter fuel of the two after
all. Flesh, with its blushes and veins, looks

so foolish beside it. It would seem
only just—the fair exchange. The fire

can take to the paper and leave you

alone. How good to know that reading
the letter would never again push
the fire inside to ignite. The hand

writing on it would simply become
black and white again, so easily
read that as you lean your head over

the flame and catch some word, some phrase for
the last time—perhaps your own, perhaps
that other name being blacked out and

flaked into smoke—your face in a light
coat of soot will begin to cool down
and be not only illegible

but after you've washed it clean, you'll see
the skin smooth out, become unlined, free
again, a new page turning over.

1988, 1990

The Line

This is not the poem, this line
I'm feeding you. And the thought
that this line is not the poem
is not it either. Instead
the thought of what this line is
not is the weight that sinks it
in. And though this image of
that thought as a weight is quite
a neat figure of speech, you
know what it's not—though it did
this time let the line smoothly
arc to this spot, and now lets
it reach down to one other,
one further rhyme—the music
of which almost does measure
up, the way it keeps the line
stirring through the dampening

air. Oh, you know you can hear
the lure in that. As you know
you've known from the start the self
referring this line's doing
was a hook—a sharp, twisted
bit of wit that made you look
and see how clear it is no
part of this line or its gear
could be the poem. Still it cast
and kept the line reeling out
till now at last the hook's on
to itself and about to
tie this line I'm feeding you
up with a knot. Referring
to itself has got the line
and us nowhere. So clever's
not what the poem is about
either. We're left hanging there
while something like a snout starts
nudging at your ear, nibbling
near my mouth—and it's likely
it's the poem about to take
the bait. From the inside ought
to be a great way to learn
what the poem is. And we'll use
this line when the poem's drawn it
taut and fine as breath to tell
what we know, where we are and
where we'll go—unless the line
breaks. How would it feel, knowing,
at last, what the poem really
is, to lack the line to speak?

1986, 1990

Offhand Song

I do not dare compare your hand
with those of a woman or boy
or with the closed wing of a bird

at rest on the table. I do
not dare compare it there even

with my own so open here as

we talk it could hold or cover
yours up. Your hand has the power
just by touching your chest to slow

or suspend the beat of your heart.
What need then would it have of touch,
of a nest or father or man?

I hold on to my cup, hold off
finishing the coffee up, not
wanting to dare the hand to hand

comparison of goodbye. There
I might be taken by the need
to embrace or follow or fly.

1991

Could Raven Have White Feathers?

Winter, I mutter, as if the word
could restrain the cold pressing in through
the window of the plane, or some old

familiar name explain that ice
feathering out across the Great Slave
Lake below us. At home when we say

Winter is coming, the word, the words
do stroke the air, leaves turning colour,
falling, mere rumours of arrival,

and we prepare, the sun still nesting
in our heads, so we don't quite believe
in winter's imminence. But today

with the sun some way behind us, and
us the ones with the destination,
the filed flight plan to some island

in a frozen ocean, it's these words,
this word that falls off my tongue and sinks
under my breath, and the stony face

of the world turning toward us that turns white
and expressionless. Yes, these are words
from some immigrant language. This place

isn't what they were made to contain.
We say Winter again and again
to no end. It's a joke or a cry

—at best it's a question. How many
years before our ears hear that one two
syllable word as incantation?

Ask the languages already here.
Does it take generations, bitter
frost honing the tongue's edges, before

the taste becomes permanent and true,
before a house, huddling on its legs,
can hope to sing? A nest full of bright

mouths opening while the wind unfolds
its bones, white shadows into wings. Yes,
language hatching out, wise as an egg.

1997

Cowboy Pictures

I want to send away
to California
for pictures of the sun.
That state of the Union
is famous for its light.
Even in black and white,
the glamor of young men
who've oiled up their skin
till it shines with the sky
is bound to make my day,

to say nothing of night.
I can't imagine what
colour could do. Or what
those guys go through to get
to that estate. Mountain
passes, the Great Salt Plain?
A still-hostile frontier
might explain why most wear
cowboy hats black and white
as the pictures. But what

explains them lacking all
other clothes? A couple
are trying the wild
Indian bit, child
faces looking paler
under the cheap feathers
and war paint. And of course
this grown-up guy as Horse
needs some explaining too.
Or at least a lasso.

All the other rules seem
the same. Whatever game
they're playing, the only
difference seems to be
the gold there was in them
there hills is now a gleam
of silver bodies, still
as any mineral.
Gold caught in shades of grey,
never aging. Will they?

Picture yourself that way
in California,
some green rancher, say, out
riding your range, without
a thought for what sweet heart
you left across the Great
Divide. Or maybe be
the little lost dogie
he cradles to his chest.
So the pictures suggest

some sentimental ways
of bondage, yes, of boys
being boys. Shining with
the sky, in skin and breath
and eye, they're the picture
of youth—their six guns are
shooting stars through the bars
of the dark that covers
more than half the planet.
Try to bite the bullet.

1997

Joan Crate   [b. 1953]

The experiences of moving from place to place, being of mixed nations (Cree and five million other things), and having been part of different socio-economic groups at different periods in my life, have made me think of the concepts of "home" and "belonging" as somewhat transitory, really existing in terms of the spirit within the universe, rather than the physical body at some address or part of some identifiable group. My work with Pauline Johnson and Shawnandithit has allowed me to feel (and hopefully express) the existence of those of the past in our present lives and as part of the landscape which they inhabit(ed), both physical and spiritual. I thank my father for his insistence on making us familiar with whichever native culture we were living near or amongst at the time, and his love of First Nations art at a time it was devalued. I thank my mother for her open heart, my sister for her loyalty, my partner for his support, and my children for the fun we have in learning from each other.

Joan Crate was born in Yellowknife, N.W.T, but grew up moving around B.C., Alberta, and Saskatchewan. She began writing as a child: "I wrote my first poem in grade two, but stopped writing poetry in my mid-teens, and didn't start again until my mid-twenties when I took a poetry workshop class with Christopher Wiseman at the University of Calgary. I haven't stopped writing (for long) since." Crate attended the University of Calgary as a mature student, earning a B.A.(Hon.) and M.A. (with distinction) in English in 1988. She has taught at the University of Calgary and is presently teaching English and First Nations Literature at Red Deer College. She has four children, one born in each decade from the 1960s to 1990s. She published *Pale as Real Ladies: Poems for Pauline Johnson* in 1989 and a novel, *Breathing Water*, in 1990. She is currently at work on a series of poems on Shawnandithit, entitled "Foreign Homes," to be published by Brick Books.

Moving frequently exposed Crate to different cultures, including First Nations' cultures. As well, her father taught her appreciation of Native art: "We lived with a wonderful collection which was destroyed when my parents' trailer home burnt down. There were always books and art around home when I was growing up, even though my parents were poor. Expression through art, writing, and storytelling was legitimate and important." She grew up within particular spiritual traditions, although she wasn't aware of it at the time: "For a long time I though my spirituality was uniquely mine (and it certainly influences my 'take' on the world), but I found out that it's pretty traditional 'native' stuff." Being poor and having her first child at age sixteen were both big influences on Crate's point of view. "I'm middle-class now, but still can't figure out a lot of middle class assumptions."

Crate remembers being amazed by Duke Redbird's *Red on White* in 1971; she was interested in Pauline Johnson from childhood. "I read 'The Song My Paddle Sings' in school, but was more caught up with the song of her life—I saw pictures of her, her memorial plaque in Stanley Park. There was a Pauline Johnson chocolates store on Granville near a movie theatre my mom used to take us to when she was playing hookey from work." Years later, Crate developed an admiration for Johnson's writings, particularly her "Indian poems," even though they were "pretty well derided" by her English professors at university. "They're still my favorites of her work. I love her sense of drama." In her poems on Pauline Johnson and Shawnandithit, Crate inhabits and is inhabited by her subjects, weaving together past and present, herself and other. In *Pale As Real Ladies*, she also works with the myths and legends told Pauline Johnson by Chief Joe Capilano which Johnson published as *Legends of Vancouver*, making readers aware of the effects of language and translation in conveying those stories.

See this necklace? It is made from the claws
of a cinnamon bear that went mad
when her young were slaughtered.
These are my poems.
The words have been scraped clean
of death and anger,
and will shine in your mouth
like a string of white pearls.

The Poetry Reading

Tonight let me tell you of
a world swallowed in one quick gulp
with only crumbs remaining,
while in one stale memory-corner
a small girl shivers on the steps
of a tar-paper shack.
Her daydreams are bruises behind her eyes,
oozing songs of suicide
children mouth in her unfinished womb.

Can you hear me?

Powdered woman in the front row
your plucked eyebrows creased with concern,
look at me, diseased,
scarred with smallpox,
seeping gonorrhea, lungs smothered with T.B.,
drunk,
pushed into a sewer, a reserve,
the weed-choked backyard
you never walk through,
listen.

I speak of a history
pieced from a jigsaw of flesh
torn from dumb tongues.
Under my skin
blood beats along roadways
barred with DO NOT ENTER signs,
walls of small scars.
I will not return to silence.
Do you hear me?

Hands twitter.
You rise to your feet.
> *Lovely Miss Johnson.*
> *And will you have tea now?*
> *One lump or two?*

You dust biscuit from the corner
of your mouth, and I remain
onstage in front of you.
I stare at the pelts
hanging from my shoulder,
and sip from fine bone china.

Gleichen

A wash-out ahead
so the train stopped for four days
on the prairie near Gleichen.
We played cards, told stories,
dined in Frogmore and St. Cloud.
Silverware, linen and china
chattered in our hands.
Like a picnic some said.

Then the Indians came,
Blackfoot, with their horses.
One dollar, their fingers sang, to ride
across the prairie and lick the sun.
Teeth glinted with sky.
But one pony fell in a badger hole
and broke its neck.
Look, said the main from Detroit,
the Indians will eat it.
They eat anything, diseased and
unclean things. Fingers pointed like
sticks of candy, laughter slapped.
The Blackfoot watched us, eyes bewildered
by sun. They rustled dry grass, vanished
into the yellow land smudge.

The gray horse bloated before us.

Story teller

Your voice
scrapes the bones of time.

At night by the fire, it is only you,
Chief Joe, who feels
a lost spring flood thirsty cells.
In the dark heat you find legends
once buried, now
damp on your dry lips.
Whisper to me and I will write you down.

I will run ink through your long wounds,
make your past flash like fish scales
under a sharp knife.
I will give names to the tricks of seasons,
tie your stories of beginnings to weighted ends
with my careful fisher's fingers,
lock your chants, spirits,
dances, your paint, your potlatches
into a language you can't speak.
I will frame your history
on a white page.

I am a Prophet

These words I speak have been given
me by angels. Moon-faced, they fall
into sight at night and spread wings
of pine needles through my skin.
Stories appear down my arms, across
my legs, they wind my waist in red haloes.

I have been chosen by Tyee
to tell of the beginning. My flesh
is a series of writhing tablets.
Let me show it to you.
I will dance without veils.
My body is a voice.
Listen.
My feet tell the story of the lost tribes
who wandered in their own darkness.
When they reached the Promised Land
they did not know it, but fell
down its wet, green gullet,
emerged as ravens, whales, eagles.
You may see their names written across my toes
for just one dollar.

But wait!
There is more. Here, along
my thighs are the virgin births.
Sand coloured maidens bathed
in mountain streams, were filled with salmon roe.

Smolts swam in their bellies.
Move closer, hear
the swell of secret waters.
The women married totem pole carvers
and bore fishers who pulled in full nets.
Each night the mothers reconstructed
the bones, threw them back to the sea,
and the salmon lived again.
Stay,
I will let you touch their fins.

Here, on my breast, see this rusty wound?
A cross marks the time the stories
dulled and Tyee took a new name
and began to live somewhere else—
across the sea in a garden where the plants
grow at the feet of men and women
and not through the trunks of their bodies.
Yes, you may kiss it.
Our garden was cleared,
and spirits shrank, hid in glass cages,
their moon faces darting through golden
liquid to burn hotly behind stupid tongues.

They will speak to you from my mouth
if you will just buy me a drink.
No, don't go yet!
You haven't seen it all.
For ten bucks I will show you
every scar on my body.
Another ten, you can make your own.
I will dance for you in a veil
of red waterfalls.
Stay, I am a prophet.
Angels visit me at night with pen knives.

It is a history, old man, that unwinds
from your long tongue glistening
in my stillborn brain. Tell it to me
so I might climb words back to a beginning.

Beaver Woman

I

All winter long there is nothing
but a membrane of ice over the pond
and the beaver lodge like a white breast
solid with unyielded milk.

I watch from the doorway
of our cabin, wait
for your feet breaking snow
from the north forest to me.

The nights are moonless and
the beaver lodge cataracts my sight.
Even when I close my eyes it remains
milk white, glowing.
I flatten my body on skins, press
into the memory of your brown hand.

In my womb, small animals unfurl

II

Spring shuffles but your footprints
remain empty.
I grow pleas on branches, hang
them over my outstretched arms
dappled with buds and sunlight.
My mouth fills with longing.
The beaver lodge stirs and breathes.
I penetrate the pond, slide
over mud, through reeds and nesting birds,
algae plugging my nostrils,
the smell of your loins.

The fur of beaver kittens is warm
even in the darkest waters,
and I cling to them when the moon is thin
and the sky white with the cold fire of stars.

III

And now you come beckoning me
with your human hands, your feet
accustomed to walking green ferned trails
plant on the shore and I gaze up
to the earth in your eyes.

You must come into the water, husband
with your words that grind like teeth
in your jaws. My tongue longs
to stutter in the hollow of your neck.

If only the winter had not been so long
with nothing left alive but me
and a dark heart pulsing
beneath the beaver lodge.
I suckled hope from the movement of wind,
and a raven's call shadowing white.
Snow drifted through my veins until I sank
beneath the descending prayers of trees.

Come into the pond with your shivering lips.
I drink meaning.
Sink.
Nothing displaces me from these water-changes
but your man's flesh,
my woman's hunger.

1991

Empty Seas

Everything gone.

But maybe next year, the fishermen say, salt ringing their sight. Maybe a silver harvest will swell these lean seas. When we are hopeless, our hunger a crust on the low tide line, a dove, a gull, (an albatross?) will wheel through deepwater skies—an omen, a sign of redemption, dear God, dear God—

I no longer look for hope on this sad horizon. Since you died, Shawnandithit, they have forgotten you. I have all but forgotten you. Once I prayed that you escaped extinction, found a lover, delivered brown babies (one little, two little, three little—

Some mornings I think I see you sleeping on the incoming tide, awaking to watch the cold shiver of our days. I've seen

that book from the library—your sketches of waiting bridegrooms, of elders growing grey, children sifting sand, falling through their futures. I see

the dry-rot boats, the food bank volunteers in the abandoned cannery, the empty nets.

I want to tell them all, that it's all gone, that there will be no more fish, just scavenger birds slowly starving, an ocean of drought until we are all sea-changed, our bellies turned together towards a dying star, until we are immortal or wise or—

> nothing, Shawnandithit.
> Until we are all like you.

2000

Departures

This winter forest
is silent as any prim bedroom.
Under snow sheets
my captors now sleep, dreaming
of complacency and murder.

I flee them on snowshoes, mark
symbols of departure across a page,
striving for just the right sound
(a howl through needles,)
the right speed
(one quick rotation of treason.)

Earth cracks with cold, the stories
of my people—acorns buried within—slowly
freeze in forever sleep. But I

skate towards some imagined Spring
when trespass is unearthed,
and their hunger feeds on the blade of my forgiveness.

When their eyes might open.

2000

Sentences: at the Cull's

After working five years at the Peyton's,
I have learned their ways, their words,
understand sentences.

What shall we do with her?

When I weakened, they moved me to the Cull's
where I sit and sketch my lives for them.
I choose graphite, refuse colours—
yellow, blue, the flowing, flowing red.

I draw twelve ghosts on the page—the ones
my sister, mother, and I left

in camp,
        starving
            and all around them
                the animals ravaged, the land devoured,
                sickness passed from mouth to mouth
                their new sustenance—a hole
                in the gut, a torn tongue.

    Let me tell you
            about our hunting fences
            constructed with just one exit,
            killers awaiting their prey
            an ocean of assailants chasing behind,
            their only choice was between slayers
            our only choice was
        nothing
            left
for me to reveal
on these vast white sheets.
                So let them find
                    my people beneath snow
                    my Beothuk husband never-to-be,
                    babies I will not have,
                    the winter I sink into quieter, cooler
                    than their disdain
            blank pages at the back of the book
            they dream in frustrated inks—
            New-found-land, the title,
            a joke, a riddle—

What shall we do with— Me:
                    A suspended sentence

                                            2000

She is crying in a corner

of my mind, next to the dirty laundry,
her skin blistered with shower mildew
and smallpox, gaze hardening
with gnawed bread crust and toil.
She is the summer wind
sucked into air conditioners,

tree, bird, fox, fish
pushed into parks, zoos, extinction,
       a disease cured by death.
She is everything that must be cleaned,
cast-out, shelved, and treasured:
kiss goodnight, midnight hunger,
hex, star, sin, promise, stone,
and so small,
just one coal in a pit of ashes
we huddle around,
       turning cold.

So small
I can hardly hear her
screams sinking like a scalpel through sense
and absence, but she is with me,
       with us all

    Shawnandithit?

                                      2000

Unmarked Grave

There is no stone, no word or prayer to mark
Our fleet lives, our staggering deaths. Everything
We were is bound in silence, buried under dark
White plots. We mourn absences: budding Spring,
Summer seed, forests full of god and meat,
Our bullet and virus bones, stripped of light.
Babies suckle, nothing but curse to eat.
Their mouths hungry for repair, bleeding bite
The soil— stolen—their flesh, futures, rage
Beneath cold contempt and new subdivisions
Of greed. We languish in sorrow and dirt, betrayed.
Stake me with fences, bullshit, provisions
Of guilt, Weed n' Feed. I am silence crowing,
Broken wing soaring, language beyond their knowing.

                                        2000

Louise Halfe [b. 1953]

Memory is Spirit. I allow this spirit to be my guide in writing. I trust it totally. It does not choose audience, does not worry about it. I listen.... I write.... For years I've gone into my Vision Quest Lodge—my Fasting Lodge—offered myself as sacrifice to earn not only for myself, but for my community as well. I love life, love people and this love, I hope, does not dictate, rather it shares itself in stories. Stories bring readers to self-discovery and whatever it is they discover, it is for themselves, and if they choose to share, I, too, become the student. Writing, if well done, lifts the veils of our own pain, our own ignorance. It may hound us with questions, confusion, joy, anger, sadness, loneliness, frustration—these are all good places to enter.

Louise Bernice Halfe, Sky Dancer, is a Cree, born on the Saddle Lake Reserve in Alberta, where she was raised by her grandmother on her father's side, Adeliene Halfe. "The reserve was twenty-five miles from the nearest non-Native community," says Halfe. "My parents were nomads who worked for the Ukrainian farmers and in the sugar beet fields." At the age of seven, she was sent away to Blue Quills Residential School in St. Paul, Alberta. At sixteen she left home, breaking ties with her family and completing her studies at St. Paul's regional high school. "I was influenced by both the negative and the positive," says Halfe. "My father was a great provider, a wonderful hunter, a skilled orator. He was also an angry man. My mother was a dancer, an excellent humourous orator and imitator, an actress, superb cook, fine sewer, skilled craftswoman in creative works with hide, hoofs. I seldom saw her anger." Both parents "were products of residential school, which took its toll on their lives and mine." Her grandparents provided stability: "My Nokhom made her medicine, my Moosoom serviced her lodge. They had mutual harmony, a peacefulness. I miss them forever." Halfe received a bachelor of social work from the University of Regina in 1991 and has practiced drug and addiction counselling. She now lives in Saskatoon.

When she was in grade nine, Halfe entered a writing contest sponsored by a radio station. She didn't win, but she received the anthology *I Am an Indian*. "That was my first taste of Native writing and I took pleasure in it" (interview with Esta Spalding). Although when she was growing up "reading was not cultivated—my parents were oral storytellers," she became addicted to reading as an adult. Halfe began writing in her early twenties, through a process of keeping journals, meditating, walking, and recording her dreams. Much of her writing "came through" as poetry: "I didn't choose poetry, it chose me and I did not fight it" ("Writing, Healing and Spirituality"). Her first book of poetry, *Bear Bones and Feathers* (1994), was nominated for the Spirit of Saskatchewan Award, the Pat Lowther First Book Award, and won the 1996 Milton Acorn People's Poetry Award. Her second book of poetry, *Blue Marrow* (1998) was nominated for the Governor General's Award for poetry. In this book-length narrative poem, Native women and men interweave their voices to form an alternative history to non-Native fur trade histories. "What was it like for my grandmothers who didn't have the language to communicate whatever they felt?" (interview with Esta Spalding).

Many influences make themselves felt in Halfe's poetry: the formidable presence of her grandmother, the experience of young Native women suffering from abuse whom she encountered as a social worker, the voice of her mother's Cree-accented English— "The dialect is my mother's tongue…. I'm not making fun of the language. To me it's very endearing" (interview with Esta Spalding). In *Blue Marrow*, her father's point of view is voiced. Halfe's poetry, evocatively sensual and physical, often expresses both anguish and humour. "Sometimes laughter . . . can confront in a safe way" (interview with Esta Spalding). The bone motif runs through both her works, with multiple connotations. "Writing, for me, can be a process of baring myself—to lick, tear, strip stories from my bones." Bones also come "from the earth. Grinding bones makes medicine. Stories are also medicine. Stories are the marrow of our culture."

Pahkahkos

Flying Skeleton
I used to wonder where
You kept yourself.
I'd hear you rattle about
Scraping your bones

I opened a door
You grinned at me
Your hollow mouth
Stared through my heart
With empty eyes.

You lifted your boney hands
To greet me and I
Ran without a tongue.

You jumped on my back
Clinging to my neck you hugged
My mound of flesh.

For a thousand years you were
The heavy bones
The companion who would not leave.

You knocked your skull
On my head
I felt your boney feet.
I dragged and dragged
I couldn't carry
Your burden more.
I pried you loose
Bone after bone.

We stood, skull to face
Pāhkahkos, your many bones
Exposed

I, lighter than I could stand.
I fed you the drink of healing
You ran skeleton fingers
Down your face and onto mine.

I gave you a prayer cloth
I wove a blanket of forgiveness
You covered us both, skeleton and flesh.

I gave you the smoke of truth
You lit your Pipe to life
You lifted it to your ghostly mouth,
To mine.

My *Pāhkahkos* companion,
My dancing Skeleton
My dancing friend.

We carry our bundles
Side by side
Bones and flesh.

1994

Nōhkom, Medicine Bear

A shuffling brown bear
snorting and puffing
ambles up the stairs.

In her den
covered wall to wall
herbs hang…carrot roots, yarrow,

camomile, rat-root,
and *cācāmosikan.*

To the centre of the room she waddles
sits with one leg out, the other hugged close.
She bends over her roots and leaves
sniffs, snorts and tastes them
as she sorts them into piles.

She grinds the chosen few
on a small tire grater,
dust-devils settling into mole hills.
Her large brown paws take a patch
of soft deer skin
and wraps her poultice
until hundreds of tiny bundle-chains
swing from the rafters.

The brown laboring bear
Nōhkom, the medicine woman
alone in her attic den
smoking slim cigarettes
wears the perfume of sage, sweetgrass
and earth medicine ties.

Nōhkom, the medicine bear
healer of troubled spirits.
A red kerchief on her head,
blonde-white braids hang below her breasts.
She hums her medicine songs
shuffling alone in her den where
no light penetrates, no secrets escape.

She bends and her skirt drapes
over her aged beaded moccasins.
She brushes the potions off her apron.
A long day's work complete
Nōhkom ambles down the stairs
sweeps her long skirt behind her
drapes her paws on the stair rails
leaves her dark den and its medicine powers
to work in silence.

1994

She Told Me

She always told me
to take a willow branch
and gently whip the spirits
out of the house
calling, calling

Āstam we are leaving
āstam do not stay.

She always told me
to put the food away at night
to cover the dishes
or the spirits
would crackle and dance
whistle in our ears
and drive us mad.

I obeyed.

She always told me
never to eat the guts of
animals while I was pregnant
or the baby would be born
with a rope around the neck.

I yearned for the guts.

She always told me
never to walk over men

while I was in my moon
or they would die from my powcr.
I thought that was the idea.

She always told me
that *Nōhkom*, the medicine bag
had given her three cigarettes.
That's why the lizards
walked around inside her head.

I watched the flicker of her tongue.

1994

Ukrainian Hour

She spins from her belly
button-lint weaving,
pulls from her mouth
finger stump stories.
She knits horse hair
whipping the stick
of laughing songs.

She weaves on her knees,
humming rabbit fur stitched
between sheets of rags,
the land filled with
picket fences and tumbleweeds.

When the coal-oil lamp dances
and the cabin fire is still
Wīsahkecāhk jigs the two step
on Ukrainian Hour,
swirling her skirt,
whirling her children
in the safety of night.

1994

Eatin' Critters

We would stand
on the skirt of the hill
survey the stubble land
as hawk eyes marked our kill.

Ears like wings on a gliding hawk
ball cap low on his brow
lard pail and killing rock
chewing gum with me in tow.

I'd wet my finger
to test the wind.
He'd scold me if I slowed
and pinch my suntanned skin.

Tilted head and twitching ears
would listen to the gopher's pierce.
We'd spot our ground-belly meal,
race to the ditch and fill the pail
and give the hole a chug-a-lug.
When the whiskers breathe,
catch the gopher's tail.

Flatten his head with my rock
throw his dripping skin in the pail
swagger my hips like a satisfied cock
clowning home with my brother's grin.

1994

Picking Leftovers

There's men in the cellar shovelling, sweeping with combs and toothbrushes, probing dental picks, doctors in surgical gloves cradling bones, jaws, teeth, skulls, brittle arms and legs. Glueing pieces through lenses thicker than god's eye, given birth dates and pencilled in bibles.

When I was a child, father would stop at sites we called picking leftovers. I've returned with pitchfork in my hand, hammer against my heart. I've offered tobacco to earth and raked layers of toilet bowls, tin cans, beer bottles, and open-mouthed refrigerators. The skin of earth peels leaking pails, stench buried in ceremony. And over there in marble fields boxes of bones cemented in white rock. I give them birth dates, carefully record locations and fax the findings to the ship docked, waiting for hundreds of years, on the eastern shore.

1994

I'm So Sorry

I'm so sorry, the pope said
I thought you were just gathering
to lift your legs, thump your chest
around that tree of old men.
I didn't know the rock and twig
you smoked.
Blueberries, and sweetgrass
were your offerings.
I wouldn't have taken your babies
and fed them wafers and wine.

I'm so sorry, I just thought
we could borrow land for a little
to plant our seeds,
raise sheep and build churches, schools.
I really didn't know how you survived
for centuries on buffalo and teepees,
praying in medicine wheels.

I'm so sorry, I should have told
the settlers to quit their scalping,
selling hair at two bits for each Indian
I'm so sorry. I'm so sorry.
Maybe I could build healing churches
chapels full of sweetgrass and drums
chase the spirits out and fill sweatlodges
full of armed angels.

1994

In Da Name of Da Fadder

In da name of da fadder, poop
on my knees I pray to geezuz
cuz I got mad at my husband for
humpin' and makin too many babies
I 'pologize cuz I mad and cried I
didn't have no bannock and lard
to feed dem cuz my husband
drank all da *sōniyās* for wine.

In da name of da fadder, poop
my husband slap, fist and kick me
I hit him back. I 'pologize poop
da priest said I must of done someding
wrong and I deserve it cuz woman is
'uppose to listen to man. I not a good
wife cuz my hands somedimes
want to kill him.

In da name of da fadder, poop
I lookit other man he is so
handsome my eyes hurt, he kind, gentle,
soft laugh and my body wants to
feel his hot face. I no geezus
would be mad he said I must not
be durty in my doughts but
poop I want smile and warm arms.

In da name of da fadder, poop
Inside the sweatlodge I shame cuz
Indian *iskwew* don't do anydin',
In church priest said all us pagans
will go to hell. I don't know what da means,
all I no I is big sinner
and maybe I won't see geezuz when I die.

In da name of da fadder, poop
I dought da geezuz kind but
I is no good. I can't read hen write.
I don't understand how come *mōnīyās* has
clean howse and lottsa feed and he don't

share it with me and my children.
I don't understand why geezuz say I be
poop, stay on welfare cuz *mōnīyās* say
I good for nuddin' cuz I don't have
wisdom. Forgive me poop I is
big sinner.

1994

Der Poop

der poop
forgive me for writing on dis newspaper
i found it in da outhouse, saw lines
dat said you is sorry
some of my indian friends say is good but
some of dem say you sorry don't walk
so i was sitting here dinking dat we
maybe dalk
say, i always want to dell you stay
out of my pissness
if me wants to dalk to trees
and build nests in house
dats hup to me
if me wants to pitch my dent
and feed da ghost bannock hen berries
and maybe drow some indian popcorn
for you geezuz dats hup to me
i don't hask forgiveness not want
hand mary's, or a step ladder to heaven
me is happy with da sky, da bird *Iyiniwak*,
four-legged *Iyiniwak*, i is happy
sorry mean dat i don't need yous church
and yous priest telling me what to do
sorry mean dat i free to dalk to *Manitou*
the spirits and plant *Iyiniwak.*
dats all for now, poop
maybe we dalk again next time i see you
in da newspaper.

1994

These are the Body's Gifts

I offer ribs, taut flesh stretched like a starving dog's. My
tits scratching sidewalks.

I offer belly, wedged in spandex. A pit of balled snakes
quivering beneath touch.

I offer buttocks, rump of deer sailing over fences.
Wēpāyōs: white tail flipping.

I offer thighs, the smoke of a .303, fingers unclenched.

Take this body of snails and leeches. Stretched babies that
have left dried creek beds across the gut.

Take it, take it, pressed tight in your beak.
Beady eyes examining its old, tender flaws.
Marvel at the rot.

Inside you, Magpie, I will be the glutton eating flesh,
curing the dysentery of age.

1994

from Blue Marrow

Bless me father, I've pierced my flesh. Dance
with the Sun. Bathe my face in blood. I didn't mean to.
Forgive me, father, I ask for absolution.
I promise to say my rosary and serve my time.
I promise to keep my hands to myself and swallow my
tongue. Amen.

We gathered in the darkened room,
bodies pressed leg to leg. Our breath
mint and garlic, sage and sweet grass
woven into my burlap gown.
We held hands, my love and I.
On each side my mother and father sat.
Blankets   tea   sugar   flour   gunpowder.

Tobacco   ribbons   blueberry   cloth.
In the dark they came.

I bring to you
these voices I will not name. Voices
filled with bird calls, snorting buffalo,
kicking bears, mountain goats.
I do not recognize who speaks.
Skin unfolds. Sag after sag.
Words squeezed through
her blistered tongues
lick till my heart stings, my
eyes swell.

Lightning flitted.
Scorched our flesh.
They tore our tongues.
When we spoke,
my love and I, darkness swelled.
Thunder became our footsteps. This
ceremonial dance of my dead.
We were wedded that night.
The night has no shadow,
her veil always an open mouth.
Listen to the bones.

*   *   *   *

We are tired, Nōsisim.
The climb down waking our bones.
Your children's tears
roused our sleep.
You have filled our scalped breast
with tobacco.
Our wombs the medicine bags
of your festering.
Listen, Nōsisim—
these stories you gather,
our Sundance songs.
Give me my cane.
I'll awake these sleeping Pipes.
Those Bundles belong to women,
the wind storms

in the stripes of our flesh.
Our breasts that hang from the belts
of prairie settlers
now sway in the hands of our men.
Oh Nōsisim, we cannot
carry your burden.
Your youthful face,
ours storm-eaten, sun-baked.
We will dance in the tepee
of your children's songs. Dream.
Dream. Nōsisim. Drum.
Drum. The Medicine lives.
It lives. It lives.

Winter rolled from her shoulder,
her song burned. My fist
sunk in earth. I became a cave
of shredded flesh.

For centuries
I've tumbled through thistles,
charcoal stars and suns,
groaning lakes and rivers,
my hairy skull
a home for mice and snakes.

A cursed man
chopped up my body,
sent my sons running.
Now he swims
in stars,
me dangling in his fist.

I'm earth
born each moon,
waxing and waning,
bleeding eggs.

I'm painted red on rock,
I swim the caves in lakes
where my head sinks
and I drink to roll again.

The boys have been running.
They are old wrinkled hearts.
They've eaten leathered flesh.
Knuckles gnawed to bone,
they run.

The medicines they've thrown
to thorn my path
I've gathered, the Bundles
given to amisk, iskotwēw
and the swan.
They run from their mother's
nursing tongue.
The flaming open womb,
the burning boiling bone
rolls round and round in
the hairy head.

Nāpēsisak, *wailing coyotes,*
run the river bends,
cast your medicines!
Nāpēsisak, *wailing coyotes,*
dust swirls beneath your feet.
The tribal bones
and swimming moon
will fly.

⋆   ⋆   ⋆   ⋆

They hobbled, limped, shuffled,
pink, purple, blues, reds, yellows,
white, black, printed blazed dresses,
shawls, kerchiefs, blankets.
Dried flowers, old sweat
and sweet perfume, they teased,
laughed, joked and gossiped.
Ran their fingers through each
swinging hand. Pipe smoke
swirled. Men drumming our songs.

I watch them. Hundreds of my husband's family.
They've travelled across Canada, the United States,
rejoice at recognizing one another, some for the first time.

Each has brought a book they've lovingly compiled.
It contains the history of their migration
from England, Norway and into the Dakotas.
They are scattered throughout Turtle Island.
They marvel at the trek of their ancestors.
The click of wine glasses echoes through the arbour
of this large family gathering. And five Indians.
I the eldest, my children and two other Indian youths.
They are not yet aware how this affects their lives.
Who are we? Adopted. I gather inward.
How many of my relatives were cattled
onto the reservation during their settlement? How
much of my people's blood was spilled for this
migration? Laughter and wonder
as fingers move across the atlas. This is where
great-granddad Arne crossed on the barge.
This is where great-great-granddad travelled
and preached the law of the land and where his
wife Isobel taught the little savages to read.
My lips are tight from stretching when my
small family is introduced alongside the
large extended family. Later, driving home,
I weave a story for my children—how their
great-grandma rode sidesaddle, waving
her .22 in the air trying to scare those relatives
away. I tell them how my relatives lived
around the fort, starving and freezing,
waiting for diluted spirits and handouts
from my husband's family. I tell them
how my little children died wrapped
in smallpox blankets. My breath
won't come any more.
I stare at the wheat fields.

    Grandfather bent over the paper leaves,
    knife men with pāskisikana *stand by.*
    This day and many others
    I've wanted those pāskisikana
    pointed, hard and straight.

    We were eating summer pups,
    buffalo heaped in sour heat—
    no rabbits,

no berries
to fill our dying bellies.
Our warriors crying,
the Sundance Tree
falling
from the pāskisikana.
Ghost Dancers in
bleeding shirts.
We were dying. We were
dying. Dying.

Grandfather talked
with Grandmother. She said,
"River blood will always be our milk.
This talk will stain the leaves."
Grandfather carried his bending,
joined the other walk-far eyes.
They shared the Pipe.
This is how it came to be.
Grandfather drawing suns
moons
lakes
winds and grass.

Snot rainbow babies.
Parliament chieftains.
Fancy dancers. Symphony.
Drummers. Ballerina.
I will breed.
Everywhere.

1998

Marilyn Dumont

[b. 1955]

I employ language to subvert, expose, empower. I am interested in experimentation with figurative language: English and Cree, symbols, themes, and forms that challenge not only our ways of defining poetry, but our ways of defining ourselves. I see language as a tool, and I do not underestimate the politics of the English language to silence us. For me, writing must be "inspired": language which has life breathed into it. It must be a dance of the intellect and passion, both emotional and spiritual, and it must be uncompromising in its manifestation.

Marilyn Dumont, of Cree/Métis ancestry, was born in Olds, Alberta. A descendant of Gabriel Dumont, she shares in a complex history of relations between Métis, Native peoples, and Euro-Canadians that is evident in her poetry. She grew up "close enough to Indian Reserves at Hobbema and Morley for townspeople to know we were Indian, but didn't live on a reserve." Being raised by bilingual parents stimulated Dumont's interest in language; she became conscious of "sound, cadence, and meaning. I would hear the difference between Cree and English and they were so very different. I noticed my parents behaved differently when they spoke Cree, so I became fine-tuned to this difference." A love of music and dance, which she inherited from her mother, also affects Dumont's relationship to language, making her aware of "rhythm, beat, and tone." When she began reading poetry publicly, she learned "to use my voice as an instrument, once I realized the power it had on people."

In her twenties, Dumont saw herself as a visual artist rather than a writer and seriously considered attending the Alberta College of Art. She worked in video production with the National Film Board for three years and then decided to complete an M.F.A. in creative writing from the University of British Columbia in 1998 (she had received a B.A. in English/anthropology in 1991). Her first book of poetry, *A Really Good Brown Girl* (1996) won the 1997 Gerald Lampert Memorial Award from the League of Canadian Poets for the best first collection of poetry by a Canadian poet. She has taught creative writing, and her interest in film continues.

Many of Dumont's poems wrestle with the problem of identity, whether one defines oneself as "Métis" in relation to "this treaty guy" ("Circle the Wagons,") or Métis as opposed to "Canadian citizen" ("It Crosses My Mind"). She subverts ideas of identity as stable and natural, while at the same time she recognizes the need to struggle for a vision of oneself against contexts that attempt to limit and devalue. Some poems, such as "The White Judges" and "Leather and Naughahyde" suggest the complexity of living within simultaneous competing identities, or represent sudden shifts from one sense of self to another, depending on social context. The form of her poems can indicate these sudden shifts by moving from prosaic description to poetry, as in "The White Judges." The elastic and seemingly unending amplification of the prose poem "It Crosses My Mind" contradicts and undermines prosaic forms which limit, categorize, and objectify. Humour is another of Dumont's strategies of subversion, evident in "Letter to Sir John A. Macdonald" and "Letter to My Mother."

While Dumont's poems can represent an inner maze of thoughts and subtle states of mind, they can also joyfully recall, through intense, sensual imagery, pleasures of the body and the "promising sky" of childhood. Dumont calls herself a "realist" and says "some of the poets I admire are realists: Joy Harjo, Sharon Olds, Adrienne Rich, Dionne Brand."

The White Judges

We lived in an old schoolhouse, one large room that my father converted into two storeys with a plank staircase leading to the second floor. A single window on the south wall created a space that was dimly lit even at midday. All nine kids and the occasional friend slept upstairs like cadets in rows of shared double beds, ate downstairs in the kitchen near the gas stove and watched TV near the airtight heater in the adjacent room. Our floors were worn linoleum and scatter rugs, our walls high and bare except for the family photos whose frames were crowded with siblings waiting to come of age, marry or leave. At supper eleven of us would stare down a pot of moose stew, bannock and tea, while outside the white judges sat encircling our house.

And they waited to judge

waited till we ate tripe
watched us inhale its wild vapour
sliced and steaming on our plates,
watched us welcome it into our being,
sink our teeth into its rubbery texture
chew and roll each wet and tentacled piece
swallow its gamey juices
until we have become it and it had become us.

Or waited till the cardboard boxes
were anonymously dropped at our door, spilling with clothes
waited till we ran swiftly away from the windows and doors
to the farthest room for fear of being seen
and dared one another to
'open it'
'no you open it'
'no you'
someone would open it
cautiously pulling out a shirt
that would be tried on
then passed around till somebody claimed it by fit
then sixteen or eighteen hands would be pulling out
skirts, pants, jackets, dressed from a box transformed now
into the Sears catalogue.

Or the white judges would wait till twilight
and my father and older brothers
would drag a bloodstained canvas
heavy with meat from the truck onto our lawn, and
my mother would lift and lay it in place
like a dead relative,
praying, coaxing and thanking it
then she'd cut the thick hair and skin back
till it lay in folds beside it like carpet

carving off firm chunks
until the marble bone shone out of the red-blue flesh
long into the truck-headlight-night she'd carve
talking in Cree to my father and in English to my brothers
long into the dark their voices talking us to sleep
while our bellies rested in the meat days ahead.

Or wait till the guitars came out
and the furniture was pushed up against the walls
and we'd polish the linoleum with our dancing
till our socks had holes.

Or wait till a fight broke out
and the night would settle in our bones
and we'd ache with shame
for having heard or spoken

that which sits at the edge of our light side
that which comes but we wished it hadn't
like 'settlement' relatives who would arrive at Christmas and
leave at Easter.

1996

Helen Betty Osborne

Betty, if I set out to write this poem about you
it might turn out instead
to be about me
or any one of
my female relatives
it might turn out to be
about this young native girl
growing up in rural Alberta
in a town with fewer Indians
than ideas about Indians,
in a town just south of the 'Aryan Nations'

it might turn out to be
about Anna Mae Aquash, Donald Marshall or Richard Cardinal,
it might even turn out to be
about our grandmothers,
beasts of burden in the fur trade
skinning, scraping, pounding, packing,
left behind for 'British Standards of Womanhood,'
left for white-melting-skinned women,
not bits-of-brown women
left here in this wilderness, this colony.

Betty, if I start to write a poem about you
it might turn out to be
about hunting season instead,
about 'open season' on native women
it might turn out to be
about your face   young and hopeful
staring back at me   hollow now
from a black and white page
it might be about the 'townsfolk'   (gentle word)
townsfolk who 'believed native girls were easy'

and 'less likely to complain if a sexual proposition led to violence.'

Betty, if I write this poem.

1996

Blue Ribbon Children

I was supposed
to be married, a wife
who cooked
large pots of potatoes,
chunks of steaming meat and
slabs of brown crusty bannock. I was supposed
to prepare meals
for a man who returned
every night like
a homing pigeon
to hot meals and a warm bed, slept
up against my flannel back and generous hips. I was
supposed to balance children like
bags of flour on my hip,
lift them in and out of
bathtubs, lather them
like butterballs, pack them safely
away in bed, then stuff them
into patched clothes for morning, and
feed them porridge as though
they were being fattened up
for prizes at a fair, blue ribbon
children, like the red rose
tea he expected hot and strong
in front of him as we sat down for supper.

1996

Let the Ponies Out

oh papa, to have you drift up, some part of you drift up through water through
fresh water into the teal plate of sky soaking foothills, papa,
to have your breath leave, escape you, escape the
weight of bone, muscle and organ, escape you, to rise up, to loft,

till you are all breath filling the room, rising, escaping the white, the white
sheets, airborne, taken in a gust of wind and unbridled ponies, let the ponies
out, I would open that gate if I could find it, if there was one
to let you go, to drift up into, out, out
of this experiment into the dome of all breath and wind and
reappear in the sound of the first year's thunder with
Chigayow cutting the clouds over your eyes expanding, wafting, wings
of a bird over fields, fat ponies, spruce, birch and poplar, circling
wider than that tight square sanitized whiteness
you breathe in, if you could just stop breathing you could
escape, go anywhere, blow, tumble in the prairie grass,
bloom in the face of crocuses
appear in the smell of cedar dust off a saw
in the smell of thick leather
in the whistling sounds of the trees
in the far off sound of a chainsaw or someone chopping wood
in the smooth curve of a felt hat, in unbridled ponies

1996

Horse-Fly Blue

'…d'you believe in god?,' I ask

>   he says, he 'doesn't
>   know,
>   care'

'But,' I say,
'can't you see that this sky
is the colour of the Greek Mediterranean,
and won't last?'

>   although I've never seen the Mediterranean
>   I have faith

'Can't you see that this light,'

>   'what light?' he says

is the same as all those other afternoons when
the light was receding like
our hairlines, when it shone through
our winter skin and we
awoke from a long nap and
it was light all the time we were sleeping?

'Doesn't this light remind you of all those other times
you looked up from your reading
and weren't expecting to see
change and nothing
did change except the way
you looked, the way you met the light,
greeted it at the door as a friend
or smiled at it from a distance as your lover?

Can't you see that the sky is
horse-fly blue?
I swear I've seen this light before;
before I was born,
I knew the colour of this sky.
When I was five
the yard I played in
had a sky this colour,' I say   'what colour?' he says.

                                                                        1996

Letter to Sir John A. Macdonald

Dear John: I'm still here and halfbreed,
after all these years
you're dead, funny thing,
that railway you wanted so badly,
there was talk a year ago
of shutting it down
and part of it was shut down,
the dayliner at least,
'from sea to shining sea,'
and you know, John,
after all that shuffling us around to suit the settlers,
we're still here and Metis.

We're still here
after Meech Lake and
one no-good-for-nothin-Indian
holdin-up-the-train,
stalling the 'Cabin syllables /Nouns of settlement,
/…steel syntax [and] /The long sentence of its exploitation'
and John, that goddamned railroad never made this a great nation,

cause the railway shut down
and this country is still quarreling over unity,
and Riel is dead
but he just keeps coming back
in all the Bill Wilsons yet to speak out of turn or favour
because you know as well as I
that we were railroaded
by some steel tracks that didn't last
and some settlers who wouldn't settle
and it's funny we're still here and callin ourselves halfbreed.

1996

Circle the Wagons

There it is again, the circle, that goddamned circle, as if we thought in circles, judged things on the merit of their circularity, as if all we ate was bologna and bannock, drank Tetley tea, so many times 'we are' the circle, the medicine wheel, the moon, the womb, and sacred hoops, you'd think we were one big tribe, is there nothing more than the circle in the deep structure of native literature? Are my eyes circles yet? Yet I feel compelled to incorporate something circular into the text, plot, or narrative structure because if it's linear then that proves that I'm a ghost and that native culture really has vanished and what is all this fuss about appropriation anyway? Are my eyes round yet? There are times when I feel that if I don't have a circle or the number four or legend in my poetry, I am lost, just a fading urban Indian caught in all the trappings of Doc Martens, cappuccinos and foreign films but there it is again orbiting, lunar, hoops encompassing your thoughts and canonizing mine, there it is again, circle the wagons....

1996

Leather and Naughahyde

So, I'm having coffee with this treaty guy from up north and we're laughing at how crazy 'the mooniyaw' are in the city and the conversation comes around to where I'm from, as it does in underground languages, in the oblique way it does to find out someone's status without actually asking, and knowing this, I say I'm Metis like it's an apology and he says, 'mmh,' like he forgives me, like he's got a big heart and mine's pumping diluted blood and his voice has sounded well-fed up till this point, but now it goes thin like he's across the room taking another look and when he returns he's got 'this look,' that says he's leather and I'm naughahyde.

1996

It Crosses My Mind

It crosses my mind to wonder where we fit in this 'vertical mosaic,' this colour colony; the urban pariah, the displaced and surrendered to apartment blocks, shopping malls, superstores and giant screens, are we distinct 'survivors of white noise,' or merely hostages in the enemy camp and the job application asks if I am a Canadian citizen and am I expected to mindlessly check 'yes,' indifferent to skin colour and the deaths of 1885, or am I actually free to check 'no,' like *the truth north strong and free* and what will I know of my own kin in my old age, will they still welcome me, share their stew and tea, pass me the bannock like it's mine, will they continue to greet me in the old way, hand me their babies as my own and send me away with gifts when I leave and what name will I know them by in these multicultural intentions, how will I know other than by shape of nose and cheekbone, colour of eyes and hair, and will it matter that we call ourselves Metis, Metisse, Mixed blood or aboriginal, will sovereignty matter or will we just slide off the level playing field turned on its side while the provincial flags slap confidently before me, echoing their self-absorbed anthem in the wind, and what is this game we've played long enough, *finders keepers/losers weepers*, so how loud and how long can the losers weep and the white noise infiltrates my day as easily as the alarm, headlines and 'Morningside' but 'Are you a Canadian citizen?',   I sometimes think to answer, *yes, by coercion,   yes, but no...there's more*, but no space provided to write my historical interpretation here, that *yes but no*, really only means *yes* because there are no lines for the stories between *yes and no* and what of the future of my eight-year-old niece,   whose mother is Metis but only half as Metis as her grandmother, what will she name herself and will there come a time and can it be measured or predicted when she will stop naming herself and crossing her own mind.

1996

Instructions to My Mother

Never list the troubles of my eight brothers and sisters
before hearing mine.

Simply nod your head and say 'uh huh,'

                            say 'I hear you,' a lot

                                    and the rest of the time say nothing.

When I am sick,
don't list your ailments
before I tell you mine. Instead
ask if I need a blanket and a book
and let me eat ice cream bars dipped in dark chocolate.

Never call
                     the names of all my sisters
before calling mine.

When I doubt my creativity,
avoid listing the talents of my siblings first.
Instead dig out my 10th grade sketch book and
homesick letters to you and
tell me they are remarkable and
that they make you cry.

And never tell me
I'm 'getting grey,'
but that I am wise in skin,
sturdy-minded in bone and
beautywise in the ways of old women.

                                      1996

The Sky Is Promising

Danny, come home
it's sunny
the ponies are frisky,
the sawdust pile is high,
the spruce are whistling and
the day rolls out before us.

Danny come home to sky
the colour of juniper berries,
it's summer and
time to twist binder-twine
into long ropes to catch the ponies,
race them to the water trough,
listen for the sound of green
poplar leaves applauding
and dream of prizes,
hand-tooled saddles
big silver buckles and
our victories assure us
we have lived our sawdust days well.

Danny come home
the berries are ripe and we've collected
lard pails for picking, We've driving
up the bench road to fill them
with sweet smelling huckleberries.
We'll meet for lunch, use the tailgate for a table,
dump our berries into buckets and
talk about the patch we found,
the deer we saw, the stream
we drank from or the bees'
nest almost stepped on.

Danny come home
the sawdust pile is high and
its slopes are sand
dunes we can slide down
at the bottom we can look
up and see only the crest
of sand and the promising sky.

Danny come home. The men
are riding skid horses into camp,
watering them at the trough,
we can get close, watch
their flared steaming nostrils
sink into the icy water,
see them chew the cool liquid,
teeth the size of our fingers,
water dripping from their chins
throwing their heads back,
harness sounds rippling,
whinnying to the horses in the corral.

Danny come home we can
walk through the warm pine smells
to where the men are falling, we can
listen to them hollering orders
to the skid horses
whose heavy hind legs
lever the still logs
into a moving universe.

1996

Armand Garnet Ruffo [b. 1955]

My writing is about fostering positive change. I'm saying that to be of Native heritage is something to be proud of, not something to be ashamed of, which has been part and parcel of colonial indoctrination. While I am certainly occupied with addressing the colonial powers that be, and advocating justice for Native people, by no means is all my writing oppositional. I firmly believe that as human beings, as children of the Great Mystery, we all share certain experiences and qualities. Love. Hate. Happiness. Sadness. These things also concern me. These are the emotions and experiences that poets have contemplated since human beings spoke and sang their first words.

Armand Garnet Ruffo was born in Chapleau, northern Ontario. "Both of my parents come from tiny communities that no longer exist," according to Ruffo. "My mother's community of Biscotasing is now basically a tourist site."

"For many years, I identified myself as half of this and half of that, until one day Wilfred Peltier corrected me and told me that you cannot be half of anything. You either are or are not. From that point on I have identified myself as Anishinabe and strived to integrate the European with the Ojibway side of my heritage, to find good in both traditions." Wilfred Peltier, the Odawa Elder, storyteller, and author of *No Foreign Land* and *A Wiseman Speaks*, "was one of my biggest influences, particularly in regard to his perspective on life. I met him when I first moved to Ottawa in the late 1970s, and we stayed in touch right up to his recent death."

Becoming a writer was not something Ruffo set out to do. Growing up in northern Ontario, he spent most of his time hunting, fishing, and guiding. When he got to York University, he intended to study biology. In a literature class, poet-critic Eli Mandel encouraged him to pursue his interest in literature by and about Native people. "From that moment, I was hooked." Leaving Toronto after receiving a B.A. from York University in 1980, Ruffo moved to Ottawa to work for *Native Perspective* magazine and became involved in various Native organizations.

At the same time, he began to write poetry in earnest. He comments: "In the late 1970s and early 1980s there was very little room for Native writers in the mainstream literary culture, and everything that I sent out was rejected. For a while I stopped writing." One day, hearing that George Ryga was writer-in-residence at the University of Ottawa, Ruffo sent him some poems. "He called me up gave me the best advice I could possibly get at the time: to keep at it and not to stop no matter what anyone said."

Ruffo's experience at The Banff Writer's Program in 1989 encouraged him to see his writing as central rather than peripheral. From there, he completed an M.A. in literature and creative writing at the University of Windsor, working with Alistair McLeod. He is an Assistant Professor of English at Carleton University in Ottawa.

Ruffo published his first book of poetry, *Opening in the Sky*, in 1994. In 1996 he published a creative biography of Grey Owl, written in poetry, entitled *Grey Owl: The Mystery of Archie Belaney*. A second collection of poems, *At Geronimo's Grave*, was published in 2001. He has also workshopped three plays. Many of Ruffo's poems investigate history from many angles. They encourage reinterpretation of the written record by incorporating and recontextualizing—often from Ojibway perspectives—the actual language of figures such as Duncan Campbell Scott, and Grey Owl. In poems such as "I Heard Them, I Was There," he looks through the eyes of a Euro-Canadian persona. In others, such as "At Geronimo's Grave," he reflects on the making of history and historical record, a problem which other poems implicitly raise.

Poem for Duncan Campbell Scott

(Canadian poet who "had a long and distinguished career
in the Department of Indian Affairs, retiring in 1932."
The Penguin Book of Canadian Verse*)*

Who is this black coat and tie?
Christian severity etched in the lines
he draws from his mouth. Clearly a noble man
who believes in work and mission. See
how he rises from the red velvet chair,
rises out of the boat with the two Union Jacks
fluttering like birds of prey
and makes his way towards our tents.
This man looks as if he could walk on water
and for our benefit probably would,
if he could.

He says he comes from Ottawa way, Odawa country,
comes to talk treaty and annuity and destiny,
to make the inevitable less painful,
bearing gifts that must be had.
Notice how he speaks aloud and forthright:

This or Nothing.
Beware! Without title to the land
under the Crown you have no legal right
to be here.
Speaks as though what has been long decided wasn't.
As though he wasn't merely carrying out his duty
to God and King. But sincerely felt.

Some whisper this man lives in a house of many rooms,
has a cook and a maid and even a gardener
to cut his grass and water his flowers.
Some don't care, they don't like the look of him.
They say he asks many questions but
doesn't wait to listen. Asks
much about yesterday, little about today
and acts as if he knows tomorrow.
Others don't like the way he's always busy writing
stuff in the notebook he carries. Him,
he calls it poetry
and says it will make us who are doomed
live forever.

                                                    1994

Some

                                        (For George Ryga)

When I read the caption announcing your death
I think of the gnarled hands of immigrants
swinging sledge hammers in dollar-a-day cold,
those same hands plowing
stubborn lives. All that steel
cutting the land, carcasses
of buffalo bleached into winter
and brown children huddled
behind wire. Old stories
rising like tobacco smoke. Some laugh.
Some do not.

And I think of myself as I was, wanting
so much to be myself, wandering
half the world. You said,
look where it began for you. Move

ahead by moving back.
North? But we aim to get out.
The train whistles a dream
south and our roots get stretched
across this country. A city chills
our blood (a kind of longing) and we turn
to drink for lost warmth. Some stop.
Some never do.

I also think of you visiting me and
going through my words. Not
one for compliment, idle talk, you
came to offer advice. You said poetry is a gift.
These days the page is an endless winter,
the words sleep soundly and do not fly
when left alone. You said our responsibility
is to speak. To speak for those who cannot.
A child grows with circles in his eyes
and looks for direction. Some find it.
Some do not.

And finally I think of your summerland,
the basket of cherries you gave
me for my journey back. I split the red flesh
with my teeth and sucked in the juice of wind,
rain and sun. We are all going somewhere.
In kindness is guidance. For a moment
I met you and now you have returned to our Mother
the Earth, to God. Do we not spend our lives
returning. Some believe.
Some know.

1994

Poetry

makes me
want to write poetry,
exotic disease I guess,
      butterfly palpitations
bursting across the kitchen table
fragrance of sweetgrass
and wild mint wafting into the room,

jasmine tea
for two
suddenly on the boil,
whistling intimacy,
warming what is inside,
perfection of nipple, im-
perfection of heart,
arc of arm,
shape of (tender?) greeting,
(bitter?) farewell,
extended from toe to thigh to infinity.
nothing to do with
I can do better
nothing like that, this honest desire
that kicks
like a new born calf
jumping up and disappearing
into its own geography.

1994

Surely Not Warriors

black leather
and pink porcupine hair
believing birth and history are against them
on the corner bumming spare change
waiting on party-time.
is this rebellion
        or resignation?
only their hairdressers know for sure.

1994

Grey Owl, 1935

You in the audience who sit in expectation cannot know.

This fear, this inexorable fear, I take with me,
so much a part of me I carry it in my blood. Picture me
stepping onto the stage and into a beam of light.
5 I look out to the audience, to you,
but I see only a curtain of black. Certainly I hear

Goldie;
mystique

your applause, the rumble of voices, the clapping of hands,
and I greet this not without a small degree of satisfaction,
but I am far from at ease (though this air I try to assume)
10 as I make my way to the podium, for here darkness is no forest
sanctuary but more a murky abyss, ready to open greedily
like the mouth that it is, with a sharp, accusing shriek.

The music has come to an end: Beethoven's "Moonlight Sonata,"
an echo of my childhood, of Highbury Villa, of Aunt Ada
15 towering over me, a music that continues to swell my past
inside me but which for some unknown reason—Call it love
—I continue to use as a prelude to my entrance.

Call it affliction.

The film is rolling; no, correction, I haven't yet given the cue.
20 After a prefatory greeting in which I tell you I come in peace,
I'm now launched into a story of my early days as a riverman,
or maybe I'm mentioning how different it was for me to move
to northern Ontario from the southern United States, to learn
the still-hunt of the Ojibway as compared to the whoop
25 and holler of the Apache buffalo hunt.

What I do know is that I'm in the middle of a sentence when
as though by lightning my words are struck down.
Without warning. From behind the black curtain
where you sit, someone is shouting: Liar! Liar!

30 Nothing but a liar.

Immediately the house lights come on with a hush as blinding
and as penetrating as the darkness which has now accumulated
in the person of the woman who stands in front of me
dressed in black with a veil masking her face,
35 as though she were in mourning. Is she?

All heads are turned towards her,
as she extends her arm and points to me.
You and the rest of the audience are aghast, struck dumb.
No one knows what to do. In the room's startled breath,
40 you could hear a leaf drop, except there are no leaves,
for this is a London auditorium, no leaves, no trees,
no place to hide.

The woman is now addressing those seated around her.
She tells you that she knows me.
45 Her? Me? Yes, me. She slowly nods, — *Goldie; mystique*
as she raises <u>her veil</u> and looks me in the eye.
She is close, so close I can see the tears,
the torn smile, her emotions mixed and ravenous,
as she fulfills her dream come true of confronting me.

50 He's both a liar and a scoundrel.
I know, I'm his wife. Here, look! She screams,
and raises her left hand to show off a wedding ring,
and then from her handbag pulls out a couple of photographs:
Ask him about these, she says amid the flashing cameras
55 to the photographers who have managed to shove their way
towards her, while two ushers try to grab hold of her.

But the audience is calling for her to continue.
Continue. And so she gives them dates and names,
the name of the church, the presiding minister,
60 witnesses, guests, and on and on.
It turns out she is not alone.
One by one others in the audience begin to stand,
begin to make their way towards me, all
bearing an accusing finger.

65 And you, whoever you are, are swept up among them.
Before I can even get off stage, find a way to escape,
<u>you have all encircled me</u> and together
are pointing and chanting in unison:
70 Archibald. ~~Archibald Stansfeld~~ Belaney.
The photographers have also surrounded me, <u>flashbulbs</u>   *imaginary indian;*
explode in my face. Blinded. There is no escape.   *turned into a public spectacle*

The haunted has become <u>the hunted</u>.

I press my hands to my ears and implore everyone to stop,
75 to let me go: for you know now who I am.
Helpless, I fall to my knees. And above me, there she is,
Ivy, the young actress <u>Belaney</u> once loved and abandoned.
And beside her, all his old Hastings Grammar School classmates
laughing at odd-ball Archie who's still <u>playing Indian</u>
80 after all these years.   *desire*

1996

Mirror

In the end
there is no escape
   (Did I say there was?)
It is always me.
No matter what I do
to change
the way I look.
What is inside is inside looking out.

I see it all (home, family, friends, wives…).

Is this the reason
I'm happiest
making miles
in my canoe—
going to beat hell
over the surface of some lake?

I dip my paddle,
pull hard,
the water ripples
and swirls,
for a moment
the mirror
I'm riding
smashed to a million pieces.

1996

I Heard Them, I Was There

Writing in 1747 about captives, Cadwallader Colden records, 'No Arguments, no Intreaties, nor Tears of their Friends and Relations, could persuade many of them to leave their own Indian Friends and Acquaintance(s).
   — *Quoted by James Axtell in* The White Indians of Colonial America

We came in droves, by wagon, by train, by boat,
womanless, ready for anything, but wanting wealth.
I was there. I saw how we howled at an empty sky,

called upon heaven to open in a beacon of rainbow
and lead us to that ever blessed vein of gold. Yes,
I remember how we toiled with bare hands, plunged
ourselves in the bosom of earth until we tore our own flesh,
split ourselves wide open like the very land we preyed upon.
It got so that we no longer even felt, we mastered the art,
and merely stuffed our pain (and memory) into our mouths
and swallowed. Nobody ever let out a cry or even a whimper.
You could say we had moved into the level of sweat.

If we had faith it was in ourselves, in our backs,
our deadened minds, forged in darkness and dream.
Our God, our accomplice, always radiant and forgiving,
left us to ourselves. At night we dreamed
golden meadows, caterpillers turning to butterflies,
storms to rainbows. Some even dreamed cities,
saloons and whisky, women and sex. What else?
We all dreamed of singing, "Those were the days my friend
we thought they'd never end," relaxing in a hot tub
with a cigar in mouth and glass in hand, and of course
with the mandatory young thing scrubbing our backs.
It's no lie. I swear. I was there in flesh and spirit.

Of course there were the other dreams. And we cursed
those who had planted them for us. I put a bottle to my lips
and found it filled with scorpions, black beetles and lice.
I threw down a hammer that had squirmed into a slimy serpent.
I woke one night to find the walls of the bunkhouse
smeared in shit and blood. But all that I must say was before
a few of us dared go deep into the forest for fresh meat.
I could tell from the start that day was ripe with omen.
Away from the pit I could hear my name stirring
in the wind, could taste the fear burn in my gut, hover
in the trees, appear in the beat of crow wings
(which made us all laugh nervously).
And then, a small red sack with a braid of something
left on a rock. We burned it, damned it devil worship.

But me. I couldn't get it out of my head
and found myself labouring over it
when I should have had my mind on my work.
When I looked at my hands I saw for the first time
they were claws. My mouth stank of blunt decay.

What did it mean this offering? Was it a message?
I went back. The rest is history. Sometimes
I still return to the edge of the clearing and watch
with eyes that see through darkness. Nothing has changed.
And I wonder what it is I am looking for sitting here
in the shivering cold. Sometimes even they ask me
as though if I explain it to them I will explain it to myself,
but I repeat I don't know. What I do know is
it has something to do with death and darkness,
disease and dream. Something to do with me
looking back at myself.

1994

At Geronimo's Grave

Fierce, tenacious, master of guerilla warfare.
It's what the history books say.
Though at his grave, out of an unyielding sun,
and into a sanctuary of leafy shade, I move
through all that is said and not said
and touch the flowers left for him,
which make me wonder if it is possible for anyone
to have the last word. And I am reminded
that it took five thousand troops to track down
what was left of his Apache, thirty-five
men, women and children. Caught,
they say herded from New Mexico to Florida to Alabama
and finally all the way to Oklahoma, to so-called
Indian territory (as if the rest of the country wasn't).

They say more.

That by time he died at eighty he had embraced Christianity
and even taken part in a Presidential inauguration.
Part of the parade I suspect, the evidence committed
to memory: last year in England, at the Brighton Museum
(of all places), I bought a postcard of him lost
behind the wheel of a Model T Ford,
looking like he had just fallen out of the sky and
onto the driver's seat. Portrait of an old Chief in a tophat.
It was my only purchase. From there to here in one fatal swoop
as though giant talons have dropped me unexpectedly

onto this site. If I could I would ask him
if he too got plucked up by something larger than himself.

Last of the hold-outs, they call him.

This morning at Fort Sill I saw the windowless cellar
they held him in (not open to the public)
and the other building they transferred him to,
the one turned into a museum and whitewashed.
A notice said he really spent little time in his cell
since he had the run of the place,
like a bed and breakfast, I am led to believe.
Yet, with wilted petals between my fingers soft as grace,
soft as old sorrow, and an even older sun overhead
guiding me beyond this arbor and back onto the highway,
I am left wondering about who he really was.
Oilfields and prairie flowers, barbed wire and distant mesas
red as a people locked behind an aging vision
telling me it is the land that will have the last word.

For him whom they also call Prisoner of War.

1996

No Man's Land

He's already asleep when he awakes to someone rapping
at the back door. The sound thunders throughout the small house
and so he creeps up out of bed and into the kitchen.

But his mother is already there in the dimly lit room peeking
through the window in the door before opening it and uttering
a short cry.

Then, almost instantaneously, she hears him and returns to her adult
self as she sharply turns and snaps at him to get back to bed.

He wilts before her fierce look, but not before almost seeing
who it is. He doesn't return to bed but sits in the shadows and
peers through the dark hallway.

In the kitchen the noise of a porcelain wash-pan being filled
and cloth ripped and soaked as he tries to understand what
is going on.

Although their words are hushed, the boy can hear his mother
ask what happened, then curse (Jesus Christ Almighty!)
between slurred sobs that make his heart pound.

He now knows who she is, he hears her trying to answer,
give some reason why she got beat up, make it sound like
an accident.

2000

Bear

A young woman crawls into his bed
warms it golden in the late afternoon.
He returns after a day's outing,
stealing honey, munching ants,
causing general ruckus.

Then, again, perhaps he's home from school.

He opens the door only to find her
scattered clothes
which he trails to her body.
She has come to be devoured.
Every morsel.

So he begins with toes, feet, moves to leg
up inside of thigh.
When he gets to the tenderest part,
she whimpers for him
to stop.

She is losing herself to his bare kiss.
But the moment he does, she whispers,
to go on. And he does,
as though together
they were retelling
an old-time story.

1997

Fish Tale

My father tells me
of catching a northern pike so big
he had to tie a cord to his canoe
and head straight for shore.
And beach the canoe
and haul the beast up
to where he could club it with an axe.
One so big!
he had trouble getting it out
to the road.

He also tells of the time
my mother caught one
and wouldn't give up.
Rolling on the beach,
wrestling fingers to fin,
covered in sand
and slime
trying to stop it from slipping
back into the lake.

He warned her if she kept it
she would carry it herself.
She did.
Slung it over her back
and dragged it a quarter mile.
She had grown up hungry
and this was the biggest fish
she ever caught.
No way
was she going to let it go.

They were young my parents,
though already with children
they both tried to keep
and lost
My mother didn't know
the fish could have bit off her hand
or maybe she just didn't care.
In her determination

to bring home food
for ones left behind.

1999

Rockin' Chair Lady

Today's the day I wake up knowing I am going to commit myself
to the memory of Mildred Bailey. To my young mother
spinning her unfashionable and unpardonable jazzy 78's
in the land of Country & Western
on her rigged-up gramophone.
Music I couldn't appreciate, let alone understand.

These days an old woman I met out west a few years ago
sends me tapes she records from her collection
spanning 70 years. The last one of Bix Beiderbecke,
the white cornet player from the 1920's
(they say he 'sounded like a girl saying, yes')
who played black and died at 28.
Bootlegged booze and love will do that.

As for Mildred, the encyclopedia says
she was 'The first white singer to absorb
and master the jazz-flavored phrasing, enunciation,
embellishments, improvisatory fervor,
and swinging rhythm of her black contemporaries.'
To put it plainly, 'the first non-black woman
to sing jazz convincingly.'

What they don't say is that she was Indian,
Coeur d'Alene to be exact,
and could party with the best of them.
In jazz things are either black or white.
Red doesn't count. Unless your name is
Red Norvo, the musician Mildred lived with
for 12 years, before she got too fat and too sick.
Diabetes (the Indian disease) and heart trouble,
or trouble of the heart, claimed her in 51,
before I was even born.

But back to Mildred's young life. Bound for the city,
she got a job with the Paul Whiteman Orchestra

(talk about ironic) and hit the jazz scene
big time, in a world of big band swing.
They called her the Rockin' Chair Lady
because she was one great swinger
who sang with the greats, Goodman,
                              Dorsey,
                              Hodges,
                              Hawkins to name a few,
and took over the airwaves on her own national show.

Imagine tuning into her voice
on your Motorola. Hot stuff in 1933.
Imagine being labeled Indian back then
and not wanting to be, because red is out,

and hearing Mildred
coming in strong and knowing she's in
all the way to the top.

                                                2000

Joanne Arnott   [b. 1955]

My parents were guitar-playing musical types. My mom painted, including a giant apple tree on our dining room wall. In each of my father's homes, musical instruments were hung on the wall in the living room. My siblings wrote, sang, played guitar, drew, and/or painted. Although I never heard the words "creative expression" growing up, it was as essential and as ordinary as snow and sunshine, part of what being human was all about. My eldest sister encouraged me to write poetry, and still does. I read a poem once, in Moosehead Review, *about digging potatoes; that was the place where my real life experiences and poetry powerfully intersected for the first time. Anais Nin and James Baldwin were two of the writers I most admired, as a young adult. Beth Brant was the writer-teacher who helped me make that transition from "I wannabe" to "I am."*

Joanne Arnott was born in Winnipeg and moved to Vancouver at the age of six. She moved, every five or six years, between the prairies, the west coast, and Ontario, attending both Roman Catholic and public schools. "When we were living with my father in the country, we were pretty isolated. I used to entertain myself writing stories that never ended, and songs that all featured the same three chords on the guitar." Until the age of ten, Arnott was a regular church-goer, and enjoyed singing in the choir.

Arnott began writing poetry at high school, in Windsor, Ontario. Her eldest sister studied at the University of Windsor and got Arnott involved in several writing groups. Arnott later studied English at the same university and received encouragement from her writing instructors and fellow students. She began to find her voice as a Métis writer during several years of co-facilitating Unlearning Racism workshops in Vancouver and western Canada. "Native identity was not talked about when I was growing up," she says. "There was anxiety about our mixed ancestry and flat-out denial for many years." A writing workshop with Beth Brant was pivotal in this process of uncovering or recovering an identity. "She gave me permission to exist as a mixed race person, and that allowed me to go forward as a writer." Arnott enjoys leading writing workshops, where she passes on some of the permission and encouragement she has received from others to those who might still be waiting to be invited in. She lives in Richmond, B.C., with her four sons.

Arnott's first book of poetry, *Wiles of Girlhood*, was published in 1991, winning the Gerald Lampert Award for the best first book of poetry. Her second book, *My Grass Cradle*, was published in 1992. Arnott has also written *Ma MacDonald* (1993), a book on natural childbirth for children, and *Breasting the Waves: On Writing and Healing* (1995), a non-fiction collection of essays and stories.

Like the piece of glass in her poem "The Shard," Arnott's poetry conveys both vulnerability and toughness, fragility and endurance. These qualities are evoked by the persona of the young girl who is often the subject of her poetry. The forms she chooses, which sometimes employ choruses or chants, can lead or enchant the reader into revelations of violence, alienation, loneliness, and fear as well as joy, love, and belonging.

Wiles of Girlhood

GARBAGE

White paper, waxed stiff and shaped into a flat-bottomed cup, and used once, and crushed. Nearby, a lid, a cracked straw, mysteriously forged, equally abandoned. The eleven-year-old with her pain-hollowed face, her weedy dark hair, passed down the street with her eyes focusing inward.

ELEPHANT PANTS

She wore a very large pair of very bright pants, peacock blue, roped in at the waist so that uncomfortable bunches alternated with hanging crevasses, the whole shifting about with every step as her toes pulled the hems. Elephant pants. When anyone said, "What's that?" she ignored the laughter and answered, "These are my elephant pants."

THE FIGHT

They were halfway down to Dennis's, by the big hedge where she sometimes stopped to eat flowers. Small yellow flowers, honeysuckles she called them, with a tiny taste of sweetness among the petals. Or maybe the bush with the hard purple berries, said to be poison. Sam was with her, and when the large angry Prince bolted across the street toward them Sam stiffened and moved in a kind of pleasure to meet him. Their lips curled and their tails twitched in formal gestures, then both broke and lunged and they whirled fiercely together.

She waded in, telling them to stop. Their backs fell against her legs and launched forward again, totally absorbed, not listening.

Someone told her to move away, threw a bucket of water on them, shocking.

FLYING

She walked down the street to school, tasting the rain and its relative freshness. On the way back up in the afternoon, she felt the wind at her back, and lifted her arms, arched her body. She knew there was a special way to do this, to send herself into the sky. She tried to, for it had a delicious sensation.

PHANTOMS

At night she was very concerned with a particular corner of the room. She threw all her concentration there, heard voices warbling in from another dimension. Wicked, angry voices, indistinct. Also a wee child's voice, she strained to hear it. None of these voices had bodies, faces. Invisible lives that would emanate from the blank shadows.

THE FIRE

She awoke to see the whole sky vivid and beautiful, and she could hear the operatic voices of the legions of angels. She ran to the window, with her sisters, and the eldest announced that it was a housefire down the street. "But what about the angels?" She shook her head, trying to shake the sound. But it remained, real, the singing.

DYSFUNCTION

They were yelling in the kitchen, she had a bad sense of it, a foreboding. She moved past the tv set, along the wall where the guitars, ukelele, tambourines and drum were hung high, into the doorway as she heard the loud steps and the banging of the back door. Her father stood wiping the grease from the automobile from between his fingers. Her younger brother and sister stood separate before him.

His look of anger was overwhelmed with purest hatred, and he picked up a child and threw it against the wall, picked up the other and threw it at the same spot so that it fell on top of the other. Then he kicked and kicked the whole mess, shouting his fury.

ENCHANTMENT

There was a ghost that came in at night and tried to suffocate her older sister. It put a large hot hand that she said she could actually feel, right on her mouth, and a great weight pressing down all over her body. This was a very evil spirit, very frightening. Though it left, it might still come back to haunt her.

1991

The Shard

I found a piece of glass
on the sidewalk, it glittered
bright in the noonday sun

o sharply glowing
o magic triangle
o hopeless one

I squatted on the sidewalk
and bore down upon the glass
with a sturdy stare. In its mirrored side
I saw the wrists of my many best friends
marked with thin, unsuccessful white scars
that spoke of despair,
and the impotent, thwarted rage
of young women

o sharply glowing
o magic triangle
o hopeless one

Its brilliance leapt out
from the sidewalk, surrounded
by a dull, pedestrian grey, the piece of glass

the struggling fragment
the shard

o sharply glowing
o magic triangle
o hopeless one

1992

In My Dance Class

because i need not hold
my pants up any
longer. the quiet
oppression of
ill-fitting clothes. she
told me,
my alignment had so
much improved since
she'd given me the
leotard. why, she
wondered. the subtle
self-deprecation that
comes
along with being
poor,
broke, unwashed,
self-critical,
unhappy. be it
signed by the
clothes that don't fit,
or the body too
rigid, or the
mind out of step.

the greatest boon occurred
the day she looked
at the unhappy face i was
trying to shield.
        she said,
it's okay to cry you know.

so i cried i bawled
my shame away as
the others pulled in
around me, we all
swayed we danced
together.

   that
energy used by us all,
once it was flowing.

1992

Manitoba Pastoral

In a peculiar way, he favoured her
She got to hold the chickens
while he cut off their heads
While I cooked and washed dishes,
she dragged the honey bucket to the bush;
it was heavy as she was
When he worked at the mushroom farm,
she had to wash his clothes out by hand, night
after night, getting the shit out.

One summer we went to a barbecue
held by a neighbour, to honour his mother.
She arrived before we did, in tears
and bruises because her boyfriend
couldn't tolerate her being honoured
in any way. Her son was enraged.
A little guy, he started drinking right away
singing "Hit the Road, Jack" over and over;
Jack was the boyfriend's name.

After we had arrived and once
the guys were sufficiently tanked up
he said Okay, let's go, we're gonna kill
the motherfucker. The men
piled into trucks and started driving
away. My father grabbed my sister
said, They're going to kill a man. You have to
come with me. We have to stop them. Off she went,

and they all ended up at our farm,
gang-raping my sister. The rest of us
women and children
passing time
watching the sun go down
waiting
for the men.

1992

Proud Belly

proud belly sits cross-legged
at the seashore, fat lotus

rosehips thicken once the petals
have spread

proud belly walks through
city streets, erect

a proclamation

when I was a child
the mothers were identified
by their eyes, blue-black
or greybrown hemispheres
below dull or intensely bright orbs
lidded with pain

the shapes of women's bodies
were mysteries, under clothes
is foreign territory—we have
forgotten where we come from

in those days
mothers belonged
to other people

I remember my mother
her coffee cup and her ashtray
balanced on the orb of her
clothes-over-belly

her cigarette a burning wand
that drew a sacred space

the smoke was an incense
I as a child would gaze across
study the overall picture
the icon
peer into that tired face
memorize
those eyes

as a virgin I looked
down on thickening breasts
on burgeoning belly

what the mystery was
I'd let through the gates
now taking shape

losing sight
of vulva, knees, feet
my part of the street

as a mother I look up
past columns of thigh
flattened mound of pubis

over waxing belly
into purple-tipped fountains
of nipple

on to a face
familiar   one of a vast array
and special

in the belly of the beast
in a structure built of
beastly bones

in a shelter of bodily fire
in a web of flesh
in a landlocked body
of water

there grows

in me
there grows

1992

Song About

this is a song patterned
after a song sung
for centuries

maybe you recognize it

it is a rhyming song, but the rhymes are
in another language

maybe you can hear them

it is a song sung
by a native mum
to her babies

maybe you recognize her

she sang it to her baby who
sang it to her baby
who sang it

maybe you remember her

she married nice gaelic men
she married herself
into the white race

maybe you recognize me

she sang it to her baby who
sang it to her baby
in silence

maybe you can hear me

this is a song patterned
after a song sung
to a baby

maybe you recognize it

it is a song about
it is a song about

a sound caught
in a mother's throat

it is a song about
it is a song about

a song caught
in a mother's throat

it is a song about
it is a song about
it is a song about

1992

My Grass Cradle

o grandmother
o grandmother wake up
o grandmother wake up with shining eyes

talk to me, grandmother
tell me all that you know
sing me the song that will make

my grass cradle
safe again

sing to me grandmother
sing to me o grandmother
sing to me o grandmother with shining eyes

1992

Like An Indian: Struggling With Ogres

Like An Indian

My family / some of us are sitting around the table, getting on for a change, peaceable, friendly. My sister, who always thought that my father was beautiful, tells him so. He hears it. She goes on, strokes his arm lightly and says, your skin is beautiful. Like an Indian. He jumps up, afternoon shattered by a girl's words saying the unsayable words, he storms from the room, a real electrical storm crackling and swirling through the rooms of our small house. Power of repression, power of lifetime and generations of denial, everything coming unhinged on an afternoon where he'd dared to relax for a moment with his children. Well you can't trust children. Never relax with them. They are crazy, and you never know what they might say.

Avalanche

My mother's side of the family is fraught with stories, the old ones lived long enough to answer the young one's questions. I first interviewed my maternal grandmother for a school paper in grade six, never forgot what she told me then, and used that information as a basis for further questions. She is French/French Belgian descended. Her husband was much less communicative, but as the years went on he and I drew close as well. I know a bit about his jobs as a young farm worker. I know a bit of the terror he felt during war. I know that his mother smoked, and that she badgered my grandmother into quitting work upon marriage because it wasn't right, that she should work and him not. I know that his father was illiterate and an artist/craftsman.

My father's side of the family may be fraught with stories too, but I hardly heard them. I first heard my father refer to his childhood when I was twenty years old. Apparently some of my father's people spoke Gaelic, within the last couple of generations. Pushing against that wall of absence and silence, having the courage to know what I know, I can tell you that my Dad's mum was also Native, as are we, her descendants. But all of these people died, you see, all the older ones were gone before I arrived and the middle generation, prematurely elder, was intensely unprepared to take on the job.

Denial

As a child in such a family, I learned a lesson quite the opposite of my elders': you can't relax among adults. You never know when they're going to flip. They'll invite you to sit on their knees for a moment, then push you to the floor minutes later because you happened to relax, happened to let on just a bit of what you really thought or felt about something. They'd get all charged up and couldn't handle it: energy like thunderstorms high winds tornadoes, suffocation under hailstorm snowstorm and blizzard, so much shame and shaming, few stories, few names, and little naming.

They'd look fine. Then they'd crack right open and ogres would spring, lunge out at you, looking for blood.

Impact

The impact of racism on my family, and the impact of family on my writing is all of a piece. Punishments for lying, punishments for telling the truth and for insubordination, erasure of all that is Indian, Christian inculcations of ethics/morality, and a deep and genuine horror of all the incongruities I have grown up with, all vie for space, urgently tell me to speak out and to shut up at the same time.

My quest in each and every poem story myth is and has been the truth, the reconstruction of a life with its interpenetrating multi-generational fragments, the wholegut truth with its frequently desperate edge, and/or/at the same time: the gut-level double-talk needed to keep hard truths at bay.

Using writing as a tool in this vast archaeology/reclamation project, being a girl and a woman who will say the unsayable and keep on saying it, is about being worthy, is about coming out as a human being. I have written a lot about shame, fraudulence, dissonance, remember/forget. Caught in the fear of being murdered, terrified of being completely abandoned, and followed about by bliss, waves upon waves.

I am not the only girl or woman of my generation/in my family learning to find safety in the truth. We struggle to unsilence ourselves, and to stop silencing each other. Not easy. We write letters, poetry, songs, and tell each other stories, from a distance, over time.

Am I an Indian? Like an Indian? Or, as a dream-man told me with a loud guffaw, "Better a little bit Indian than not Indian at all!" I am a woman who was a girl, Native and European, a parent who was a child who struggles with ogres.

Now and then, Now and again.

1992

Migration

The most recent thing

simply tugs on a rope a long
chain of similar
things that
were we trees and cut in half
you could read by the rings

these things

incident upon incident linked
by the essence
the message
or by an image
sensation

because you are female
because you are Indian
because you are smaller than me
because you inconvenience me
because you're handy

you are in danger
I am your danger

roots

the fingers we plunge into the soil
of our worlds

everytime that I cried and was safe
everytime I was endangered and saved
each and every gentle human contact
that is made

one of my roots is the moon

another is the taste of cold weather
the feeling of a warm sun
the sound of rain
and of thunder
the feeling of a strong wind
big sky
snow
earth
the colours of plants and trees
the quiet crackle of autumn
the feeling of me
the sound or scent or sight
of favourite people

and these are the chains

the curve of a white shoulder
white breasts
a man's round belly
something approaching fast from above
or before or behind
not believing me
looking disgusted by me
no one looking at me
everyone looking at me

the forest
should stand
many lifetimes

but sometimes I just can't

in preparing to go

for the first time I am pulling
my roots up gently

rattling my chains on purpose
not ripping up and tearing off

only to be brought up short
in a stunning cessation

2000

Protection

where is the flower
within whose petals softly folding
i may sleep safe, hidden
from the great night

so small and vulnerable am i
these delicate legs and wings
require profound and golden light
to carry me

tasting nature's menus
through each day, averting
certain dangers and inviting
certain play

still, at nightfall
when flowers sleep
i am too naked to survive
and starlight too weak

2000

MidLife

I am an old woman
nestled in the arms
of a wide-eyed girl

feeling tired
seen enough

I am happy to drowse
through the last years of my life
I like to watch the sky
through my curtains
gaze upon a quiet bush
in my lone back yard

then the girl starts up
caught by some heady fragrance
a scintillating sight
some inner rush of springtime
urging her out
passion sweeps through
and she carries me off
in swift pursuit
of life's offerings

she is a young woman
and strong enough to carry
this bone-tired girl

2000

Beachhead Dreaming

Under my clothes
is a land
where you are always
welcome

landscapes unfurling
under the fingers
of morning
sun

bright lit and
shadow hit
small animals and birds
awaken

crow walks
on mud flats

hungry
searching

under the kiss
of a soft salt wind
orca stretches
and arcs

up from the ocean
dips down
into the ocean
again

seabirds drop
and hunt across the waves
for morning
has broken

under our clothes
is an ocean
sweet tides
of desire

flow
with simple power
to wash over
then ebb

2000

Connie Fife

[b. 1961]

I believe that it is a poet's role to bear down on the simplest of truths. Poets are able to put into a language that which is not only seen but unseen, and to make it real and tangible. Poetry is what binds the heart and mind together to create an internal shift. Poets can also be nasty, snarky creatures. We jump off the cliff's edge and look for splintered light.

Connie Fife is Cree. She was born in Prince Albert, Saskatchewan. Adopted by an Anglican minister's family, she was educated in Saskatchewan until the age of ten and then travelled to England and Fiji where her adoptive father carried out missionary work at the Pacific Theological College. "I grew up within the walls of the Anglican Church," says Fife. Looking back, she credits her schooling in England for helping to foster her love of literature. "Literature was always my favorite subject." At the age of eight, she told her English teacher she was going to be a writer. "I have always written."

While she was growing up, Fife was "trying to find my way home." She left Fiji and returned to Canada at the age of eighteen. Once back in Canada, she became involved in radical politics. "I fell into the arms of really powerful Native women." In the mid-1980s, Fife joined a collective of women who founded the Native Women's Resource Centre in Toronto, an organization which "became the catalyst for the Native women's movement in Canada. The collective honed and sharpened me." She attended the University of Toronto during 1984-85, and in 1986 she edited the Native Women's issue of *Fireweed* magazine (No. 23, 1986). Moving to Winnipeg, she received a degree in business administration. In 1990, she became a full-time creative writing student and part-time writer-in-residence at the En'Owkin International School of Writing in Penticton; in 1991, she edited that institution's journal, *Gatherings 2*. In 1994, Fife moved to Vancouver where she ran the Outreach Program for Aboriginal Youth until 2000. She lives in Vancouver today with her son, Russell.

Fife's first book of poetry, *Beneath the Naked Sun*, was published in 1992. In 1993, she edited the anthology *The Colour of Resistance*. Her book of poems, *Speaking Through Jagged Rock* (1999), won the Prince and Princess Edward Prize in Aboriginal Literature for "talents and achievement in literature." That work broke a five-year silence, during which "my voice had changed. Earlier my writings were very political. Right now, my main concern is bringing the heart and the intellect together."

In short, continuous phrases, Fife's earlier poems, such as "and dance they will" and "This is not a metaphor" drum out painful recitations of injustice and cruelty, as if to relentlessly confront the reader with what he or she ignores. In some poems, such as "the revolution of not vanishing" shared pain is transmuted into sisterhood and strength. The symbol of the stone, which runs through her work, suggests remedies for the world's pain: endurance, the storing of time and memory, immanence, survival. In a later poem, Fife writes to "dear walt." Like Walt Whitman, she takes on a prophetic voice, as in "i have become so many mountains." In other poems, such as "the naming" she reveals more intimate and sometimes humourous glimpes into her life.

Ronnie, because they never told you why

twenty eight years old
at an age where
to be told
is to understand
yet on this dark
night you are
locked in a
vice grip of racism
condemned by a court
system that leaves
rooms taking its
small barred cells
to the streets where
white men prowl
like starving dogs

not finding a guilty party
they settle
for the innocent
stopped
you question
their investigation
and
receive only their
special looks saved
for indians who believe
we never lost
the war of the west that
they are sure they
are still fighting

until our total annihilation
not one of us
is above suspicion

this time it is you
who is taken to
their station and
enclosed behind steel
obstructions released
early the following day
you are finally entitled
to knowledge of your crime
you are guilty of being
brown indian lesbian woman
you are criminal in
your nature because
you do not
believe in your guilt
like they do
will sign no confession
instead swearing to fight
back against a system
that wishes for your silence
and eventual death
though as long as you
do die they will
allow you to scream

you dare to walk down
sidewalks of cold concrete
alone deep into the night
in the belief that you
are entitled to be
anywhere on this continent
left to you by your
grandmothers and grandfathers
worse than this attitude
you travel where and
when you want

your skin is not white
and you say you are
proud to be

indian
prouder still of your
love for women
so you carry your head
raised always to the sun
back straight
you break all laws
by not lowering your
eyes to the stares of
white people
by not cowering in dark corners
meant for rats and alcoholics
safe in their drunken stupors

you are charged with
two counts of assault
and one of robbery
but not until you
have been hurled
against the police car
handcuffed
while they try to
steel your dignity
still you say you
will
fight back

1992

Communications class

if i drop out of your educational system
do not fool yourself that i have fallen
off the face of the earth and
am just another statistical write-off.
this act will cause you embarrassment and
i am familiar with the feeling of
being caught turning red in the face.
tomorrow if you do not find me, again,
dozing during another one of your lectures
do not think firstly that i have disappeared
amongst sheets of paper shelved in
a reference library....

instead picture me wide awake at 3:00 a.m.
throwing ink upon blank white squares
creating with your own language
a universal formula for change.

1992

the revolution of not vanishing

i sit here and read your work
    the colour of your words
    the shape of your heart
alone i follow the lines captured
between the spaces of letters i
stop when there is a dark dot   but
only to gulp in the breath needed
for me to continue   i fall off the
page when a gap appears into a
lake of salt water tears and i
swim its length i re-emerge when
each new sentence begins ready to
follow the path you have bulldozed through
the jungles of this city   this place
that is not a home   my legs give way
and i am on my knees   my blood splatters onto
the ground while more gravel embeds
itself into my flesh   i weep torrents
of water creating an ocean now as
i am taken to my place of remembering
    while anger and resistance become sisters
    while i journey towards sunlight   i run
into the border of a blank white square
and celebrate
    and i celebrate
    to the drumbeat
    resounding out of
    the skin of your heart
    then i dance

dedicated to Chrystos
1992

This is not a metaphor

today from romania there were pictures released
     photographs brought across the ocean images
children trapped between a fascist regime and resistance
     most of them were my son's age
     though I could see five and six year olds
I looked closer falling into their eyes   looked at
scars on their heads as the result of experiments
     each body was starved   most had no clothes on
and what was there was torn and blood riddled
     the bodies I had seen before   starving children
seem so common-place   poverty a given   I looked into
the eyes of a child and saw nazi germany   starvation is
a blank look   rags offer little warmth   I searched my
memory and found nothing to compare   crouched in a
corner   shaking so hard I expected to hear bones
rattle   a child cowered as if she   he could escape
the probing camera   I recall the names given to me
     my anger in response I look back into my childhood a
beating
could feel gentle depending how hard I was hit   my sons
tears yesterday at being called halfbreed   still
I find nothing that screams the terror carried by
the mute child   wide eyed and starved
     I looked farther back   across the landscape of my history
according to the books   as told by white colonizers   I look
into the effects of columbus being lost and
find the truth   it is not me that is savage
     or primitive   or doomed to your hell   it is not me
that takes the spirits of her children and replaces it
with terror   it will not be me
who takes responsibility for your savagery

                                                     1992

Stones memory

translucent stone murmured of my beginnings
whispered the secrets of my origins
called me home following nights of darkness
cried out for my return to sunlight
urged me to bring memory forward
compelled my circle to become complete
round curve of mountain's face
showed herself to me in a blanket
of blue and green expression
stories passed from palm to palm
trickled down my throat
etched their essence upon my heart
embedded their words within my ribcage
settled amongst my blood
i remember her face
recall her tone
i remember my relatives
their journey from water to land
i am reminded of every stone
who has ever spoken
ever wailed
ever celebrated
every stone whose birth
is evidence of creation
whose death harbours
new journeys on wind's voice
i remember every stone
i have swallowed
every stone i have
ever held
every stone that
has crossed my path
and cleared the way
footprints

beyond the plush green embankment
the smooth body of sand touches the
fingertips of water
here there are no words
just sound in constant motion

caught in a place between
the blue and brown
here too exists the voice inside of colour
they are whispering secrets to me
as i dash across the earth
i am determined to find the
exact moment and place where
sound birthed song

1992

We remember

We live
     within the fine line
     between the underworld and the sky
We have been here
     since Thought Being
     gave birth to shape
We have no choice
     but to listen to the voices
     caught between our
     joints as they struggle
     towards sunlight
We will know
     when it is time
     by the movement
     birthed within our ribcage
We have not forgotten
     our journey
     towards this moment

1992

i have become so many mountains

standing on the shoreline of history
pondering the forthcoming sunrise
or the very impossibility of it
i have become so many rivers
not a single current but many
leading to a whirlpool of countless places
i have become so many women

waking each morning with jaws clenched
determined to bite down on the impending day
i have become so many men
wondering which mask to remove
afraid of flailing skinless in the wind
i have become so many forests
whose tears slide down hillsides
then come to rest in shimmering pools of ice
i have become so many ancestors
who dance through empty houses
windows blown out by our laughter
i have become so many photographs
framed and frozen behind glass made of lies
whose eyes hold the truth despite the distortion
i have become so many songs
slipping off the tongues of entire nations
who sing me into the existence of memory
i have become so many landscapes
scarred by the hands of the uncivilized
whose open wounds now swallow them whole
i have become so many poems
whose fingers caress me with their desire
while fighting for our lives breath by breath
i have become so many mountains and rivers
so many women and men singing
so many ancestors
so many photographs carried in my lungs
so many landscapes acting in revolutionary fashion
i have become so many movements
without having made the slightest motion
standing in solitude on the shoreline of history

1999

dear walt

it must have been difficult
to be caught in the grip
of strong willed metaphors
who dictated that you
live as an outsider
in a country you so
wanted to breathe into

dear walt
i imagine you actually
believed that poetry can
make a democracy smeared
with the blood of others
into some kind of beauty
now you have become the dust
you wrote about us being
so little has changed
we who are poets
still believe we shift hearts
while speaking through the voice
of stone and water
not even paralysis drove
your spirit away
nor the illness of a brother
in a world without compassion
dear walt
is it ever possible to escape
metaphor or change a democracy
whose foundation digs into the bones of her original people
i would like to know walt
if there is a place for dead poets
where we can lie among leaves of grass
then laugh at how little has changed

1999

the naming

half breed
half breed
squaw
princess mini ha ha
    voices caught between my bones
    writhe and twist between my joints
    following years of my being force fed by crow
    i push them up afraid of death by drowning
half blood
half breed
squaw
princess mini ha ha
    i place in my pockets two hands

one brown one white (both callused)
i pull out words sung in ceremony
turning them over in my palm
examining their faces (re-examining my own)
half blood
half breed
squaw
princess mini ha ha
there were songs sleeping in my throat
throughout my school years
whenever the history books tried to rape me
half blood
half breed
squaw
princess mini ha ha
i stayed drunk an entire summer
determined to go back to a place i'd never been
traveling through my corridors
caught in the grip of an ugly poem
half blood
half breed
squaw
princess mini ha ha
helen betty osborne's killers got off
i live in a country run by murderers
no wonder i cried for hours when i turned thirty
i still don't care about my father being french
half blood
half breed
squaw
princess mini ha ha
where i come from you can still hear the dinosaurs
moving slowly toward the other side of the world
once a year i go back to sniff out their trail
its still clear despite the roads and cities
half blood
half breed
squaw
princess mini ha ha
there's a painted feather in my beaver top hat
that i wear to remind myself to laugh
folks are let down when i tell them its pigeon
pedestals are boring and the ordinary is where the sacred sits

half blood
half breed
squaw
princess mini ha ha
    i don't want to live in a teepee
    not when my apartment's warm
    with heat and the smell of fresh ground coffee
    I'd rather book into a local hotel to remember who i am
half blood
half breed
squaw
princess mini ha ha
    voices caught between my joints
    they cry out with each new poem
    knowing that i'll go on living
    long after they are dead

1999

Joseph Dandurand [b. 1964]

i think what influences me most is what i see every day, every bird, every child, every moment gives me something. [as a writer] you need to know what to see and what to share in your work, watch every thing, you may use some or all you just never know, store it and use and reuse, make it fit into you and what you see. sometimes images are gifts and you should share them, other times they need to be kept inside for you.

Joseph Dandurand, of Kwantlen heritage, was born on the Kwantlen First Nations Reserve #6, "near Fort Langley, B.C., about 20 minutes up the Fraser River from Vancouver." In 1990, he received a Diploma in performing arts from Algonquin College in Ottawa and in 1994 received a B.A. in theatre and direction at the University of Ottawa. Playwright and poet, Dandurand has produced plays for Native theatre companies in Canada and the U.S. which include "Crackers and Soup" (1994), "No Totem for My Story" (1995), "Where Two Rivers Meet" (1995) and "Please Don't Touch the Indians" (1998). His poems have appeared in numerous journals and anthologies and are collected in *The Upside Down Raven* (1996), *I Touched the Coyote's Tongue* (1997), *burning for the dead and scratching for the poor* (1998), and *looking into the eyes of my forgotten dreams* (1999). Commenting on the writing process, Dandurand says "I write the same whether I am writing poetry or drama. It's an explosion followed by quiet followed by worry followed by quiet. And then I store up all my emotions and the images I have seen and then when I just can't hold it in any longer…explosion followed by quiet followed by worry followed by quiet." He counts among the writers who mean a lot to him the poets charles bukowski and Leonard Cohen and in drama, "the greats" and particularly Sam Shepard.

Dandurand has described himself, besides poet and playwright, as "fisher, researcher, archeologist. I left home when I was sixteen and have been failing ever since but in that failing I have survived, I have made it, you know. And I have found my home, my life, my spirituality, my daughter, my meaning, if I was ever to have one. And that meaning is to be a fisherman. My people are from the river and so I fish when the Canadian government allows me." Dandurand also works to protect his people's past "from those who continue to use our lands for their profit." Currently, he is drafting a heritage management plan to protect over 60 villages sites that are under the water of reservoirs created by B.C. Hydro.

In poems such as "Fort Langley," "Before me," and "One Year," Dandurand's poetry brings the past sharply into the present by evoking a dreamlike hyper-awareness which dissolves boundaries

between past and present. Neither the past nor nature are roman-
ticized in pellucid images which sometimes have the force of night-
mare.

This was One of Them

The train pushed slowly
through the old fort

Encased in the box
were the bones of a great chief

Professor Muncy carried it
with kindness to his house
upon the hill

His wife greeted him with
a smile and a bosom so round

They ate the fish caught by
George the nice indian

As his wife cleaned the dishes
the professor went to his study
with his box of bones

He opened the box
touched the bones
and a chill went screaming
to his spirit

His wife cried all the way
to the graveyard and she
wailed when they placed
his box into the ground

As they went home
the rain carried on
and George stepped out
from the trees
and he went to the new bed
of the professor

And here he placed some tobacco
and a feather given to him
by a great chief

1994

I Touched the Coyote's Tongue

paw prints lead on to
the woods where my father
stored his life

up old tree was where
he placed the rope

wind blowing
from the west

his feet almost touching
the soft spoken
earth

whispers lick
at the moon
and the black-eyed
owl awakes for its
evening feed

wings stretched
allowing the air
to caress mice as they run
to safe warm holes

creaking tree
still stands
alone

coyote pisses
on its mighty
trunk

a sort of remembrance
for my father

1994

Someone

there is someone walking away from me
disappearing over the edge.

never seen him before or since.

it's like that somedays
never knowing what you just witnessed.

never knowing.

in ways I am like the earth:
dirty and shallow
and weak
and crumbling on the edges.

in another way I am like nothing at all:

just a disappearing figure
of someone else's
imagination.

1998

Fort Langley

you can see the fort from where I live.

wooden walls,
trees,
desperate voices.

they call to me,
come on over,
come on over,
come on.

shut up,
I say.
shut up and stay over there.

used to drink at their bar,
used to sip whiskey,
used to fight,
used to be blind from it all.

now
I stare at their walls.
wooden walls.
thick with history.

many men and women never made it home.
they found them trying to climb over the walls.
whiskey bottles broken and empty roll down to the
river,
laceless shoes sit silent as if waiting to fit someone else,
a picture of someone's mother blows away and over the
walls,
the gate is closed.

the fort.
over that way.
over past the mass grave.
smallpox.
you ever seen smallpox?
pretty ugly.
not as pretty
as wooden walls.

1998

One year

there seemed to be a quiet moment
here on this island.
not sure why.
maybe because the indians
all left long ago.
just bodies of drink and smoke
re-telling tales
of woe and false glory.

(he drops the rope down far enough
so they cannot see him hanging there.

he jumps and snaps away his worries.
little children place flowers on his grave
and try and remember who he was.
a father? a son? a man?)

(she covers her baby in wet leaves
and sharpens the fishing knife for
her own throat and slips away from
the desperate voices that yell at her
to just go ahead and die.
no children come to her grave.
old people come and shake their
heads in disbelief and try to remember
this girl and her child and they try
to remember the old days when
dying was so much quicker.)

this is one reserve of a thousand others.
here they fish and laugh and hide
from the spirits that walk and fly in
and about the cedar trees.
the world and water passes by.
the moon and sun creep over mountains.
animals and birds talk and stare.
everything is quiet in this moment.

a small girl walks towards the river filling
her pockets full of ancient stones.

she steps over the edge and is gone forever.

1998

Before me

read a book about the past.
it seemed real enough for me to go there.
so I went.
1900, something or other.
old time.
back then.
before me.
before.

river looked the same,
treacherous,
silent,
unforgiving.

more trees than now.
more eagles,
deer,
salmon,
humans with faces.

saw them.
they wore the paint,
not like now,
not like humans now.

I tried to talk to them
but the river came and got me,
it took me down,
shit,
I think my shoes fell off.
my toes touched the bottom.

I woke up as the ones with paint
came to me and told me never,
never tell.

"tell what?"

no answer.

"tell what?"

only water.
I found my shoes,
they were next to my bed,
right where I left them.

the past.
before.
before me.
so clouded,
so uneven.

future.
after.
after me.
eternity,
I think.

eternal water.
the paint.
faces.
human with paint on their faces.

brothers and sisters.
crying the song.
drumming the past.

never.
never read a book about your past.
it becomes you.
you become it.

my face,
it has the paint.

my voice,
it has my song.

my eyes,
they have never,
ever,
let go.

1998

Feeding the hungry

blue jays nest beside my legs.
flying to eat winter bugs juicy with nectar.
black birds squawk at me and my day.
telling me that I should've stayed in bed.

spring.
day.
mid-afternoon.

quiet.
no one about.
just me and the island.
no one drunk on the side of the road,
not even me,
not even my spirit.

blue jays eat big worms.
choking on their hunger.
chewing too quickly.
throwing up the day.
the day.
quiet.
no one dead.
everyone alive.
even the old ones in the trees.
they squawk at the warm wind.

blowing dust into the eyes of birds:
blue and black.
tired and hungered by the length of the winter months.
skinny birds nest in swampy waters,
their wings too weak to fly
they stand and stare at the owl as she dives for unsuspecting mice.
the cracking of their skulls echoes around this island.
this island where everyone is alive.
this island where spirits eat you.
you can hear their songs pounding in the trees.

can you hear them?

quiet.
owl dives.
cracking bones.
drum.
whispers of the old ones.
something touches my arm.
I open my eyes.
it was my spirit.

someone forgot to feed him.

1998

Kateri Akiwenzie-Damm [b. 1965]

My work is a way of attempting to express beauty, truth, joy, and love. It is a way of connecting with those around me, of sharing what I am learning, of dreaming, of praying. For me, writing is ceremony. I write to tell something of who we are, to remember, to celebrate life, to transform the injustice and hatred and lovelessness around me into something creative and positive. Words are powerful. They can change the world. My work expresses the beliefs and values of my people. It is influenced by the literary tradition of my people: the songs, stories, chants, prayers, invocations, oratories and poetry handed down to me. As always, I am inspired by the land, by the sky, by my dreams, by my ancestors, by the friends and lovers and enemies who have been my teachers. I give love and thanks to my family, to my community, to the web of Native writers, orators and storytellers that sustains me, and especially to those who share my crazy beautiful life. To the ones I have loved and been loved by, for teaching me the most important and difficult lessons of my life: chi meegwetch. K'zaugin.

Kateri Akiwenzie-Damm is an Anishnaabe writer of mixed ancestry from the Chippewas of Nawash First Nation. She lives and works at Neyaashiinigmiing, Cape Croker Reserve, on the Saugeen Peninsula in southwestern Ontario. Born in Toronto, she attended grade school there, then moved to the Cape Croker area in 1976 where she attended first a Catholic grade school, then a public high school. She received a B.A. in Honours English from York University in 1987 and an M.A. in English from University of Ottawa in 1996. That same year, she taught creative writing at the En'owkin International School of Writing in Penticton, British Columbia. After a trip to Aotearoa (New Zealand) in 1991, Akiwenzie-Damm has come to see that land as her "other home." In 1993, she established a publishing company, Kegedonce Press, to support the work of Indigenous writers, artists, and designers, and, with her company DammWrite! continues to work as a communications consultant with First Nations organizations. In 1999 she set up NiSHin Productions, which promotes and produces performing arts projects by Indigenous performers and artists. She is currently editing an anthology of erotica entitled "Without Reservation: Indigenous Literary Erotica." She has also edited *Skins: Contemporary Indigenous Writing* (2001), an anthology of indigenous writing from North America, New Zealand, and Australia; it is co-published by Kegedonce Press and an Aboriginal Australian publisher, Jukurrpa Books.

Akiwenzie-Damm's first collection of poems, *My Heart is a Stray Bullet*, was published in 1993. She has a long-standing interest in the spoken word; her poem "stray bullets," she writes, "tends to be one that I 'perform' rather than 'read.'" She has performed readings in Canada, the U.S., Australia, and Aotearoa and on national radio in Canada and Aotearoa, as well as on the WTN network, and her poetry has been recorded on various audio-cassette compilations. An experimental spoken word/music piece entitled "2 Spirited Nanabush" was broadcast on CBC's Out Front program in November, 1999. She is currently working on a CD of poetry and music, including the work of musicians Raven Polson-Lahache and Te Kupu (a Maori spoken work artist, rapper, and producer of the Upper Hutte Posse, a Maori hip hop group), as well as indigenous collaborators from Canada, the U.S.A., and South America. Early interest in the connection between song and poetry and a comment on Canadian literature from an Anishnabe perspective can be seen in her "poem without end #3."

Besides experimenting with sound and rhythms, Akiwenzie-Damm plays with visual form. In "my grandmothers," for example, she creates a structure which suggests the interconnection of the two grandmothers within her life, memory, body. In her later work, Akiwenzie-Damm is less interested in "the look of the words on the page" and more involved in "the spirit of them, in breath, in speaking, in the power of words."

stray bullets   (oka re/vision)

my touch is a history book
full of lies and half-forgotten truths
written by others
who hold the pens
and power

my heart is a stray bullet
ricocheting in an empty room

my head was sold
for the first shiny trinket
offered

my beliefs were bought cheap
like magic potions at a travelling road show
with promises
everyone wants to believe
but only a fool invests in

my name was stolen
by bandits in black robes
my world was taken
for a putting green

1989, 1993

my grandmothers

anna   irene
there are so many memories
shaping   your words
my image of you
my love for you
my history of us   are a life line
in toronto i remember
eating the chocolate bars that marked every visit
and shopping in eaton's bargain basement
trying to keep up   i cling to
to
you   like i would cling to your warm hands
and i remember you
telling the butcher on eglinton
i was your grandmother   when i was a child walking with you to church
and how straight and smiling you stood
and how shy and secretly proud i was
i remember being with you
in your bachelor apartment on bloor street
when i first realized i was woman   and you had a way of speaking
i remember   so words would hook in my brain
your voice awakening me
with the eerie
pain full cries that snuck out in the dark
from that secret secure place you held them
in the daylight
and even now
i remember buying you five star brandy
and the thanksiving mom jo-anna you and i
went rummaging through flea markets
where you bought me a pink rhinestone pin
for two dollars
then
when we had dinner
i remember

how you had too much wine
and when i think
of how we all laughed together
        i can feel your gentle tug
then i remember you
so relaxed and smiling
i remember too how much i took you for granted
i remember my ears burning from listening
while you recounted your days
and how many times i wasn't really listening   at the other end
because i'd thought i'd heard it all before
and was young enough to believe i'd always remember it
now this is all i can say   of my thoughts

1992, 1993

poem without end #3

nanabush is an english professor
sitting in an ivory tower
looking down upon the masses who go herd-like to their classes
writing books that no one looks at
reading poetry on money
drinking tea and eating crumpets with the dead men who turn women into bone

nanabush is a landlord who turns off the heat in winter
and a tenant who throws parties while the babies are fast sleeping
the one who keeps you laughing even when your heart is breaking
and the one who tells you stories when it's wisdom you've been seeking

nanabush is a singer
she's a heavy metal drummer
she cheats and swears and talks of death
then lets you meet her children
she throws pearls onto parliament hill
dresses men in clothes of sheepskin
then she sits alone and drinks cheap wine and cries into the table
while she prays for gods' forgiveness because she can't forget the sabbath
she's a lonely wooden goddess on a path into damnation

nanabush knows jesus
he plays tricks on paul and peter
he unlocks the gates and steals a peek

and cannot keep the secret
he will shit in darkened hallways
pull your pants down to your ankles
he will take your love and steal your life
and give you dreams and laughter

nanabush is a trapper who wears sealskin pajamas
he eats fish that have been poisoned
speaks a language now forgotten
and when he jumps into the river
half crazy with survival
he tries to touch the bottom to create a new religion
but he floats up to the surface
and his hands are cold and empty
so the animals give him shelter because they know the winter's coming
and when he wakes they wait together for the storm that is approaching

silent   nearly frozen   they turn into a monument of stone

1990, 1993

my secret tongue and ears

i
  as dusk falls from this autumn day
  (like a blood red leaf)
  the darkness whirls madly to the earth
  carried by windfury

  still
  i sit alone
  against the lamp's dim light
  staring at the hieroglyphics in my skin
  thinking
  if i could simply read these symbols
  tell my own story to myself
  and know i had spoken a truth
  but these lines mean nothing to me
  except a number of years gone by
  and a certain lack of understanding
  so
  sadly as the day flies
  the truth remains
  a secret i keep from myself

ii

in a second of silence
raindrops pellet
the roof and walls
echoing off
the tin and glass and brick
like a verbal assault
that i cannot say i understand
though i would cross a sterile desert
or stand naked in a december snow
to gain that wisdom

iii

so another day passes unceremoniously
while i sit like a fool
in this easy chair
the stars shining above
(like asterisks to some important note)
tempting us to close our eyes and forget the rhetoric of hate
that was spoken
moments before
in the space
between us

iv

but
i cannot let sleep steal away
my secret tongue and ears

in the darkness
of my house
i seek
perfection vision clarity
within my own deaf silence
i strain to hear
syllables unspoken

v

and still i don't understand
the intricate design
of raindrops rolling down my face at dawn
or the map of my vision against my skull
still
i have not learned the language of my quest

even as sunrays sneak past shadows
and i wake in a shower of falling stars and your
light caress
still
i have no words to say

1989, 1993

from turtle island to aotearoa

(i - new arrival)
morning shatters
like ice in our lungs
shallow breaths hanging ragged
above our heads
the tent is swimming
as women men children
twist turn
in a joyous rush to feed together
nniichkiwenh and i emerge slowly
from our cocoons
spinning in transformation
but unlike the caterpillar
we carry hope in our dull heads
as we shake off our old selves
to join the waves of maori
lapping at the shore of the marae

(ii-answering a call)
yesterday
the convoy that was mataatua waka
led us eastward to this place
where i finally come to understand
being called from home by voices i do not recognize
(but perhaps my true ears heard them
carried on the wind
or my true eyes read them in driftwood
like messages in a bottle)
and now i am aware
of slow cautious steps taken
inside this gate
where songs of family lines are cast
like nets across a sea of faces

(iii-drifting)
my moccasins step timid
on this part of mother earth
waiting for the pounding of other like-covered feet
my ears swivel but cannot hear the spirits whispering
"so this is what it is to be
a stranger in another land" i think to myself as foot follows foot

but feeling the pull of my ancestors
i am like someone walking against the current

while all the while
my head drifts slowly home
where i know the bending of the trees
and the sounds of undeveloped places
where my sister's children dream
and my grandparents' bones are cradles by ahki
where the lost spirits roam
and the heartbeat echoes
where my words are
(buried under rocks hidden in snow drifts
resting in flower beds
floating on clear bay waters
filling the forest)

here i am the quiet one
here i must reach across an ocean to find the right words

(iv-gathering stones)
once more under the moon
and the words of these people
do not jangle like jagged rocks in my head
the steady rhythmic pounding of voices
is wearing the sounds smooth
so that now the strength of the tide is apparent
even to one who stays close to the shore
tomorrow aotearoa will be waiting
with more gifts
and new stones to harvest
but tonight with only my own hollow thoughts for company
sleep overtakes me
carries to the place of dreams
every echoing sight and sound and smell

(v-an awakening)

the morning sky breaks
i wake
stretching into a new day
that yawns before me like a mother's child
i wake
peel off my blanket shell
to air so cool and gray
i retract and re-cover
listening as bits of conversation tell me
the house is awake

i am still
but my thoughts are bats in a cave
settling in dark corners of the room
as i sink deeper into the pillow
like a footprint in the sand

weeks from now
i will fall through the sky to turtle island
clutching a bit of papatuanuku in my fist
i will create a new beginning for myself
on the solid back of canada

(vi-long-distance connection)

now the day hangs directly overhead
and my sister's voice is sap running in my veins
though our words are nothing more than
leaves falling from sturdy limbs
feet firmly planted
i call for my sister's daughter
who pours out the drops of knowledge
she has gathered to share with me
so that suddenly i am a woman drinking under arid midday sun
thus revived i offer stories to her safe-keeping
showering with love the signs of new growth
later we are all embraced
by the child's grandmother   my mother
who grows more and more like her mother before her

"everyone is fine" she says

the roots are well protected

(vii-actionsong)

    far into another aotearoa night
    stories are told so the young ones will remember
    in turn
    i make simple gifts of gathered words
    but if i could sing
    i would sing songs of thanks
    to all our relations who guide our steps
    to the whakapapa whispered on the waves
    to the tangata whenua who have not challenged my being here
    or my attempts at poetry
    to the earth winds sky water
    to moon stars and sun
    to creatures of land and air and sea

    if i could dance my actions would say
    what my voice cannot

1992, 1993

partridge song

    come to me
    my love
    i am calling

    hear my song
    sweet one
    i am drumming

    near the reeds
    dear one
    i am waiting

    come to me
    my love
    i am calling

1996, 1997

frozen breath and knife blades

the village is asleep

      there are strangers living with us
      there are strangers drifting in and out of the dull edges of my sight

and the village is asleep

      there is a man who stares and calls me sister
            as if he was born to do so
     he walks among us and the people fall silent around him
              it's as if they can't remember their names in the face of his
strange words
                 his eyes are knife blades
        and i can't tell if it is love or hate he carves into me
            but i know he is cutting through us
     this man we call Father is watching
            I feel his eyes cutting into me

and the village is asleep

      the man he brought with him
   is like the frozen breath of his words
                     sometimes i glimpse him
but he vanishes
   like a strange spirit
   who has wandered far from home

the village is still sleeping

          and i wonder who will be tangled in the web
of my dreaming
      when i awake
               1997. 1998

hummingbirds

i am hummingbird
        darting
    into
luscious wetness
    your dulcet tongue
spilling nectar
while a brilliant flower
sprouts
    in thick damp
        moss
then my heart
becomes
hummingbird's
        wings
    as i hover above you
hungering for the
honey-
suckle
taste
of you
                and now
        you are my hummingbird
                pushing
        a hard thick tongue
                into
            the unfolding
                petals
                of my
            succulent
                    flower

                                    1997, 1998

night falling woman

this is as it was meant to be
for if one footstep misplaced i might have
walked past someone at some other table
brushed against some other arm or knee and found myself
walking backwards at daybreak instead of counting the moons i found

when your hand touching my arm opened a hole in the sky
and i jumped or was pushed or was pulled

and i keep falling

hummingbirds hovering turn translucent
bats diving fireflies a token sign of life's lesser gods
lighting the trail of tears you once cried
for all the displaced people who came true in you
she who is born of many grandparents

now makinak and negik medicine i gift you
blue clay seemah cedar sweetgrass and me
while marten bearing the weight of other-being
sleeps and dreams

be still

in your arms the weary traveler finds shelter
by you the hungry are nourished
and though dodem says we are not kin
we wander like sisters walking twin planets
though you move as though music fires your soul
while i stumble graceless as a newborn doe struggling
to her feet

but nothing in life is reasonable not life itself
nor the trajectory of running that leads us home again
so who can say we don't share the same blood
or that you are not the child of a dream
i imagined several lifetimes ago?

here time swallows its own tail and our spirits laughing
recall Shawnee chief and Muskoke leader fixing the morning star
two horses breaking free a battlefield of brilliant red berries returning
                    ever turning
towards daybreak waking two fireflies escaping and it is here
and i know you beyond logic or a single lifetime
remembering with each falling star that moment
your touch broke open
the sky i fall into

                                              1998

Gregory Scofield [b. 1966]

My voice is the voice of many communities, a voice that sings one small song in a community of powerful singers.

Born in Maple Ridge, British Columbia, of Cree, Scottish, English, and French ancestry, Gregory Scofield was raised in Saskatchewan, northern Manitoba, and the Yukon. He went to school in the Lower Mainland of B.C., near Vancouver, until the age of fifteen. In 1985, he attended the University of Regina's Gabriel Dumont Institute. He began writing in 1988, after returning to the west coast. His first piece was a radio drama entitled "The Storyteller," produced by CBC Regina. From 1988 until 2000, when he moved to Edmonton, Alberta, Scofield lived on the west coast and continued to write.

"When I was growing up, my role models were my mother and my Aunt Georgina," Scofield says. His mother, Dorothy Scofield, who was a voracious reader–"she read everything from the *National Enquirer* to *The Tibetan Book of the Dead*"—also wrote poetry. "She instilled in me a love of literature." His aunt, Georgina Houle Young, gave her nephew "traditional knowledge—medicines, sharing, traditional languages, both Cree and Michif."

Scofield published his first book of poetry, *The Gathering: Stones for the Medicine Wheel*, in 1993. Three more followed in the same decade: *Native Canadiana: Songs from the Urban Rez* (1996), *Sakihtowin-maskihkiy ekwa peyak-nikamowin/Love Medicine and One Song* (1997), and *I Knew Two Metis Women* (1999), a tribute to his mother and aunt. In 1999 he also published his autobiography, *Thunder Through My Veins: Memoirs of a Metis Childhood*.

Scofield sees his own work reflecting "a process of growth and maturity. My books represent different stages in my life and voices within the community." The Cree language was particularly important to *Love Medicine and One Song*. "The language is rooted in the earth. So much of the book is about nature and our human bodies coming from mother earth." Writing in Cree allowed Scofield to draw on the particular connotations of the language as well as its sounds. "The language is lyrical, soft, melodic—it is gratifying as a poet to be able to work with the language." Scofield translates the meanings for non-Cree speakers. "I attempt to convey the connotations, although they can't be exact. The poems that incorporate Cree will be experienced differently by Cree speakers and those who don't read or speak Cree."

Many of Scofield's poems suggest autobiography, moving through phases of protest, exploration, and acceptance. While the erotic poems from *Love Medicine* depart from the earlier, more political poems of his youth, the poems from *I Knew Two Metis Women* form a counterpoint. They offer new perspectives, which move back into early childhood and the lives of the women who raised him. In his poems from both *Love Medicine* and *I Knew Two Metis Women*, Scofield experiments with song—traditional song in the former and country music in the latter, each with its own connotations and emotions.

What a Way to Go

Middle of the month
 We're so hard pressed
  Hunting through every pocket

Hoping I stashed
 A little something away
  Teasing gum wrappers show up

My lucky prize jingling
 Deep down between the lining
  Escaped coins just frustrate

What is her majesty
 Doing for supper tonight?
  Fry bread sounds good

We might have moose
 If we were bush Indians
  But our appetite is city cuisine

Back home our elders
 Have ancient taste buds
  Wintertime they stock up

Long distance hunting stories
 Confirm who is a good grandson
  Staying put keeping freezers filled

Coming together to feast
 It all seems so simple
  Taking from the land, being thankful

In the city we hunt each other
    Looking to borrow some flour, sugar, tea
        Just enough to get by til the end of the month

1993

God of the Fiddle Players

The wilting sun catches them centre stage, taking a
Well-deserved breather. Safely shielded by the big top,
Easy for me to applaud for more. An old-timer's
Favorite, my mom would say.

Surveying the dance floor, my generation is damn-near
Lost. Even me, I don't know how to promenade
Properly, let alone that quick heel-toe-on-the-spot
Step. Gyrating to a techno-beat is more my history.
Then again, who can dig roots in the city?

I have to ask a friend about being Métis, what there is
To be proud of. Because she's an elder, she says just
Watch, listen. Later, we join the pilgrimage to the
Graveyard, go to the museum.

They have a special show using mannequins to
Re-enact the Northwest Resistance. Weeping openly, I
Got to meet the heroes I was ashamed of in school.

That summer, the God of the Fiddle Players visited
Batoche. I bought my first sash; wearing it proudly
Around the house, practicing the ins & outs of jigging.

1993

Cycle (of the black lizard)

It was a priest
who made him act that way
so shy he wouldn't say shit
if his mouth was full of it.
At least that's what his
old lady said
each time her face got smashed
with his drunk fist.

The last time
he just pushed her around
then passed out.
Later, her *kôhkum* said
a lizard crawled inside his mouth
and laid eggs.

It was a black lizard, she said
the kind who eat the insides
feasting slowly
until their young are hatched.
Already his tongue was gone
from so much confessing.
Other boys at the boarding school
never talked out loud
for fear the lizard
would creep into their beds.
At first it just moved around
inside his head
manoeuvring serpentine
like a bad dream.

Then one night
his brain caved in & oozed out
his ears, nose and mouth.

It was his mouth
that caused so much trouble.
In there was rotten teeth
and stink breath
made by that gluttonous lizard.
Morning Mass
he swallowed hard to rid the slime
but nighttime it just returned
and slithered around.

Another boy, only older
had the same trouble.
Recess
they eyed each other's dirty holes
and spit, spit, spit.
Once they got caught
and had to scrub the stairs—
and neither said shit about it.

At school, the teacher
noticed his kids had dull eyes
and never spoke or laughed.
The girl was ten
and developed for her age.
When asked in class to tell an Indian story
she went crimson in her face
and cried.
Every few days
her brother got sent
to the principal's office.
They thought he was just naturally rough,
like all Indians.
What they didn't know
was in her pee-hole, his mouth
a lizard crawled around
leaving eggs
during the Lord's prayer.

1996

Unhinged

Sure
I've imagined you,
my unkempt soldier
alone in your room
pulling up all your heated secrets,
coming unglued
like the dovetail joints
of my antique dresser.

You are exquisite at this hour,
pure milkweed,
opalescent as the moon
turning down her blind eye.
And always, dangerous.

Sure
I've slipped the curve
of your backside, slipped between
your thighs,
my seasoned lips mouthing
the peach song

beneath your scrotum.
So, sing my breather, play me
the whole black night.
Sing me, anoint me
with your musk, ear wax,
your navel dew.

Sure
I've imagined you
alone in your room,
alone with me
in a phone booth, a theatre
the back seat of a bus
travelling somewhere so solitary
the landscape has no memory.

Sure, my unkempt soldier
I've dreamed you unhinged
and raging,
your seed exploding like a bullet,
my death
merely a fading pulse.

1997

Pawâcakinâsîs-pîsim
December • The Frost Exploding Moon

And where did we start?
Was it the summer
of my seven year moulting,
the day I thought
another man's body beautiful?
Or was it the spring
and the night
your eyes passed over my naked feet
and lingered such an infinite time?

Perhaps neither.
Perhaps it was only a day
no different from the ones
haphazardly strung together
like the silver bones

of the wind chime
rubbing the night's cool finger.

And though the day eludes me,
I remember that love
galloped in on the backs of horses,
kicked up dust in my heart,
their drumming hooves
carrying you, the dreamrider,
the four corners of the earth
tied together
in a sacred bundle.

But this is the day
of your hateful absence.
last night stars fell from the sky,
and moon, with her winter cough
hacked all night.
Now I wonder did we kiss good-bye
and was this the last dream?

Tonight there is no trace.
I've searched every valley,
every canyon, every mountain.
You are gone. The horses are gone
and the earth is cold
with all the things I cannot say.

Now
what name is to be given
to the moon?
Coyote has torn her to shreds,
dances wild from the blood of her
to the cracking of the trees,
the frost and my heart exploding.

1997

Pêyak-Nikamowin • One Song

At the break of dawn
the spirits I call
to the west, the south,
the north, the east

I am looking
like them I am looking
calling to my love.

âstam ôta nîcimos
ôtantâyan, ôtantâyan
hey-ya-ho-ho
hey-ya-ho-ho
hey-ya-ho-ho
hey-ya-ho-ho

In this dream
he is across the river
standing upon the bank
just over there
my sweetheart.

kâya mâto nîcimos
kinîtôhtan, kinîtôhtan
hey-ya-ho-ho
hey-ya-ho-ho
hey-ya-ho-ho
hey-ya-ho-ho

I am going to cross
to where he is
cross that river
for my love
but he is gone
and the reeds are weeping.

kakwêyahok nîcimos
ninêstosin, ninêstosin
hey-ya-ho-ho
hey-ya-ho-ho
hey-ya-ho-ho
hey-ya-ho-ho

Now all I have are
rainberries and tears to give
as I sit here
watching where he stood.

pekîwêyan nîcimos
nî-mâtoyân, nî-mâtoyân
hey-ya-ho-ho
hey-ya-ho-ho
hey-ya-ho-ho
hey-ya-ho-ho

âstam ôta nîcimos
ôtantâyan, ôtantâyan:

come here my sweetheart
I am here, I am here

kâya mâto nîcimos
kinîtôhtan, kinîtôhtan:

don't cry my sweetheart
I hear you, I hear you

kakwêyahok nîcimos
ninêstosin, ninêstosin:

hurry my sweetheart
I am tired, I am tired

pekîwêyan nîcimos
nî-mâtoyân, nî-mâtayân:

come home my sweetheart
I am crying, I am crying

1997

T. For

Texas, T. for Tennessee,
T. for Texas, T. for Tennessee,
T. for Thelma
That gal that made
A wreck out of me
If you don't want me mama,
You sure don't have to stall,
Lord, Lord,
If you don't want me mama,
You sure don't have to stall
'Cause I can get more women
Than a passenger train can haul . . .

and the needle would catch,
slide into
its well-worn groove,
refusing to budge
like Fat Paul the bootlegger
our very own
small-town Buddha.

Even weighted with pennies
and promises
it wouldn't move
so T. was always for Texas,
Tennessee, for Thelma
that invisible gal
that made a wreck
out of the record, so

T. ended up
strummed in D, sung in C minor
D. for Desmarais, Alberta,
C. for the Carter Family
and Harry…

If you don't want me daddy
You sure don't have to call,
If you don't want me daddy
You sure don't have to call,
Cause I can get more neecheemoosuk
than a dog sled can haul

and the needle and Fat Paul
scratched
and waited, stubborn
as hell,
thinking it was damn funny
till they
both got busted.

> —lyrics sung by Jimmie Rodgers, "Blue Yodel
> No. 1," from *Down the Old Road*

neecheemoosuk: sweethearts

1999

Not All Halfbreed Mothers

for Mom, Maria

Not all halfbreed mothers

drink

red rose, blue ribbon,
Kelowna Red, Labatt's Blue.

Not all halfbreed mothers
wear cowboy shirts or hats,
flowers behind their ears
or moccasins
sent from up north

Not all halfbreed mothers
crave wild meat,
settle for hand-fed rabbits
from SuperStore.

Not all halfbreed mothers
pine over lost loves,
express their heartache
with guitars, juice harps,
old records shoved
into the wrong dustcover.

Not all halfbreed mothers
read *The Star, The Enquirer,*
The Tibetan Book of the Dead
or Edgar Cayce,
know the Lady of Shalott
like she was a best friend
or sister.

Not all halfbreed mothers
speak like a dictionary
or Cree hymn book,
tell stories
about faithful dogs
or bears

that hung around or sniffed
in the wrong place.

Not all halfbreed mothers
know how to saddle
and ride a horse,
how to hot-wire a car
or siphon gas.

Not all halfbreed mothers

drink

red rose, blue ribbon,
Kelowna Red, Labatt's Blue.

Mine just happened
to like it

Old Style.

1999

True North, Blue Compass Heart

Twenty-eight years, drenched to the bone
she talked about Wabasca,
the old days, mud-caked roads
and muskeg forever

a blue compass heart
pointing north, lost
like moose tracks
in the snow

on this wet, grey coast
where other women like her—
true bush and tough—
outlasted city streets,

phantom whitewomen
who floated ever so delicately
behind shaded windows,

drinking herbal tea,
poisoning their children
neatly to sleep.

She told me of a place
in Wabasca
so sacred it couldn't be named,
a clearing in the bush
thick with Jack pine, spruce
moss earth beneath her feet.

One time, she said,
she got lost.
Still as the dead
she stood there and was lifted,
carried like a leaf
to the road back home.

"Seepwaypiyow," the old people said
and this became her name,
stuck long after
TB ate her lungs, long after
the sanatorium closed
and the Wabasca, the people,
the wild roses of her childhood,
became stories
that skipped across the kitchen table,
sung over strong tea
brewed in a blue enamel pot.

One night
we were out walking, picking cans.
"Hey, you fucking squaw!" some kids
yelled from a car.
"Never mind," she said,
taking my small hand.

I don't remember getting home.
Only that we were
standing on the steps,
all the lights burning inside.

Down south
she joked about snaring rabbits,
checking her trapline
which in the end
ran through the cemetery,
grew wild with clovers, dogwoods

over her
a plot of hard earth
sinking and settling,

claiming the north, the sun
in a distant land

spooked with strangers.

Seepwaypiyow: She flies away
1999

I've Been Told

Halfbreed heaven must be
handmade flowers of tissue,
poplar trees
forever in bloom,

the North and South Saskatchewan rivers
swirling and meeting
like the skirts, the hands
of cloggers
shuffling their moccasined feet.

I've been told

Halfbreed heaven must be
old Gabriel at the gate
calling, "Tawow! Tawow!"
toasting new arrivals, pointing
deportees
to the buffalo jump
or down the Great Canadian Railroad,
like Selkirk or MacDonald.

I've been told

Halfbreed heaven must be
scuffed floors and furniture
pushed to one side,
grannies giggling in the kitchen,
their embroidered hankies
teasing and nudging
the sweetest sweet sixteen,
who will snare the eye
of the best jigger.

I've been told

Halfbreed heaven must be
a wedding party
stretched to the new year,
into a wake, a funeral
then another wedding,
an endless brigade of happy faces
in squeaky-wheeled carts
loaded with accordions, guitars
and fiddles.

I've been told

Halfbreed heaven must be
a rest-over for the Greats:
Hank Williams, Kitty Wells,
The Carter Family
and Hank Snow.

It must be
because I've been told so,

because I know
two Metis women who sing
beyond the blue.

Tawow! Tawow!: Come in, you are welcome!
1999

Randy Lundy [b. 1967]

I have heard it said that poetry is about passionate attachment to the world and/or ecstatic attention to the world. What does that mean? I grew up in northern Saskatchewan within a five-minute walk of the confluence of three rivers: the Fir, the Etamomi, and the Red Deer. Whenever I needed solace or refuge, I sought it among the animals, birds, rocks, plants, trees, and waters, all of them animate and articulate. It was under the tutelage of these creatures that I first studied the confluence of the mind/soul/spirit, the body, and the landscape, including all of the creatures to whom it is home. Nothing I have seen or experienced since has convinced me that reality is other than a confluence, all things flowing into and out of one another and an inseparable part of one another. The living landscape, the earth and sky and all the creatures in between, has been and continues to be the greatest influence on my writing. When we live in a landscape for an extended period of time and pay attention, we develop an attachment. The place gets inside of us and lives there, just as we live within that place.

Randy Lundy was born in the month of November, in Thompson, Manitoba. He is a member of the Barren Lands First Nation, Brochet. He suspects that being born in the midst of winter in an isolated northern community has left an indelible impression upon his being.

After a brief sojourn in the interior of British Columbia, Lundy, at age nine, moved to Hudson Bay, Saskatchewan, where he lived until he began post-secondary studies. It was in Hudson Bay that Lundy began writing poetry, primarily out of the desire to relieve boredom and loneliness—"it didn't work, but I continue to try." In 1987 he attended the University of Saskatchewan in Saskatoon, where he studied religion, philosophy, "and, after learning to laugh at metaphysics, English Literature." Lundy completed an honours B.A. and an M.A. in English, focussing on Native Canadian Literature. "Among my favorite authors were too many poets to mention, though I will name Gregory Scofield and Daniel David Moses. Other favourite poets include Pablo Neruda, Patrick Lane, Tim Lilburn, Margaret Atwood." Lundy has worked as a graduate teaching fellow at the University of Saskatchewan, a sessional lecturer at the Saskatchewan Indian Federated College in Saskatoon, and a writer-in-residence at SIFC in Regina. He currently lives in Regina, where he is a lecturer at SIFC and shares a home with "a fat, agoraphobic cat named Cricket."

Randy Lundy's poetry has appeared in literary periodicals "from coast to coast—but not in Nunavut, which seems to have a dearth of such publications." His poetry has also been broadcast nationally

on CBC Radio, and his first book, *Under the Night Sun*, was published in
1999 by Coteau Books.

my lodge

this will be my lodge
skin stretched tight over bone

this I will call my home
sacred place I cannot leave

no light visits me
in this womb
thick with hot, stone-breath

moonlight beats
in the ear of the world

stars wonder
where I have gone

trees lean listening

my soft voice centred
      rises
      and
      falls
with the wind

2000

ritual

this is a ritual, this uncovering of flesh
we shed clothes like tired skins
frost presses its face against the window

what are the words we should recite
the words this ceremony demands?

our tongues stir
deep roots reaching into earth
with no memory of sky

our hands move
new light on a landscape
coaxing a sound from silence

three thousand miles away
birds are beginning to flock

2000

ghost dance

I

at sand creek, at wounded knee creek
the valleys are filled with bones

after the first green shoots of spring
when the wind stirs
the leaves and knee-high grasses
they will come, a gathering of many tongues

Violence
nature

to hear of new soil coming like a tide
to greet the return of the buffalo
the herds of wild horses
the sound of thunder on the plains

they will dance and chant
from dawn until dawn
they will dance and chant
until they feel the earth move

II

the wind whistles a dry song
the sun touches the valley floor
the hills breathe a dusty breath

there is a shaking and rattling
tired bones coming together
each scattered part finding a place

brittle fingers gather
flesh of roots and moss
eyes of rounded stone

the laughter of the coming storm
shakes the world with its voice

2000

an answer to why

if you were to ask me
would answer

it is the fault of the season

as the flesh of the trees is torn away
birds flee with the sun
removing their voices
far from our helpless ears

as the river moves toward stillness
bears dream themselves thin
among roots and stones

we too are part of this

2000

a reed of red willow

a reed of red willow
stripped by the teeth of a beaver

white as stone in sun
slender a flute

the notes it sings
into black night

white and slender
as a bone

in the wrist of a woman you love

2000

Ayiki-pisim
the Frog Moon (April)

these voices rise with the moon
waxing and waning in their throats

bright stone from the centre of the earth
rising through branches and bones

she is the song they sing
moon-song, song of slow light

pale asphodel
blooming in the night

2000

Pawacakinasisi-pisim
The Frost-Exploding Moon (December)

i would like to say

nothing is forgotten
because nothing moves

then moon moves from behind
a heavy bank of snowclouds

the frozen landscape explodes
into light and silence

the green branches of a pine
the only voice in the night

2000

stone gathering

stones gather in circles
on moonlit hilltops

with bowed heads they meditate
upon the things stones know

deep in forested valleys
there is singing and dancing

wind and shadows
honour these gathered stones

the stones inhale
ten thousand days

the stones exhale
ten thousand days

into stone-sized
indentations in the earth

if we wait this long
will the guardians of beetle and worm

speak the secrets
of mountain and bone?

2000

deer-sleep

this place does not require your presence
and beneath the staring stars
you have discovered
your offerings are meaningless

you are left with nothing
but silence

you have forgotten why you came here
you were looking for something

the wind wanders among willows
muttering forgotten stories
it has been everywhere
and cannot keep quiet

you must learn
to listen, to be alone

only then
will you bed down with the deer
to sleep in the long, deep grass
wrapped in the warmth
of slender bodies
of slow-moving breath

each time you awaken with the dawn
stars and moon fading memories
the deer will be gone

all day you carry with you
the sound of their sleeping

the howling song of coyotes
the common dream
that binds you

2000

Acknowledgements

[All unpublished poems are printed with permission of the authors.]

KATERI AKIWENZIE DAMM. "stray bullets," "my grandmothers," "poem without end #3," "my secret tongue and ears," "from turtle island to aotearoa" from *my heart is a stray bullet*, (Cape Croker, ON: Kegedonce Press, 1993). Reprinted with permission of the author. "partridge song," "frozen breath and knife blades," "hummingbirds," "night falling woman" published with permission of the author.

MARIE ANNHARTE BAKER. "Granny Going," "Penumbra," "Moon Bear," "Bird Clan Mother," "Pretty Tough Skin Woman," "Trapper Mother," "Boobstretch," "Raced Out to Write This Up," "His Kitchen," reprinted from *Being On The Moon* (Winlaw BC: Polestar Press, 1990) with permission of Polestar Press. "Coyote Columbus Café," "Tongue in Cheek, if not Tongue in Check," "Coyote Trail," "Bear Piss Water," "I Want to Dance Wild Indian Blackface" reprinted from *Coyote Columbus Café* (Winnipeg: Moonprint Press, 1994). All poems reprinted with permission of the author.

JEANNETTE ARMSTRONG. All poems from *Breath Tracks* (Penticton: Theytus Books, 1991) reprinted with permission of Theytus Books, except the following. "In-Tee-Teigh" was originally published in *Many Voices: An Anthology of Contemporary Canadian Indian Poetry*, eds. David Day and Marilyn Bowering (Vancouver: J.J. Douglas, 1977). "Reclaiming Earth," originally published in *Gatherings, Volume III*. "Apples" and "Right It" originally published in *West Coast Line* 25, 32/1 (Spring/Summer 1998). All poems published with permission of the author.

JOANNE ARNOTT. "Wiles of Girlhood," from *Wiles of Girlhood* (Vancouver: Press Gang Publishers, 1991). "The Shard," "In My Dance Class," "Manitoba Pastoral," "Proud Belly," "Song About,""Like an Indian: Struggling with Ogres" from *My Grass Cradle* (Vancouver: Press Gang Publishers, 1992). Reprinted with permission of the author. "Migration," "Protection," "Midlife," "Beachhead Dreaming," reprinted with permission of the author.

PETER BLUE CLOUD. "Alcatraz," "When's the Last Boat to Alcatraz," "Ochre Iron," "Sweet Corn," "Bear," "Dawn," "Crazy Horse Monument," and "Yellowjacket" all originally appeared in *Turtle, Bear and Wolf* (Roosevelt Town, NY: Akwesasne Notes Press, 1976). All poems published in *Clans of Many Nations* (Fredonia, NY: White Pine Press, 1994). Poems reprinted with permission of the author.

BETH BRANT. "Her Name is Helen," from *Mohawk Trail* (Toronto: The Women's Press, 1985). "Telling," *Food and Spirits* (Vancouver: Press Gang Publishers, 1991). "Honour Song" and "Stillborn Night" were originally published in *Native Women in the Arts*, "in a vast dreaming," 1997. All poems reprinted with permission of the author.

SKYROS BRUCE / MAHARA ALLBRECT. "when the outside is completely dark," "eels," "in a letter from my brother, atlantis," all from *Kalala Poems* (Daylight Press, 1973). "in/dian," first published in *The Malahat Review* 26 (April 1973). "For Menlo," "the mountains are real," "in memory of fred quilt," "her husband is a film maker," first published in *TAWOW*, Vol 3.3 (1974). All poems reprinted with permission of the author.

JOAN CRATE. *"See this necklace?,"* "The Poetry Reading," "Gleichen," "Story teller," "I am a Prophet," "Beaver Woman," from *Pale As Real Ladies: Poems for Pauline Johnson* (London, ON: Brick Books, 1991). Reprinted by permission of Brick Books. "Empty Seas," "Departures," "Sentences: At the Cull's," "She is crying in a corner," "Unmarked Grave," published with permission from the author.

BETH CUTHAND. "Zen Indian," "Seven Songs for Uncle Louis," "Were You There," from *Voices in the Waterfall* (Penticton, BC: Theytus Books, 1992). "Post-Oka Kinda Woman" and "This Red Moon" originally published in *Gatherings Volume V* (1994). All poems reprinted by permission of Theytus Press and Beth Cuthand. "Confluence" and "For All the Settlers Who Secretly Sing" published by permission of Beth Cuthand.

JOSEPH DANDURAND. "This Was One of Them," "I Touched the Coyote's Tongue," from *I Touched the Coyote's Tongue*, chapbook by Joseph Dandurand; "Someone," "Fort Langley," "One year," "Before me," "Feeding the hungry" from *looking into the eyes of my forgotten dreams* (Cape Croker Reserve: Kegedonce Press, 1998). Reprinted by permission of the author.

MARILYN DUMONT. All poems from *A Really Good Brown Girl* (London, ON: Brick Books, 1996). Used by permission of Brick Books. All poems reprinted by permission of the author.

CONNIE FIFE. "Ronnie, because they never told you why," "Communications class," "the revolution of not vanishing," "This is not a metaphor," "Stones memory," "We remember," from *Beneath the Naked Sun* (Toronto: Sister Vision, 1992). Reprinted by permission of the author "i have become so many mountains," "dear walt," "the naming" (Fredericton: Broken Jaw Press, 1999). Reprinted by permission of the Broken Jaw Press.

CHIEF DAN GEORGE. All poems from *My Heart Soars* (Surrey, BC: Hancock House Publishers, 1971). Reprinted by permission of Chief Leonard George.

LOUISE HALFE. "Pahkahkos," "Nōhkom, Medicine Bear," "Ukrainian Hour," "Eatin' Critters," "Picking Leftovers," "I'm So Sorry," "In Da Name of Da Fadder," "Der Poop," "These are the Body's Gifts," "She Told Me," from *Bear Bones and Feathers* (Regina: Coteau Books, 1994. Used by permission of Coteau Books. Excerpts from *Blue Marrow* (Toronto: McClelland and Stewart, 1998) reprinted by permission of McClelland and Stewart. All poems reprinted by permission of the author.

RITA JOE. "I am the Indian," "Your buildings," "Wen net ki'l/Who are you?," "When I was small," "Expect nothing else from me," "She spoke of paradise," from *Poems of Rita Joe* (Abanaki Press, 1978). Reprinted by permission of the author. "I Lost My Talk," "The Legend of Glooscap's Door," from *Song of Eskasoni*, (Charlottetown: Ragweed Press, 1988). "Demasduit," "The King and Queen Pass by on Train," "Migration Indian" from *Lnu and Indians we're called* (Charlottetown: Ragweed Press, 1991). Poems reprinted by permission of Ragweed Press and the author.

LENORE KEESHIG-TOBIAS. "(a found poem)" originally published in Beth Brant, ed., *A Gathering of Spirit: A Collection of North American Indian Women* (Toronto: Women's Press, 1984). "At Sunrise," originally published in *Poetry Toronto* (March 1987). "New Image," originally published in *Trickster* (1988). "He Fights" first printed in *The Colour of Resistance*, Connie Fife, ed. (Toronto: Sister Vision, 1993). "In Katherine's House," first printed in *Native Women in the Arts*, "sweetgrass grows all around her" (Toronto, 1997). Poems reprinted by permission of the author.

GEORGE KENNY. All poems from *Indians Don't Cry* (Toronto: Chimo Publishing, 1977). Reprinted by permission of the author.

WAYNE KEON. "nite," "an opun letr tu bill bissett," "a kind of majik," "the eye of the raven," "moosonee in august," "Kirkland Lake, Sept. 21" "eight miles from Esten Lake," reprinted from *Sweetgrass* (Elliot Lake, ON: W.O.K. Books, 1972). "in this village," "for donald marshall," "smoke nd thyme," "i'm not in charge of this ritual," "if i ever heard" reprinted from *Sweetgrass II* (Stratford, ON: The Mercury Press, 1990). "Spirit Warrior Raven: Dream Winter" reprinted from *Storm Dancer* (Stratford, ON: The Mercury Press, 1993). "the apocalypse will begin," "replanting the heritage tree" reprinted from *My Sweet Maize* (Stratford, ON: The Mercury Press, 1997). All poems reprinted by permission of the author.

EMMA LAROCQUE. "Incongruence," "Commitment," "The Beggar," and "The Uniform of the Dispossessed" originally appeared in *Writing the Circle: Native Women of Western Canada*, (Norman: University of Oklahoma Press, 1990). Reprinted by permission of the author. "Nostalgia," "The Red in Winter," and "Progress" are reprinted by permission of W.H. New, ed., *Native Writers and Canadian Writing* (Vancouver: University of British Columbia Press, 1990). "Long Way From Home" originally published in *ARIEL*, Vol.25.1 (1994). Reprinted by permission of the Board of Governors, University of Calgary. "My Hometown Northern Canada South Africa" originally appeared in *Border Crossings* (Fall 1992). All poems reprinted by permission of the author.

RANDY LUNDY. "my lodge," "ritual," "ghost dance," "an answer to why," "a reed of red willow," "Ayiki-pisim/the Frog Moon (April)," "Pawacakinasisi-pisim/The Frost-Exploding Moon (December)," "stone gathering," "deer-sleep," from *Under the Night Sun* (Regina: Coteau Books, 1999). Used by permission of Coteau Books. All poems reprinted by permission of the author.

LEE MARACLE. All poems from *Bent Box* (Penticton, BC: Theytus Press, 2000). Reprinted by permission of Theytus Press. All poems reprinted by permission of the author.

RASUNAH MARSDEN "Father," "Condolences for Marius," "Three Objects" originally published in *Voices* (Jakarta, Indonesia, 1986). All poems published by permission of the author.

DUNCAN MERCREDI "my red face hurts" originally published in *Gatherings II* (1991). "Morning Awakening," Blues Singer," from *Spirit of the Wolf* (Winnipeg: Pemmican Press, 1990); "back roads," "He Likes to Dance," "something you said," from *Dreams of the Wolf in the City* (Pemmican Press, 1992); "born again indian," "searching for visions,"

"Searching for visions II," from *Wolf and Shadows* (Pemmican Press, 1995); "dreaming about the end of the world," "racing across the land," "yesterday's song," "the duke of windsor" from *The Duke of Windsor— Wolf Sings the Blues* (1997). Reprinted with permission of Pemmican Press. All Poems published with the permission of the author.

DANIEL DAVID MOSES. "Song in the Light of Dawn," "A Song of Early Summer," "October" from *Delicate Bodies* (Sechelt, BC: Nightwood Editions, 1980). Reprinted by permission of Nightwood Editions. "The Sunbather's Fear of the Moon," "Twinkle," "Ballad from a Burned-Out House," "Of Course the Sky Does not Close," "Crow Out Early," "The Persistence of Songs," "The Letter," "The Line" from *The White Line* (Saskatoon: Fifth House Publishers, 1990). "Offhand Song" first published in *ARC* 26 (Spring 1991). "Could Raven Have White Feathers?" first published in *The Dramaturgical Works* 23, Playwrights' Workshop, Montreal (Winter/Spring 1997). "Cowboy Pictures" first published in *The Church-Wellesley Review, Xtra's Literary Supplement* (Toronto, 9 October 1997). All poems reprinted by permission of the author.

DUKE REDBIRD. All poems reprinted from *Loveshine and Redwine*, 1981. All poems reprinted by permission of the author.

ARMAND GARNET RUFFO. "Poem for Duncan Campbell Scott," "Some," "Poetry," "Surely Not Warriors," from *Opening in the Sky* (Penticton, BC: Theytus Books, 1994). Reprinted by permission of Theytus Books. "Grey Owl, 1935," "Mirror" from *Grey Owl: The Mystery of Archie Belaney* (Regina: Coteau Books, 1996). Used by permission of Coteau Books. "At Geronimo's Grave," "No Man's Land," "I Heard Them, I Was There," "Bear," "Rockin' Chair Lady," "Fish Tale," from *At Geronimo's Grave* (Regina: Coteau Books, 2001). All poems published by permission of the author.

GREGORY SCOFIELD. "What a Way to Go," "God of the Fiddle Players," from *The Gathering: Stones for the Medicine Wheel* (Vancouver: Polestar Press, 1993). Reprinted by permission of the publisher. "Cycle (of the black lizard)" from *Native Canadiana/Songs from the Urban Rez*, (Vancouver: Polestar Press, 1996). Reprinted by permission of the publisher. "Unhinged," "Pawācakināsîs-pîsm, December • The Frost Exploding Moon," "Pêyak-Nikimowin • One Song" (Vancouver: Polestar Press, 1997). Reprinted by permission of the publisher. "T. For," "Not All Halfbreed Mothers," "True North, Blue Compass Heart," "I've Been Told" (Vancouver: Polestar Book Publishers, 1999). Reprinted by permission of the Polestar Book Publishers. All poems reprinted by permission of the author.

SARAIN STUMP. All poems except "Round Dance" reprinted from *There is My People Sleeping* (Sidney, BC: Gray's Publishing, 1970). "Round Dance" first printed in *TAWOW*, Vol. 4.3 (1974). All poems and illustrations reprinted by permission of Linda Jaine.

GORDON WILLIAMS. "The Last Crackle" first printed in *I Am An Indian*, 1969. "Lost Children," "Dark Corners," "Ernie," "The Day Runs" first printed in *The White Pelican* (1971). "Justice in Williams Lake" first appeared in *The Malahat Review* 26 (April 1973). All poems reprinted by permission of the author.